JULIA!

**YOU'VE HEARD THE STORIES.
NOW FIND OUT THE TRUTH ABOUT
JULIA ROBERTS:
AMERICA'S PRETTY WOMAN—**

THE COVER-UP OF THE DECADE:
The *real* story behind her troubled family life!

HER ILL-FATED AFFAIRS:
Kiefer Sutherland and Jason Patric

**HER CONTROVERSIAL TWO-YEAR
DISAPPEARANCE:**
Was it publicity ploy or hushed-up scandal?

HER BIG COMEBACK FILM:
The blockbuster movie that has Tinseltown talking!

HER SURPRISE WEDDING TO LYLE LOVETT:
Was it a match made in Heaven or Hollywood?

AND MUCH, MUCH MORE!

PINNACLE BOOKS HAS SOMETHING FOR EVERYONE —

MAGICIANS, EXPLORERS, WITCHES AND CATS

THE HANDYMAN (377-3, $3.95/$4.95)
He is a magician who likes hands. He likes their comfortable shape and weight and size. He likes the portability of the hands once they are severed from the rest of the ponderous body. Detective Lanark must discover who The Handyman is before more handless bodies appear.

PASSAGE TO EDEN (538-5, $4.95/$5.95)
Set in a world of prehistoric beauty, here is the epic story of a courageous seafarer whose wanderings lead him to the ends of the old world — and to the discovery of a new world in the rugged, untamed wilderness of northwestern America.

BLACK BODY (505-9, $5.95/$6.95)
An extraordinary chronicle, this is the diary of a witch, a journal of the secrets of her race kept in return for not being burned for her "sin." It is the story of Alba, that rarest of creatures, a white witch: beautiful and able to walk in the human world undetected.

THE WHITE PUMA (532-6, $4.95/NCR)
The white puma has recognized the men who deprived him of his family. Now, like other predators before him, he has become a man-hater. This story is a fitting tribute to this magnificent animal that stands for all living creatures that have become, through man's carelessness, close to disappearing forever from the face of the earth.

Julia:

THE UNTOLD STORY
OF AMERICA'S PRETTY WOMAN

Aileen Joyce

PINNACLE BOOKS
WINDSOR PUBLISHING CORP.

PINNACLE BOOKS are published by

Windsor Publishing Corp.
475 Park Avenue South
New York, NY 10016

First Printing: December, 1993

Printed in the United States of America

ACKNOWLEDGMENTS

My profound thanks to all these people whose recollections helped make this book a reality; and my heartfelt gratitude to Guy d'Alema, Paula Ann Lintz, Hilda Simms, Vivien McKinley, Karen Jackovich, and the late James C. Strayhorn, for their assistance and friendship during the many months it took to research and write this story.

Aileen Joyce
September, 1993

Introduction

In the summer of 1991 a friend suggested perhaps I should consider doing a book on Julia Roberts who, having starred in two back-to-back box office bonanzas, *Steel Magnolias* and *Pretty Woman,* was at the zenith of her popularity.

I had quickly dismissed the idea. "There just isn't that much to write about," I'd responded, recalling the many stories I'd read about her happy, idyllic upbringing in tiny Smyrna, Georgia. "Julia Roberts," I had smugly explained, "doesn't have any substance. How could she? She's only twenty-three years old. And without substance, there's no book."

As it turned out, I was greatly mistaken.

The following summer, I was assigned by a major magazine to uncover the reasons behind Julia's eighteen-month disappearance from the Hollywood scene. In pursuit of the truth about "America's Number One Sweetheart," I traveled to Julia's hometown, where I discovered, to my astonishment, that virtually everything previously written about her family and childhood was little more than a carefully woven tapestry of half-truths, all of which had been dutifully recorded and subsequently reported by an unsuspecting media.

What you are about to read is based on never-before-published information gleaned from court records and from exclusive interviews with family members and friends, as well as previously published interviews with Julia, her brother, Eric Roberts, and her mother, Betty Roberts Motes. The result is a fascinating portrait of a family divided, ripped asunder more than twenty years ago by forces beyond their control that have nevertheless molded Julia into an intriguing personality, both on screen and off.

The Untold Story of America's Pretty Woman is, quite simply, the truth behind the oft-asked question, "Who *is* Julia Roberts?"

Chapter One

There was nothing to distinguish Saturday, October 28, 1967, from any other late fall day in Atlanta. The top headline in *The Atlanta Constitution* reported a U.S. raid on Hanoi and the loss of three American jets. IBM had closed up at $597.50 a share and Notre Dame had beaten Michigan State, 24–12. Jackie Gleason was still television's Saturday night King of Comedy; and Lawrence Welk was still entertaining the Geritol set with an hour of his brand of champagne music. Even the temperature was normal—partly cloudy, with a high of 65 and a low of 40.

In the maternity ward of Crawford Long hospital in downtown Atlanta, however, thirty-three-year-old Betty Roberts was not watching television or reading the newspaper. She was recuperating from the birth of her third child, a baby girl whom she and her husband, Walter, had decided to name Julia Fiona.

By the time Julia was born, Betty and Walter Roberts had been married for twelve mostly unhappy, largely poverty-stricken years. During that time Walter had never been able to fully support his growing family, if for no other reason than he couldn't hold a job. He was too argumentative, too arrogant to work for anyone else. Besides, Walter Roberts' dream was to become a well-known writer and producer. Any other type of employment therefore was beneath him.

So Betty had always worked to help keep a roof over their heads and food on the table. It was a difficult situation, which is why the couple waited ten years to have a second child after the birth of their son, Eric. As a result of their on-going financial problems the couple had spent years squabbling over money and, in fact, were so short of funds at the time of Julia's birth that Coretta Scott King, the widow of Martin Luther King and a close family friend, supposedly paid the hospital bill.

Despite her heartfelt adult recollections of an idyllic childhood filled with "a lotta hugging, a lotta kissing, a lotta love," the truth is Julia's remembrances are more fantasy than fact, more wishful thinking than well-grounded reality. She was *not* born into a happy family and when that family unit disintegrated only four years after her birth, Julia's life took an even more unpleasant dysfunctional turn.

"We were really lucky," Betty once told an interviewer. "We had no teen horror stories in *our* family." That's true. They were all *adult* horror stories.

Julia's mother, Betty Lou Bredemus was born August 13, 1934, in Minneapolis, the daughter of Elizabeth and Wendell Bredemus, a football coach-turned-salesman

10

who, despite uprooting his family to a dozen towns in as many years, never earned enough money to offer a college education to either Betty or her older brother, John. "He got sick and the money just sort of disappeared," Betty later offered as an explanation of why she had decided to enlist in the Air Force when she was nineteen years old.

A short, bubbly blond of German and Scandinavian descent, Betty's life-long dream had been to become an actress. But the fact that she displayed a natural dramatic flair, and had received praise for her performances in a variety of school productions, did not impress her parents. They were less than encouraging about her theatrical ambitions because, she explained, "There was no money in it."

So Betty took the advice of her older brother, John, and, as he had years before, enlisted in the Air Force on August 27, 1953, a year after graduating from the Austin (Minnesota) Public High school. She planned to study drama through the G.I. Bill of Rights when her enlistment was up. But fate had other plans.

After basic training in San Antonio, Texas, and a brief transfer to Chanute Air Force base in the Midwest, Betty was assigned to Keesler Air Force Base in Biloxi, Mississippi, where she was happily attached to Special Services, dividing her time between working in the library and performing in variety shows at Keesler and other nearby bases.

Then one afternoon Betty encountered Walter Roberts, a handsome young Georgian with coal black wavy hair, finely chiseled features and dark, brooding eyes, who was a would-be writer of short stories. An Airman First Class and a year older than Betty, Walter had served as a medical corpsman in Korea, and had only been at

Keesler a few weeks before meeting Betty in the library. The two quickly discovered they shared the same passionate interest in theater arts but, unlike Betty, Walter was not interested in being an actor. Instead, his dream was to write, direct, and produce. "Actors are mindless," he'd explain.

Years later, long after Walter had died, Betty would relate to interviewers how Walter had "caught the acting bug" only after hanging around her, trying to win a place in her heart by learning how to build sets and paint scenery. However, this is inaccurate. Walter is remembered by high school classmates as having been an incredible actor, a "natural" performer whose appearances in high school productions always guarranteed a sold-out crowd.

It was while at Keesler that Betty and Walter, whom she always insisted on calling Rob, met Rance Howard and his wife, Jean, and their four-month-old son, Ron, who would grow up to become Opie on *The Andy Griffith Show* and then a top Hollywood film director. Together the foursome, along with Ron's dog, Gulliver, began traveling to bases throughout the Southeast, merrily putting on shows to entertain the servicemen.

A year later, when Rance Howard's tour of duty was up, and he and Jean were moving to Los Angeles, they tried to convince Betty and Walter to join them. But Walter still had a year of his enlistment left and couldn't go. So Betty stayed behind with Walter and, as she would later explain with a sigh, "chose to marry instead."

Thus Betty Lou Bredemus and Walter Grady Roberts got a marriage license and were united in holy matrimony by the Reverend Victor Augsburger of the First Presbyterian Church in Biloxi on July 1, 1955, in a fellow librarian's home on the base. Twenty-five days later, Betty received her discharge, but she continued living on the base since Walter still had a year left to serve.

The following April the couple had their first child—a son whom they named Eric Anthony. Betty would later laughingly confide to friends that Eric's birth on April 18, 1956, only nine-and-a-half months after her marriage, had "kept everyone counting on their fingers."

When Walter received his discharge a short while after Eric's birth, the couple and their infant son moved to nearby New Orleans. Walter enrolled at Tulane University, where he studied psychology and English literature, and Betty worked at an insurance company, and later a chess and game shop in the French Quarter, to support the family. At one point, Betty also attended night classes at Tulane, majoring in English literature, too.

Then, only three months short of graduating, Walter angrily dropped out of Tulane. "He had a great deal of animosity toward the professors and was convinced there was nothing more they could teach him," Betty explained. Since Walter wanted to return to his roots, the couple moved from New Orleans to the Atlanta area, where Walter had been born, one of two children of Beatrice and Walter Thomas Roberts, a construction worker.

Years later, Betty would tell friends, that Walter had been estranged from his family most of his life because he didn't fit in with their rural middle-class existence. Walter had a high IQ and was an intellectual, two qualities that separated him from the average person and as an adult lead to his tremendous drive and subsequent frustration.

"He came from nothing and was going to be something, make something of himself. He didn't want to leave Georgia," Betty once explained, "so he stayed and beat his brains out. He was a very talented, brilliant man who was in the wrong town to be doing what he was doing. That was his downfall. Also, he expected everyone to work as hard as he did, be as committed as he was."

The couple first settled in Decatur, a small town just outside the perimeter of greater Atlanta. Betty went to work as a secretary in the public relations department of Emory University and Walter found a job as a wholesale milk salesman with the Atlanta Dairies Co-op. In 1965, the year Betty gave birth to the couple's second child, a daughter, whom they named Lisa Billingsley Roberts, Walter launched his first Actors Workshop—in the living room of the couple's Decatur apartment on Scott Boulevard. By that time Walter had gone through several jobs, including a stint as publicist for the Academy Theater.

"Walter Roberts was one of the most charming people I've ever met," recalled Frank Wittow who, as head of the theater, had hired Walter. "He was extremely good-looking, sort of like Armand Assante, and had very dark, piercing eyes. He was very dynamic, very verbally adept, and, since he had some background in theater, he seemed well-suited for the position."

But Walter didn't last long in the job. "I became aware that he clearly had other interests, which were distracting him from doing the job," Wittow explained, adding that Walter's relationship with the Academy Theater had ended within a year.

"Walter decided to have an art exhibit in the lobby of the theater, which was a converted Baptist church then," Wittow said. "The lobby was less than sixty feet in diameter and not conducive to an art exhibit. But Walter wanted to have an exhibit and then pretend one of the

14

paintings had been stolen, which he believed would get a lot of publicity. He left shortly afterward.

"He was very bright and he was king, where his family was involved," Wittow added, "but he was somewhat manipulative and I felt he had some emotional problems."

Wittow was not alone in his assessment of Walter's standing within his own family. Another witness to the couple's lifestyle described Walter and Betty as having "a Fifties kind of relationship, where the husband is king."

After departing the Academy Theater, Walter wound up working at the Harrington Scenic and Lighting Studio which, only a couple of blocks away from where he would launch his Actor's Workshop within a year.

"He just walked down here and introduced himself to Mr. Harrington," recalls Charles Walker, who now owns the studio, "and the next thing I knew he was working here, building scenery."

Walter and Edith Russell Harrington hit it off almost immediately, probably because they were both interested in theater. Mrs. Harrington, in fact, had founded the Civic Children's Theater years before. "As I recall he worked his way into the theater, got her mailing list, and then went out and started his own theater," Walker confided. "I remember her being quite upset about it, saying 'that renegade so-and-so tried to take our kids!' "

As in the case of the Academy Theater, Walter's affiliation with the Harrington studio did not last more than a year. "He was kind of like a butterfly," Charles Walker explained. "He seemed to want to dig in, but then he'd fly away." Walker also recalled Walter as being a "moody fellow."

"He was alright unless you crossed him," Walker

said. "He was a bit pompous and I remember he got on Mr. Harrington's nerves. He had very definite political ideas, especially about the Vietnam War, and he enunciated everything perfectly. When he talked, it was better than listening to the radio."

With or without Edith Harrington's list, Walter opened his Actors and Writers Workshop in a large, two-story, white frame Victorian house at 849 Juniper Street in the heart of midtown Atlanta. The Workshop took up the entire first floor and the family lived on the second. "It was Walter's idea, and I went along with it," Betty would later admit, referring to both the move from New Orleans to Atlanta and the opening of The Actors and Writers Workshop.

"The house stood high above the street," recalled Philip De Poy, who attended the workshop throughout its five-year duration, "so you had to climb up ten or fifteen steps and then five steps more up to the front porch.

"Once you were inside, immediately to your left was a library. There was a staircase going upstairs, where the family lived, and on the right were a large dining room and a sun room, as well as a kitchen and oversized pantry, which is where they stored the costumes. I remember that each of the rooms had sliding wooden doors and lots of woodwork. The house seemed enormous to me at the time."

In the late Sixties and early Seventies midtown Atlanta was a "happening" neighborhood filled with hippies, off-beat theater productions, street vendors, and artists, all bound together by an avant garde pursuit of free-flowing creativity. As a result, the neighborhood atmosphere resembled that of San Francisco's Haight Asbury district.

By the mid-Seventies, however, the flagrant freedom of the Sixties had disappeared, taking with it entire blocks of the area which were demolished to make way for an urban renewal project that, failing to materialize, left in its wake bleak stretches of vacant lots where houses filled with life once stood. Thus, all that remains now of the house Walter and Betty rented is a large remnant of a graffiti-filled granite retaining wall.

When Betty and Walter brought Julia home from the hospital in early November, 1967, however, the house was alive with the sounds of young actors in the making. One of them was Julia's eleven-year-old brother, Eric, who had begun appearing in workshop productions from its inception.

Eric was an unusually beautiful child, small and blonde and very shy. Yolanda King, one of Walter's older students, remembers Eric as having a lot of energy and being "very, very skinny. He was not quiet, but he was very introspective, very thoughtful," she recalled.

By the time he was fifteen years old, Eric was a seasoned actor who had appeared in more than eighty stage productions. "I started acting as a baby and that's always been part of my advantage," he would later explain to interviewers. "A lot of what I do now when I am working comes as habit, I've been doing it so long."

Ed Danos, a veteran Atlanta actor, once saw Eric in a local production of *Othello* and remembers being fascinated by the artistry shown by the fifteen-year-old actor. "He had a strong man's voice and, truthfully, was better than some Shakespearean actor's I'd seen," Danos said. "He was head and shoulders above everyone else in the play. Nobody had that kind of voice at his age, with that kind of resonance and stage presence."

* * *

Walter's original intention in founding The Actors and Writers Workshop had been to create a Lee Strasberg-like theater company and workshop. But he soon discovered his major appeal would be not to adults but to parents who believed their off-spring had a future in the theater. One of those parents was Coretta Scott King, wife of Martin Luther King. With three of her children involved in the workshop, Mrs. King quickly became one of the Roberts' staunchest supporters, enrolling all of her children—Yolanda, Martin Luther, Jr., and Dexter—in various classes. "She was very supporting, both emotionally and financially," Betty would say of Coretta Scott King many years later.

"My mother *was* immediately attracted to the workshop because it was an integrated group," recalled Yolanda King, who attended classes there from the time she was nine years old until she was fifteen, studying speech, movement, and drama, as well as appearing in more than forty of Walter's productions.

As one of the workshop's older students, Yolanda remembers the Roberts' battle to keep the theater group intact. "It was a constant struggle to get funds to keep going. My mother was very much committed to them. But it was always a case of just barely getting by, paying the rent, getting the costumes."

Although the workshop was an odd mixture of avant garde theater being incongruously performed by an integrated cast of young people, it was for this very reason that Walter managed to land a $2,500 grant from the prestigious Guggenheim Foundation shortly after mounting the Workshop's first production, *Othello,* which starred Walter in the title role and Betty as Desdemona.

With the Guggenheim money in hand Walter produced his own adaptation of the traditional Chinese fable, *The Nightingale*, followed by a production of his adaptation of Joel Chandler Harris' "Uncle Remus" stories, which featured Eric as Bre'r Rabbit, Philip De Poy as Bre'r Fox and Yolanda King, covered from head to toe in green food coloring, as Ma Alligator.

The following summer the Workshop landed a federal grant through the Economic Opportunity Act and toured Atlanta's ghettos and low-income neighborhoods in a "showmobile"—a stage built atop a flatbed truck. "When we toured that summer," Betty would recall, "I would put Julia in a stroller while I set up the sound system. In the ghetto areas the kids would come up and ask, 'Can I take her for a walk?' And I'd say 'Sure.' Then one time someone said, 'Are you sure she's coming back?' But the black children were fascinated with her because a lot of them had never seen any white children. She was about two years old, and she had all this soft blonde hair.

"It didn't get us a lot of publicity," Betty added, referring to the Showmobile tour, "but it was a wonderful summer, and it covered our expenses."

Despite tuition from its classes, ticket sales to its productions, and its infrequent grants, however, the Workshop never yielded a genuine income. Instead, after paying the rent on the Juniper Street house, the family was forced to live on fifty dollars a week, far below the poverty level, during the first six years of Julia's life.

"We dealt strictly with volunteers, which could be very difficult because Walter felt they should work as hard as he did," Betty explained. "We made our own costumes, which meant I used to spend a lot of time in thrift stores, buying them that way. When Julia was just a baby, I'd put her downstairs in a playpen, while I worked twenty-four hours a day making costumes for the next production."

Although it has always been difficult to earn a living from such a venture, the family's livelihood was further diminished by Walter's inability to deal with people. As beloved though he was by his young students, he was apparently anything but revered by a majority of the adults he encountered, especially those involved in local theater. "Basically," explained a former friend, "Walter's problem was that he got into theater late so he had no patience with the people he had to work with."

A less charitable opinion is that Walter was too opinionated, too argumentative, too domineering to deal with anyone more knowledgeable and less malleable than an impressionable young student.

"Walter Roberts had more dreams than talent," opined Stuart Culpepper, a well-known veteran Atlanta actor. "He was one of those men I didn't want to pursue a friendship with because I never quite trusted him. He was quite pompous, something of a con man I think. Anyway, he just didn't fit in with anything. It was a workshop for kids. I don't think there was any substance there at all. My impression was that it was a very shoestring operation, run by family members and close friends."

Another veteran of the Atlanta theater scene echoed Culpepper's assessment of Walter. "Whenever I talked to Walter I had an idea in the back of my head that he didn't really know much," Ed Danos confided. A former director and one of the founders of The Pocket Theater, Danos was on the scene throughout the years Walter and Betty operated The Workshop.

"Walter was somebody on the fringes of society and, frankly, I didn't have a good impression of him. There

20

was something about him that was not quite on the up-and-up. He was a little sleazy, a little oily. He seemed like somebody living hand-to-mouth. And I remember his clothes never seemed pressed, and he always seemed to be wearing the same baggy, nondescript dark suit.

"But his assurance had to come from somewhere, not just from his family," Danos concluded, referring to Walter's overwhelming self-confidence.

One of the few people to take both Walter Roberts and his workshop seriously was Terry Kay, veteran drama critic of the *Atlanta Constitution*. "The Workshop was a real serious attempt to create the first repertory company in Atlanta," Kay said. "Walter had a tremendously intense feeling toward theater, and a zest for what he was doing, so ultimately it hurt him deeply that he did not get the attention he wanted. But, truthfully, although his ideas and ambitions were good, his productions didn't live up to them. He never had enough time, enough talent.

"He was a tough man, very short-tempered," Kay recalled, adding, "I liked him and respected him, but I also thought he was unreasonable at times. He felt he knew more about theater than anyone in Atlanta. He was passionate and temperamental, and he didn't like criticism. Walter was the kind of guy who argued with you because *his* interpretation was the *only* interpretation," Kay continued. "He had a drive to teach because he was ambitious. He was trying to establish a school that would have his name stamped on it. But he was headstrong, the kind of guy who would fight the system too head-first."

Despite the difficulties Walter had in dealing with adults, and they were obviously legion, he had an incredible impact on his young students, most of whom idolized him.

21

"Rob didn't act like an ordinary adult we'd ever seen," explained Philip De Poy. "He was outside mainstream adult behavior. To us, he was an *artiste*, something most of us had never met before. He didn't put on a suit or go to an office. He wore sweat shirts or a shirt, jeans, and loafers. He was absolutely the coolest man I'd ever met."

Yolanda King, who considered the Roberts clan to be her "second family" and who often babysat for tiny Julia and Lisa, also recalled Walter being a "larger than life person."

"He was a cauldron of energy. He seemed to be bubbling over with it," she said. "I remember feeling very comfortable with him, never intimidated, even though he had a temper. He would scream and rant, but I think he was very paternal, very protective. I think he represented a father figure to me."

So, regardless of his financial difficulties, the late Sixties were heady days for Walter, who was acting out his dream of writing and producing plays as the titular head of the Workshop, with Betty at his side, directing many of the productions, handling the costuming and also teaching.

It wasn't until after Julia was born, that Betty began devoting more of her time to running the household than she did the workshop, although she remained in charge of costumes and continued to act as the Workshop's publicist. "I wore out shoes taking press releases around personally to the newspapers so they couldn't say 'Oh, it must've gotten lost in the mail,' " Betty would later recall, adding she had spent hours begging for publicity. "We built the Showmobile with our own hands," she once said, "but nobody ever cared to take a picture of it."

In the six years the theater group was in existence,

the students performed throughout Atlanta—at Piedmont Park, at nearby Stone Mountain, at various shopping malls and, of course, in the black neighborhoods of downtown Atlanta. In 1966 Walter even produced a local television kiddie show, a thirteen-week Saturday morning series on Atlanta's Channel 11, starring Betty as a character called Bum Bum.

And yet, despite the sacrifice, the originality and the hard labors of both Betty and Walter, the workshop never garnered any true attention; and Walter's dream of making a name for himself never became a reality. Nor did he ever gain the respect he felt he deserved from his peers within local theater circles. "It was children's theater," explained a former acquaintance, "and that just didn't add up to much, really."

Not true, said Philip De Poy. "The Workshop may have not been financially successful but it created a lot of artists. Kids came out of it with their lives in the arts. It's absolutely no coincidence that Eric is such a fine actor. He started acting when he was just a little kid and it was difficult for him because he was smaller than the rest of us. But," De Poy added, "he was the cutest kid in the entire universe. I remember Rob telling me one time that the most memorable moment in his life was when he was holding Eric's hand, running down a hill towards a ferris wheel. Eric and Rob *did* have a special relationship."

De Poy had no idea as to why Walter and Eric had such a special relationship. Nor could he have known that it had been forged in the fires of unhappiness. In fact, it wouldn't be until years later that Eric, after having undergone several years of psychoanalysis, would begin to discuss his childhood, the first five years of which he claims were spent in silence.

According to Eric, he did not speak until he was around five years old. Then, when he did begin talking, it was with a pronounced stutter, something he still works to overcome. Whether it's genetic, since Betty also has a stutter, or the result of some childhood trauma, is unclear. But the speech impediment made Eric's life a virtual nightmare as soon as he was enrolled in elementary school.

The children laughed at his stuttering whenever he was called upon to read aloud, something he dreaded and which, of course, made him stutter that much more. "Then one day my father discovered me in my room memorizing things and talking into a mirror," Eric explained not long ago. "He realized that when I memorized words I was less afraid to present myself. Otherwise, I would just go off into my little peculiar world."

Thus, in an attempt not to be the butt of his classmates joke, Eric began memorizing everything he thought he might possibly have to read aloud in school. "If I didn't get it memorized first, I thought I would stutter and the class would laugh. But what really bothered me more than that," he explained, "was that I was always so much shorter than the other kids. I was short until I was fifteen and then I grew six inches in ten months."

So while the other students read their allotted passages, Eric strained to commit his to memory. This worked well, except for the times the teacher would inexplicably call on students in an order Eric hadn't anticipated. In those rare instances, Eric learned to master his upcoming passages at breakneck speed. Although this made him a quick study, which proved useful as an actor in later life, the tension of awaiting his name to be called filled him with anxiety and made him want to retreat from the cruelty of his tormenters. Thus he claims to have spent much of his early years in an imaginary world, peopled by imaginary friends and an imaginary playmate, a smooth-talking, non-stuttering pal whom Eric named "Jimmy."

Then during a Saturday afternoon matinee at a local movie house Eric saw the classic John Wayne western, *Red River*, and his fantasies changed. He pictured himself as a cowboy, someone who was respected and lived by their own rules and cared not what anybody thought of them. Of course, those cowboys didn't have a father. And Eric adored his father. Walter Roberts was then, and remains to this day, the one person Eric idolized, the one person whose opinion desperately mattered, the one person who loved him unconditionally and without reservation.

"My father was a gentle giant," Eric has told all who would listen. "My father was the most educated man I've ever known. And because I didn't talk so well when I was a kid I got into reading. We didn't even have a TV. I had to go over to a friend's house to watch 'Leave it To Beaver.'

"Anyway, I remember my father always spoke with such wisdom, but in a way that was never condescending. I was only eight years old when I read *The Glass Menagerie* and when I got older I realized I had become educated peripherally because of books.

"My father was my book pal. He was my best friend, my teacher, my dad, and I loved him."

To all who beheld them, Betty and Walter Roberts appeared to have an incredibly solid relationship. They lived together. They worked together. They performed together. And they balanced each other. Walter was intense, moody, somber, and always frowning, while Betty was the exact opposite, an outgoing dishwater blonde with a ready laugh and a great smile.

"I liked Betty," said Terry Kay. "She was always very lively and had more personality than Walter. He was too wrapped up in his sincere intentions to be a great teacher and director. I think she tried to bridge the distance Walter had set up. She was responsible for a lot of the attention Walter received."

"Betty looked like a movie star," recalled Philip De Poy. "She had luxurious hair and a glamorous attitude. She was just a really neat person and Walter was very handsome, very intense. They seemed to be the perfect couple."

Beneath the perfect exteriors, however, there rested great discontent within both Walter and Betty. He was frustrated by his inability to achieve recognition. She was dissatisfied with their lifestyle and tired of their poverty-line existence. As their individual frustrations grew, the couple's late-into-the-night arguments grew more frequent and increasingly nasty until there was a wide gulf, rather than love, between them.

In February, 1971, in an apparent attempt to appease Betty, Walter purchased a modest three-bedroom, one bath, white brick and stucco home at 432 Eighth Street, just across the street from Grady High School, where Eric was enrolled as a sophomore. But it was too late to save the marriage. It had already disintegrated.

On June 13, only four months after Walter took possession of the $17,800 bungalow, Betty filed for divorce. A month later the couple reached an agreement regarding the support and custody of the children, who were to live with Betty. In an attempt to keep the children's lives intact, Betty was to assume the mortgage on the house,

26

and to receive the couple's 1968 Volkswagen. Walter agreed to provide $195 in monthly child support payments and in return was granted generous visitation rights.

"We lived as a family unit until I was twelve. Then Mom took the girls away," Eric would bitterly explain years later. "There will be very much debate over this fact."

From all outward appearances, however, the dissolution of the sixteen-year marriage seemed amicable. Whatever rancor the two felt toward each other had been set aside, probably for the sake of the children. Thus it was a smooth road that lead to the couple's final divorce decree, which was issued on January 28, 1972.

"I never saw any trouble," De Poy admitted, "but I also wasn't shocked when they split up. The relationship seemed more like two artists working together who incidentally happened to be married."

Not long after Betty filed for divorce, Walter mounted a final Actors Workshop production, an innovative and controversial adaptation of *The Owl and The Pussycat*, in which he cast Yolanda King starring opposite a white male actor. Unlike his other creative stretches, such as when he rewrote Shakespeare's *Taming of the Shrew* and set it as a western in Texas, *Owl* was a daring ploy in the deep South of the Seventies and was not well-received by either the local drama critics or the theater-going public, white *and* black. "People were saying my father was turning over in his grave," Yolanda recalled. "People even threatened to leave my father's church. My grandfather, the Rev. Martin Luther King, Sr., decided he was not coming. But, at the last minute, he did come to the premiere.

"I think Walter saw *Owl* as a way to rejuvenate the

company," Yolanda confided, "but it was too daring. It was artistically successful, but financially it was not."

After a two-week run, the play closed, taking with it Walter's dream of a successful career in the theater. Instead of fame and recognition, he found a steady income a few months later as a vacuum cleaner salesman at Rich's department store in downtown Atlanta.

"My dad ended up selling vacuum cleaners and my mom got a job as a secretary," Julia would reflect years later. "They never got rich and they never got famous, but they showed me that you do things for a purpose, and if it treats you well, then all the better. But if it goes away, you won't die. You must move on."

And so Walter and Betty moved on in entirely different directions, each of them ending tragically in their own way.

Chapter Two

After vacating the Eighth Street house shortly after Betty filed for divorce in June, 1971, Walter had moved into a comfortable apartment in Ansley Forest, a large complex of brick and white frame colonial apartments not far from the house and the children. Life, it seemed, had returned to normal.

Since Betty had begun dating a man named Michael Motes within a month of receiving her final divorce decree, she often left the children with Walter on the weekends, which was fine with him because, above all, Walter Roberts loved his children. Together the foursome—Walter, Eric, Lisa, and Julia—would sing songs, play games, go to "flicks," as Walter loved to describe movies, draw with crayons, and just generally have a good time.

More than twenty years later, Julia would still remember those happy days she spent with her father. "I had a great relationship with my dad," she told a writer in early 1991. "Nothing intellectual, just really caring and fun, singing the Oompa-Loompas song or drawing and painting."

One summer day, not long after he'd moved into his new apartment, Walter was walking down the sidewalk of the complex, holding Lisa by one hand, Julia by the other, when they encountered one of Walter's neighbors, a pretty young woman named Eileen Sellars. The two stopped to briefly talk, at which point Julia reportedly introduced her father, telling Eileen: "This is my Daddy. His name is Walter. But you can call him Daddy!"

Several weeks after this exchange Walter asked Eileen out on a date. Julia, as it turned out, had been a matchmaker at age five. The first few months of 1972 were happy ones for Walter. Not only did he have a pretty and exceptionally nice young girlfriend, he had unlimited access to his children. For the first time in his life, he also had a regular job and was actually making money. He had to, of course, because he was supporting his children, a deeply felt responsibility he had taken on without qualms.

Five months into the new year, however, trouble reared its ugly head when according to court documents filed by Walter, Eric and Michael Motes, Betty's boyfriend got into a physical altercation. Two nights later, on a rainy Saturday night in May, Betty ordered Eric out of the house. By that time Betty was no longer living in the Eighth Street house, having been unable to keep up the mortgage payments. Instead she was living with Motes in his hometown of Smyrna, a rural community about a half hour's drive northwest of Atlanta.

Unable to reach either his father or Eileen, who apparently were out on a date, in desperation Eric called Eileen's mother, Virginia, whom he was very fond of, and asked her if she could pick him up. Somehow the skinny fifteen-year old had managed to get from Smyrna to downtown Atlanta.

Getting in her car, Virginia Sellars drove downtown and picked up Eric. "I felt so sorry for him," she later told her sister. "He couldn't get in touch with his father and he didn't have any money. He was just soaking wet and he was so upset he was stuttering something awful."

Years later Eric would claim that upon hearing what had befallen him, his father had immediately gone to the police and had Motes arrested. But there is no record of Walter Roberts having ever pressed charges against Motes or of Motes having been arrested.

After the incident, whatever dislike Eric had previously felt for his mother became magnified a hundred fold. The two would rarely speak from that time forth.

Eric never lived under Betty's roof again. Instead he went to live with Walter. Returning to high school after that fateful Saturday night, Eric would begin telling classmates his parents had died in a boating accident and that he was living with an aunt and uncle. Several years later, in early interviews he would tell magazine writers that his mother was dead. Thus that one rainy night in Georgia marked the beginning of the end for any semblance of closeness the Roberts family might have continued to enjoy in the future. Eric finished his sophomore year at Grady High School, then flew to London, where he studied acting during a summer session of the prestigious Royal Academy of Dramatic Arts. "My father busted his butt selling vacuum cleaners so that I could study acting with the best teachers after I told him I wanted to be an actor," Eric would proudly explain years later.

Not long after Eric departed for London, Betty bundled up Lisa and Julia and, without Walter's knowledge, took them to Minnesota to visit their grandmother in Minneapolis, and then for a two-month stay at her brother's summer camp, Camp Birchwood, at Cass Lake. When she returned to Atlanta on September 13, 1972, she had become Mrs. Michael Motes.

One month later, Walter sued to gain permanent custody of his children. In his petition, Walter cited the fight between Eric and Michael Motes, claiming Motes "struck without cause our minor son, Eric, and injured him," and that Betty had subsequently "ordered Eric from the home and refused thereafter to care for him."

According to court documents, Walter further alleged that Michael Motes "has and continues to mistreat our minor children" and that "during the winter months our daughters had colds, appeared extremely tired and listless, and had fevers." The petition also stated that Betty had "neglected the minor children by staying out late at night without providing any adult care and supervision" during her absence.

Betty's response was to quickly file her own petition, accusing Walter of having removed "a large number of items from the house, including furniture, appliances, clothing, and art objects" and of being "delinquent" in his child support and of "telling malicious lies to the minor children concerning her behavior in order to prejudice them and induce them to leave her custody."

A court order, issued on October 30, awarded Betty temporary custody of Lisa and Julia, while Walter retained custody of Eric. At that time the court also ordered Michael and Betty and Walter to meet with a court-appointed psychologist to determine the final custody of the children. Two months later Betty was awarded permanent custody of the two girls and, although Eric was to remain with him, Walter received only limited visitation rights to his daughters—two weeks during the summer and either Christmas Day or Christmas Eve.

The same month, January, 1973, that Betty was awarded custody of Lisa and Julia, the family's former home on Eighth Street, which Betty had received in the divorce, was auctioned off to the highest bidder on the Fulton County courthouse steps after having been foreclosed upon for non-payment of its $136 a month mortgage. By that time, of course, Betty and the girls were living in Smyrna.

If Betty believed she was bettering her life by marrying Michael Motes, she was soon in for a rude awakening. Michael Motes was in worse financial straits than Walter Roberts had ever been. In fact, two months after their September wedding, Michael Motes was sued for $260 in back rent on an apartment he'd leased in Smyrna. It was the first of more than a half dozen lawsuits that would be filed against either Michael or Betty Motes over the next ten years.

Ironically, Betty was sued by an insurance agency for non-payment of a bill only five days prior to being awarded custody of Lisa and Julia on January 31, 1973. Had Walter known of Betty's dire financial straits he might have been able to win the custody battle. But he didn't know. No one knew, except for Lisa and Julia, who often overheard their mother and stepfather arguing loudly late into the night. It wasn't until the girls were older, however, that they realized the root of the on-going disputes had been money, namely a lack of it.

Why Betty married Michael Motes, who is eleven

years her junior, and only eleven years older than Eric, was a mystery to everyone who knew either of them. It's now apparently also a puzzle even to Betty who several years ago proclaimed the union to have been "the worst mistake of my life." But at the time she apparently was quite smitten with him.

The couple first met when Betty appeared in a Smyrna community theater production of *Arsenic and Old Lace*, and Michael, then a writer assigned to the drama desk of *The Atlanta Constitution*, was in the audience. Whether he reviewed the play or not is unclear. But he was introduced to Betty that night and the two began dating soon afterward. Oddly enough, it would be the only play Betty would appear in for many years. "I never felt it was fair to the kids for me to work all day, and then spend all evening in rehearsals," she would explain. "I did it and I enjoyed it, but I came home and said 'This isn't fun.' I was working all day and I had no time for the kids."

Tall and somewhat heavyset, with a pale complexion and horn-rimmed glasses, Michael Motes was the antithesis of Walter Roberts, who cut a dashing figure with his intense, brooding good looks, flashing dark eyes and eloquent dissertations on everything from the Vietnam War to the stupidity of the Atlanta Arts Council. Perhaps it was precisely because of these differences that Betty was attracted to Motes.

Not only was the bespectacled Motes unprepossessing in appearance, he was for the most part remembered as quiet and withdrawn, a "weird-acting, weird-looking" fellow with little ambition, more remembered by his co-workers for the obvious hairpieces he wore than for anything else.

According to a former school classmate, Michael Motes was always "strange . . . a sissy type. He was totally bald even in high school. With a round, clean-shaven face and this dark brown hair piece, he was definitely weird."

The childhood victim of alopecia, a disease which causes severe hair loss, Motes was self-conscious about his resulting baldness, a situation no doubt especially embarrassing during his teen years, which is when he apparently began wearing hairpieces.

"They weren't very attractive and they were very obviously hairpieces, sort of reddish colored," recalled a former Motes associate. "I remember he came into the office one day with a different hairpiece. Same color but obviously a different hair piece. But he didn't seem to care. He was a funny guy with sort of a comedian's look, sort of your typical second banana. He was the comic relief.

"Anyway, he wore those wigs until Betty convinced him not to, I guess, because after they were married he stopped and just went around bald."

According to a former co-worker, "Motes was a rather laid back and casual kind of guy who didn't seem to have much ambition. He had sort of a rumpled look, not the kind of guy who posed for magazine covers."

Born and raised in Smyrna and, like Lisa and Julia, a graduate of Campbell High School, according to an acquaintance, Michael Motes has spent most of his adult life shuffling from job to job, enduring lengthy periods of unemployment during which he invariably would fall behind in his bills, only to be rescued from the brink of financial disaster by his hard-working mother.

Thus, with or without his hairpiece, Betty's union with Michael Motes was anything but a marriage made in heaven. It was fraught with turmoil and angst from its bad beginning to its nasty end. In the process, it became fertile ground for the seeds of dysfunction which, initially sown during Betty's first marriage, would ultimately yield an emotional instability that would haunt Eric, and victimize Julia, in varying degrees and various ways, throughout their adult lives.

"After my parents divorced, we pretty much stayed in Smyrna—me, my mother, and sister Lisa," Julia would explain to reporters inquiring about her childhood. "Atlanta isn't far, but we didn't go there much."

Indeed, Betty and the girls did move to Smyrna almost immediately after the divorce. They then spent the first five years of her eleven-year marriage to Motes living in a series of low-rent houses there while fending off a variety of creditors' lawsuits.

One of the more intriguing lawsuits, because it underscores the severity of the Motes financial situation, was filed on March 21, 1974, by Rich's department store and involved a bad check written by Michael Motes the previous December. Although the check was for the paltry sum of $23.33, neither Michael nor Betty apparently made any attempt to settle the debt—until Betty had her wages garnished on June 18.

It must have been an embarrassing situation for her, since she was then working at the *Georgia Bulletin,* a newspaper produced by the Catholic Archdiocese in Atlanta, but she made her peace with it. She continued to live with Motes for another ten years.

Unlike the nearby community of Marietta, with its quaint town square filled with restaurants and antique stores, Smyrna is a loosely knit community of shopping malls and yuppie apartment complexes with no real core. It's a sleepy Atlanta bedroom community.

In 1988, shortly before the Democratic convention was to convene in Atlanta, *National Geographic* deemed

Smyrna to be "a redneck city," a label loudly protested by the local gentry, who prefer to think of their town as "the jonquil city" in honor of abundantly blooming flowers that cover its hillsides during spring.

Other than the fact that Julia Roberts once lived there, Smyrna's only claim to fame is that the Battle of Smyrna on July 4, 1864, was the last major Confederate battle fought before Sherman's assault on Atlanta. In fact, it was from the top of nearby Vinings Hill, the highest point in the area, that Sherman watched the burning of Atlanta. It was into this quiet, rather lifeless, habitat that Betty moved herself and her two young daughters upon her marriage to Michael Motes, a long-time member of the Sons of The Confederacy and an avid collector of *Gone With The Wind* memorabilia.

While Betty and Michael Motes were trying to balance their checkbook in rural Smyrna, Walter was enjoying life, even though he remained concerned about the girls' welfare. He was dating Eileen and had worked his way up from department store salesman to being the Eureka vacuum cleaner rep for the Macy's chain of department stores in Atlanta.

A legal secretary with an English degree from Georgia State University and a Masters degree from Florida State, Eileen was the opposite of Betty, not only physically but in personality. Whereas Betty was a bubbly outgoing blonde, Eileen was a quiet and studious brunette who, with her dark brown hair, brown eyes, beautiful smile, and perfectly aligned teeth, bore a certain resemblance to Mary Tyler Moore.

"Eileen was a very shy person, a very conservative person in both her manner and her dress. Walter brought her out,'' explained Eileen's aunt, Vivien McKinley. ''She was like a flower that bloomed. He liked her to wear her hair down. He even bought some of her dresses, things that she would never have bought herself. I often thought maybe she had a calming effect on him. He was so upset about the girls, you know, that he saw them so seldom. But he seemed crazy about her and they seemed happy together. I think they adored each other, really. Walter was very likable, very charming, and handsome. He was really a delightful person, a good conversationalist, and *very* dramatic.''

On April 4, 1974, Walter and Eileen were married in a quiet civil ceremony. Walter was forty. Eileen was twenty-eight, only ten years older than her newly acquired stepson, Eric.

After Eric graduated from Grady High that summer, Walter no longer needed to reside in the neighborhood. So the couple moved to an apartment complex in Stone Mountain, Georgia, where they rented a three-bedroom apartment and blended Eileen's antiques and Walter's contemporary furniture into the sophisticated look of a New York apartment.

Several months later, apparently believing his new marital status might make a difference in his quest to regain custody of Lisa and Julia, Walter made one final attempt to dislodge the girls from Betty's grasp. He filed a second petition on June 20, 1974, only two days after Betty had received notice of her garnishment, seeking greater visitation rights with his two daughters.

While the Cobb County court was busy determining the merit of Walter's petition, and Betty's counterclaims against it, a bizarre bit of further bad luck found its way to the Motes' home, which was then a small brick bungalow in need of repair, situated next door to a service station, almost directly below a huge round water tower, at 154 Privette Road in Smyrna.

The entire family was sound asleep when suddenly there was a series of loud insistent knocks on the front door. When Motes opened it, he was confronted with members of the local narcotics squad, search warrant in hand, who were looking for drugs after receiving a tip that if they went to that address they would find a stash of drugs secreted in a hollowed-out Bible on the living room coffee table.

Sure enough, according to Troy Ballinger, one of the police officers who was present during the raid, there on a coffee table in the living room was a Bible, its hollowed-out core containing the drugs. Despite the evidence, however, neither Betty nor Michael were arrested.

"The husband started crying," recalled Ballinger. "He got really upset and began wringing his hands, saying he had young children in the house and how he would never have drugs around them. And then the wife said the stuff had probably been planted by her ex-husband. As I recall, they were involved in some court problems at the time.

"Anyway things just didn't fit. So we never charged them, and the whole thing was dropped. I do remember, though, that the house was kind of dumpy on the outside, but the furnishings inside were nice and the house was well-kept."

Whether or not Walter had planted the drugs in the house in a desperate attempt to win custody of his daughters is unknown. There is no evidence that either he or Eric, at that time at least, had any connections into the world of drugs.

Although Ballinger does not recall appearing in court on behalf of Betty during the custody hearing conducted a short while later in mid-July, chances are the subject of the raid was introduced because Walter was subsequently restrained from going near the house, or even being on the block of Privette Road where the house was located.

According to a final court ruling issued August 8, 1974, Betty was ordered to notify Walter through her attorney on a semi-annual basis what provisions she had made for the supervision of Lisa and Julia during the hours they were not in school, provide a list of clothing purchased for them, and obtain medical and dental examinations for them on a regular basis.

With his visitation rights still restricted to Christmas Day or Christmas Eve, plus two weeks in the summer, the only gain Walter made in this last futile attempt to spend more time with his daughters was that the court granted him one Wednesday night fifteen-minute telephone call to each child between seven and seven-thirty P.M. on a weekly basis. But even then, Betty often managed to keep the children from talking to him, either by hanging up on him or by not telling the girls their father was on the line.

"It was terrible, just plain meanness on her part," recalled a friend of Walter's. "She kept the little girls away from Walter's parents, too, for the most part. But I know that whenever Mrs. Roberts, Walter's mother, was allowed to see them, which wasn't very often, Walter would either call and talk to them, or sneak up there to see them. I don't know how they managed to keep that a secret from Betty, but somehow they did."

"It tore him up," confirmed Vivien McKinley, Eileen's aunt, referring to Walter's inability to spend time with Lisa and Julia. "It tormented him that he didn't get to see the little girls. And that upset Eileen. I remember

40

her saying 'It's just not fair. He's a good father. He needs them and they need him.' "

According to a friend of the couple, Walter was obsessed about having been cut off from the girls. So was Eric. Together the father and son spent hours talking about their dream of someday getting the girls back and being a family once again. "Walter and Eric were both obsessed with that dream," recalled a friend. "I remember Eric used to talk about how he was going to go to Hollywood and become a big star and they'd all live together happily ever after. But, of course, even though Eric did become a movie star, it never happened, did it?"

According to people who knew him then, Eric was a handsome young man with total confidence in his ability to become a movie star. "He was very confident of what he was doing, and very keen on what he was doing, and believed he was going to be successful," a close family friend recalled, adding, "I remember Eric telling his father, 'I'll win an Academy Award and we'll all be in Hollywood together.'

"A lot of the conversations between Walter and Eric were about Eric becoming an actor. Walter was very proud of Eric's achievements and looking forward to him being a big success."

With the exception of his frustration over the girls, Walter seemed happy and content in his new life with Eileen. "Whenever I met him after the divorce there was never any mention of Betty," recalled Philip De Poy. "It was like she had never existed."

Together Walter and Eileen went to Atlanta's various art houses to catch a late night offering of a new avant garde film, Walter's favorite film genre. Often they entertained at home, preparing the food together, like they did for their first wedding anniversary. "Walter liked to entertain," said Eileen's aunt. "He enjoyed good wine and he liked to cook, which was good because Eileen wasn't much of a cook, although Walter did manage to teach her a thing or two about it."

In 1976 Walter had the opportunity to buy a townhouse in the Atlanta suburb of Riverdale, and he grabbed it. It was only the second home he would ever own and he and Eileen were as excited as kids about having their own house.

By then, Eric was residing full time in New York, supposedly living at a YMCA, slowly making his way up the ladder of success as a stage actor, while working at odd jobs to support himself. One of his brief ventures, he would later confess, was into the world of books at a New York bookstore on the corner of thirty-fourth and Broadway. But it didn't last long. He was, he later told a reporter, fired for stealing some of the merchandise.

By the end of 1975, Eric had appeared in several off-Broadway productions and at Joseph Papp's prestigious Public Theater, as well as in a roadshow revival of *A Streetcar Named Desire* in which he starred opposite Shirley Knight. Then, in December, 1976, he got his first big break by landing the recurring role of Ted Bancroft on the NBC soap opera, *Another World*. Six weeks later, however, he was let go.

"I kept falling over furniture," he would later laugh. "I would walk across the set and break a chair. I was the world's worst soap opera actor."

Walter was quite naturally entranced by Eric's daily appearances on *World*. He would stop whatever he was doing at the appointed hour and head straight to the Macy's electronics department, where he would stand spellbound, watching his son, pointing him out to co-workers and anyone else who ventured by. "My dad was so proud," Eric would recall years later, "he'd go into department stores and watch me on eight TVs at once."

It was in a teen magazine interview during his brief stint on *Another World* that Eric first told a reporter his mother was deceased. "Eileen was surprised by that, and so was I," her aunt recalled. "But Eric was so bitter against Betty that I thought, well, maybe in his mind she *is* dead."

Despite his frustration with Betty who had managed to wrest total control of the girls from him, Walter was determined to enjoy life as much as possible. One year he agreed to be the voice of Macy's Talking Christmas Tree which, prominently placed in the store's window, would speak to the children as they stood there in wonder. It was the only performance Walter ever gave after shutting down The Actor's Workshop following his divorce.

Another year Walter and Eric spent almost six months building a huge dollhouse together as a surprise Christmas present for Lisa and Julia. "Most of their year was planned around those two weeks in the summer. Eric and Walter spent hours talking about when the girls were old enough to choose, maybe they'd want to live with Walter," recalled Eileen's aunt.

"Eileen told me that Eric used to say 'When I'm famous I'm going to buy a big home in Hollywood and we can all live out there.' They were the dreams of a kid, of course. But it really saddens me to think about how much Walter put into that dream with Eric and how he never lived to see any of it."

Since his time with Lisa and Julia was so limited, Walter wrote the girls letters, one of which Julia has managed to hold on to through the years. It was written only months before his death. "I have a letter from my daddy that he wrote to me on July 6, 1977," Julia said not long ago. "It's the only letter I managed not to lose as a child. If anybody ever took that away from me, I would just be destroyed. It doesn't mean anything to anybody else, yet I can read that letter ten times a day and it moves me in a different way every time."

The letter was written around the time that Walter took Lisa and Julia to New York to visit Eric, who by then was becoming an established actor. The four spent two weeks together, with Eric showing them the sights. It was fourteen days that Julia, even though she was not yet ten, would never forget.

Returning to Atlanta, Walter sadly dropped the little girls off to be picked up by Betty and drove home to Eileen. He was despondent over the realization that he would not get to see them again until Christmas. But Eileen cheered him up, reminding him that they had made plans to spend an upcoming September weekend at Lake Lanier.

Vivien McKinley vividly recalls the Friday afternoon Eileen and Walter departed for the lake, where Walter had rented a houseboat. "They stopped by my office and Eileen was real excited because she was going to study to be a court reporter and had bought her machine the night before. I always remember her saying to me 'Do you think I'm finally on my way?' because she really hadn't found what she wanted to do. But, after working for lawyers, she'd really gotten interested in being a court stenographer.

"Anyway, I could see out the front door into the parking lot and Eileen's green Maverick was out there with a canoe strapped on top of it. Since I knew she couldn't swim I said 'Now, Eileen, don't you get in that boat. You know how easily those things tip over and you can't

44

swim.' And she said, 'Oh, don't worry, I've got a life jacket.' "

Sunday, September 18, 1977, dawned bright and sunny and unseasonably warm, which is probably why Eileen and Eric, who was in Atlanta visiting his father, decided to go for a canoe ride. It was around 9:30 a.m. when they paddled away, leaving Walter still inside the houseboat moored in a cove in the Six Mile Creek area of the Lake Lanier. So Walter never saw the speedboat that created the waves that began violently rocking the canoe. He never saw Eileen jump up in a panic and fall overboard. He didn't know that Eileen had decided not to wear a life jacket because "it was too hot." He only heard Eric screaming for help, and by then it was too late. Eileen never surfaced.

According to the police report, Eric made numerous attempts to save his stepmother, but they were to no avail. "She slipped away," he told the reporting officer. Although the rescue unit arrived within fifteen minutes of being notified of the accident, and immediately began dragging the lake, it was several hours before Eileen's body was located.

Three days after the accident Eileen Roberts was laid to rest clutching a small nose gay in her folded hands. She was thirty-one years old and, her aunt Vivien recalled, "looked beautiful, just like she was sleeping." The tiny nose gay was from Eric.

Walter was inconsolable after Eileen's death. Four days after the funeral, he telephoned Vivien McKinley to tell her Eric would be bringing over some of Eileen's clothes and began crying so uncontrollably that he had to hang up the phone almost in mid-sentence. About a month later, Walter called Vivien again. He had been on a weekend retreat, he said, adding he was "a little more at peace with himself." However, he also confided he hadn't been feeling well, physically. He still had the cough that had been worrying Eileen for months and he was having difficulty swallowing.

At first believing that Walter's throat problem might be a psychosomatic reaction to Eileen's tragic death, his doctors sent him to a psychiatrist. When that proved not to be the problem, he went into the Emory University hospital for tests. "After I'd talked to Walter that last time, he was supposed to call me. But I didn't hear from him for several weeks," Vivien recalled. "Then one day his mother called and told me Walter was in the hospital. 'They're doing some tests,' she said, 'and he wanted me to let you know he hadn't forgotten you.' "

Vivien never heard another word from either Walter or his mother. One Sunday morning, not more than a month later, Vivien was reading the local newspaper and stumbled across a death notice. Walter Roberts had died of throat cancer on December 3, 1977, less than three months after Eileen had drowned. He had gone into the hospital two months before and had never come out. He was forty-three years old and had never smoked a day in his life. Eric, who had been at his father's bedside throughout the ordeal, was emotionally devastated by Walter's death. Yet he somehow managed to take care of all the funeral arrangements.

"It was more a celebration of Walter's life than a funeral," recalled a friend. "People he'd known stood up and told anecdotes about him. And the music was lovely. I remember they played one of Walter's favorites, the theme song from *Romeo and Juliet*. He would have loved it because it was theatrical, not at all your typical funeral.''

Accompanied by Betty, Julia and Lisa attended the funeral. Although Julia was then barely ten years old, as an adult, she would often refer to her father's death and what a distinct impact it had made on her.

"My childhood was real weird to me," she would confess years later. "I feel likc I grew up twice. Once till I was about ten. After that it was completely different. My father died around then, which probably changed me a lot more than I realized. I don't think I'd be what I am today if that hadn't happened. It was just a rough time.

"I miss my dad," she'd added. "I don't feel that boundless injustice over his death anymore, which is good, because that's not a fun bag to carry. It was just something that happened to me. It's funny that I said that," she continued after a lengthy pause, "because his death happened to a lot of people. But when I was nine years old, it felt like this was done to *me*. Now I look at it as, I can talk to him whenever I want. He's everywhere I go."

There is no question that Walter's death left a tremendous void in ten-year-old Julia's life. As the years passed, however, it becomes clear that he also became an idealized father, an ethereal figure, a protector who could be summoned up at will to offer support and comfort in an otherwise cruel world. "I believe my father is with me every minute of the day, a force watching over me," Julia confided several years ago. "I feel I have a little extra guidance somewhere that maybe other people don't have."

Despite Julia's pain, and no doubt Lisa's as well, it was Eric who suffered the most because only he was old enough to truly realize how alone he was in the world. After all, within five years he had lost everyone he had ever loved, either by death or divorce.

"I remember after my father died," Eric would recall years later. "I was up in the attic at the house and I saw this old pile of trophies I had collected as a runner. It was difficult, but I resolved it all by telling myself that it 'ain't nothing but a memory.' And that's all anything really is, isn't it? A memory."

In the mid-Eighties Eric would be arrested for assaulting a police officer who was trying to prevent him from battering down the door of a New York apartment. He was drunk and incoherent, and was found to be in possession of two glass vials of cocaine. And yet, among the many bizarre statements Eric made to the arresting officer that night, was the comment, "My father died ten years ago today and he was cremated." The date of Eric's arrest? December 3, 1987, exactly ten years to the date of Walter Roberts' untimely death.

Chapter Three

By the time Walter Roberts had died, Betty and Michael Motes were the parents of a daughter, whom they'd named Nancy Dabbs Birmingham Motes, and the equally proud owners of a relatively expensive three-bedroom brick ranch situated on an acre lot on a tree-lined, kudzu-choked blacktop road meandering along the rural outskirts of Smyrna.

How they managed to scrape together enough money for a down payment, as well as find someone who would loan them money with their credit record, is unclear. The couple took possession of the Maner Road house in September, 1977, the same month that Eileen drowned.

Since Eileen had died without a will, all of her worldly possessions had automatically been inherited by Walter, who also had never bothered to prepare a will, most likely because he never had anything much to leave behind. But

Eileen had been frugal and had also inherited some money from her mother, Virginia Reeves Sellars, who had died only eighteen months before her daughter's own tragic death.

Thus, only two days before he died, Walter had weakly scrawled his signature on a last minute will, leaving everything he possessed to his children. The will, which was signed from his hospital bed and witnessed by two attending nurses, appointed Eric as guardian and trustee of the girls, as well as executor of his estate, which then amounted to $20,000 in certificates of deposits and whatever the couple's personal possessions would yield.

Following his father's last wishes, three weeks after Walter's funeral Eric petitioned the court, asking that the will be probated and that he be named guardian of Lisa, who was then twelve, and Julia, who was ten. Court documents reflect that a sheriff went to the Motes' residence to personally hand Lisa and Julia the court papers requesting their presence at a February, 1978, hearing.

On January 17, 1978, less than three weeks after learning of Eric's bid for executorship, Betty filed an objection on behalf of Lisa and Julia, seeking to overturn Walter's will and, in the process, have herself named trustee and guardian of the property. Betty's second choice was to have a bank appointed to that position. Her last option was that if Eric was allowed to serve in that capacity he be required to post a bond equal to double the amount of the estate.

"Eric Anthony Roberts is not a fit and proper person to serve as guardian and trustee," Betty explained in her petition. "He is a New York City actor with no regular income and caveators (Lisa and Julia) fear the waste of their inheritance."

In her objection Betty also stated that, since she had

50

not received "certain household goods, furniture, and furnishings" as outlined in her 1972 divorce from Walter, those items still belonged to her and that "by his failure to make mention or provision" of those items, Walter was "under a mistake of fact as to the estate he was able to bequeath."

Nine days later Eric petitioned the court to be named Eileen's executor. In the meantime, the scheduled February hearing was repeatedly continued and didn't take place until April 4, 1979, almost a year and a half after Walter's death.

In the interim, it had been discovered that, as the sole heir of her mother's estate, Eileen was worth almost five times more than originally estimated, thanks to a quarter interest she had inherited in a downtown office building which was in the process of being sold to the Georgia Department of Transportation. That was the good news. The bad news was that upon learning of Walter's will, another heir to the building, Barbara Louise Floyd Wood, had filed suit to have Walter's children dismissed as Eileen's legal heirs, which is how, of course, Betty and Eric discovered the true value of Eileen's estate.

Filed on February 22, 1978, the Wood lawsuit took up time and money. When Eric, Lisa, and Julia's claim to Eileen's estate was upheld by the Cobb County Superior Court, Barbara Wood filed an appeal. When that appeal failed in a Georgia district court, the case was then heard before the Georgia Supreme Court which, in a December 12, 1979, upheld the ruling of the lower court. Eric, Lisa, and Julia were declared to be the rightful heirs of Eileen Roberts. As such they were to receive $90,000 to be divided equally among them.

Shortly after having discovered their $90,000 windfall, Eric and Betty had resolved their differences about the girls' guardianship by having a Cobb County attorney, C.R. Vaughn, appointed to that position by the court. As a result, by the time Walter's will was finally probated, Betty had withdrawn her objections clearing the way for Eric to be appointed executor.

By the end of 1979 the money had been dispersed and placed in a trust fund under the control of C.R. Vaughn. Julia, then twelve years old, was worth more than $25,000.

After putting Walter and Eileen's condominium on the market, having their possessions either sold or stored, and filing his petition with the Clayton County court, Eric returned to New York. He would not return to Atlanta until 1984, the year his high school class had their reunion. "We gave out campy awards at the reunion," recalled Jeff Beck, a classmate. "And I remember Eric received an award for having grown the most because he was just a little guy when he was in school. I think he was about four-foot-eleven inches and weighed 100 pounds when he was a freshman."

Within a week of returning to New York Eric landed his first big movie role, and by February, in what must have been a bitter irony to him since his father had died only two months before, was appearing before the camera in *King of the Gypsies*. In what would turn out to be a strange coincidence, Susan Sarandon, who is now one of Julia's best friends, starred opposite Eric as his fortune-telling gypsy con-artist mother in the highly acclaimed film.

"The first time I saw *King of the Gypsies* was with my manager, Bill Trevsch, and I walked out into the parking lot with him afterwards and sobbed because it was such a shock," Eric would admit years later. "I had no idea if I was bad, good, or indifferent—it was just bigger than I was, and it made me nervous.''

When the film was released in 1979, it made Eric one of the hottest new faces in Hollywood. He was, as everyone who had known him as a youngster had predicted, well on his way to becoming that Hollywood movie star of his and Walter's dreams.

In rapid succession, Eric portrayed the romantic serviceman who brightened Sissy Spacek's life in *Raggedy Man*. He earned rave reviews for his performance opposite Mariel Hemingway in *Star 80*, the tragic story of Dorothy Stratten, the Playboy model, and more praise for his portrayal of Paulie in *The Pope of Greenwich Village*. He followed this with an Academy Award nomination as Best Supporting Actor for his work in the 1985 Andrei Konchalovsky film, *Runaway Train*.

Along the way to these heights, Eric also became the personification of an ''angry young man,'' routinely savaging his body in a series of accidents, heavy drinking, and drugs. Interestingly, in 1984, Eric's creative outlets and dreams of the future closely resembled those Julia would later espouse. He was, for instance, writing poetry and fantasizing about having children and living on a farm. Unlike Julia, however, he was also in the fast lane of life, recklessly fleeing his inner demons on motorcycles, Jeeps, and horses.

On June 4, 1981, for example, Eric was nearly killed in a freak accident while on his way home from visiting his then-girlfriend, Academy Award-winning actress Sandy Dennis, whose house was not far from his in Wilton, Connecticut.

According to Eric, he was driving a Jeep with the doors off, with Sandy's German shepherd beside him in the front seat. When the dog seemed to be falling out of the car, Eric tried to catch him and took his eyes off the road. When he looked up there was a tree directly in front of him. That was the last thing he remembered. The dog landed on its feet, but Eric remained hospitalized, near death and in a coma for three days.

When he finally awoke he had numerous broken bones and his face was swathed in bandages. His nose was smashed almost beyond repair and his face was slashed with large gashes. Despite four months of plastic surgery to rebuild Eric's face, his nose is crooked and he still carries a deep scar across his left eyebrow.

By the mid-Eighties, after having clashed with big talent agencies, alienated star-making producers and directors, Eric's star began descending. Even Mickey Rourke, another Hollywood bad boy, who co-starred with Eric in *The Pope of Greenwich Village*, supposedly referred to him as ''Eric the Strange.'' Thus, just as Julia's star began to rise, Eric found himself playing character actor instead of leading man, more often than not in low budget motion pictures and TV movies.

So Eric turned Walter's dreams of his success into a reality. The other half of that dream, however, was never to be. Lisa and Julia and Eric would never be a family in the truest sense. In fact, more than six years would pass before the three were reunited, and then only during brief visits, hardly enough time to re-establish a relationship that had been so abruptly ripped apart years before.

Eric would later claim that after his father's death, Betty had kept him at a distance and isolated from the girls. In a 1985 *Playboy* magazine article, Eric bluntly told an interviewer inquiring about his relationship with Betty that ''There has never been a relationship between us. I just don't like the woman.'' He'd added, ''It's as simple as that.''

But it isn't simple at all. It's never been simple. If it had been, Eric probably would not have almost destroyed what started out as a brilliant acting career through his violent, self-destructive behavior.

Since beginning psychoanalysis several years ago, Eric has apparently gained a much-needed insight into the negative forces that have driven him to anger and despair most of his adult life. Within the past eighteen months, he has begun confiding to people that his childhood was filled with physical abuse which stopped only after he exhibited his bruised body to his disbelieving father.

Whatever the truth—and the truth is known only to Eric himself—something certainly drove Eric to the brink of destruction, and it's doubtful it was only his parents' divorce. ''I've made plenty of mistakes and I don't want to make excuses for myself,'' Eric told a reporter last year, ''but so much has been unresolved in my life because of my mother and because my father died before I came into my own. I realized now those things left a huge void in me, which I filled with artistic creation and, at the same time, self-destruction.''

Despite this newly acquired perception of the causes behind his own emotional instability, Eric still remains estranged from his mother and, sadly, from Julia who remains her mother's staunchest ally, refusing to believe there is any merit in Eric's recollections of what occurred within the family before—and after—the divorce.

So, despite his decades-old dream of being reunited as a family, the truth is that, with almost a dozen years of age difference between them, Eric and his two sisters followed different paths and grew up as virtual strangers.

Lamentably, by the time Lisa and Julia had become teenagers and were able to make their own decisions, they discovered they had very little in common with their older brother. Indeed their only real common bond was their love of acting.

"I love Julia dearly. Julia's very beautiful, she's very bright, she's very everything. I see what I like to think I helped her accomplish and what she accomplished on her own. I'm nothing but proud," Eric told a reporter in 1992. And yet, although Julia has publicly described their relationship as being "complex but close," the truth is, alienated by their conflicting feelings about Betty, the two have not spoken in several years. Nor was Eric invited to Julia's wedding to Lyle Lovett last summer.

It's difficult to imagine the emotions that must have flooded over Eric, when he learned from news reports that his baby sister had married and that, despite his decades-old dream of being a family again, he had not been extended an invitation to the ceremony, a rejection made even more glaring by his mother's gratuitous comments to the media.

"Julia's brother Eric wasn't there," Betty had explained to inquiring reporters. "He wasn't invited. Julia was afraid he would make trouble."

What an apparent triumph for Betty and what a sad ending to the saga of the Roberts family, a house divided by twenty-one years of acrimony, jealousy, half-truths, and myths.

Although Eric had always been interested in becoming an actor, as a young girl Julia was far more absorbed in becoming a veterinarian. In fact, Betty would recall,

"That's all Julie ever talked about for a long time because she just adored animals—still adores them in fact, especially dogs."

"I thought I was Dr. Doolittle," Julia would later confess. "I was convinced I could talk to the animals. But then I went to school and discovered science, which I hated, so that went out the window." It would not be until years later that Julia would admit the thought of being an actress "was just kind of there in my mind all the time."

In the summers, drawing money from their trust funds beginning in 1980, Lisa and Julia, who was always called Julie by her family and, later, Jules, by her friends, would escape the Georgia humidity by spending a week or two at Camp Birchwood, which was owned and operated by Betty's brother, John. It was at Camp Birchwood that Julia first learned to play tennis, the only competitive sport she ever embraced.

After having decided that science was not her forte, Julia began seriously considering a career in journalism, which is why she entered a speech-writing and oratory contest sponsored by the local Optimists Club when she was in eighth grade. "That was probably the first inkling of Julie doing anything in the limelight" confessed Maddox Kilgore, a school classmate and long-time friend of Julia's, who wound up winning the contest.

"What I remember most," he later recalled, "is that Julie wrote and gave a speech that was not on the subject matter. "I remember her talking about women's roles in America and women's rights. The whole thing was really feminist-oriented but, then, Julie was always pretty outspoken. I had several classes with her and while she was not a stand-out student, you always knew she was clever in whatever she had to talk about. In any discussion or confrontation you knew Julia could stand her ground with the best of them.''

The one person Julia could not stand her ground with was her stepfather, Michael Motes, whom she both despised and feared, according to friends. As a result, although as an adult Julia would portray her family life as having been a warm, close-knit, loving existence, the truth was that behind the brick walls of the Maner Road house, no matter how much of a smiling mask Betty and her two daughters presented to the world, there existed vast amounts of unrelenting tension, anxiety, and hostility.

Yet, despite all evidence to the contrary, Julia has consistently painted a picture of domestic tranquility, an idyllic youth filled with joy and happiness. "I come from a real touchy family," she told *Rolling Stone* in an August 9, 1990, interview. "A lotta hugging, a lotta kissing, a lotta love. 'You're going to the market? See you later, I love you.' And it's funny to bring that outside of the Roberts' house and into the real world.''

However, when Julia refers to ''family'' she has never once mentioned Michael Motes, someone with whom she shared a household with for eleven years. This learned pattern of denial, her survival technique, has allowed her to move on without looking back whether she's distancing herself from an unhappy childhood or a failed romance.

Like Julia, Betty, too, has always preferred to overlook the negative and emphasize the positive, whether it existed or not. The result has been nicely edited, carefully manicured images of a bucolic life filled with frolicking good times, of which in reality there were few. ''The girls were easy and they were fun,'' Betty has often told interviewers. ''They took care of each other. They were close and very close in age. Julia was pampered. I think she would tell you that she was the last in line in the pecking order.

"I'm closer to the girls than I am to Eric," she'd added in a carefully worded moment of understatement. "Eric was fifteen years old when his father and I divorced and he took it the hardest."

And yet, despite Julia and Betty's recollections of a fun-filled childhood, according to friends, Michael Motes showered no love on either of the girls, choosing instead to constantly find fault with them or to totally ignore them. Considering Motes' physical characteristics and what has been termed an irascible personality by people who have known him, it is difficult to imagine Julia and Lisa having peaceful times at home with him and Betty.

As a result of their friction-filled home life, Lisa and Julia forged a strong bond, with Lisa assuming the role of protector and, later surrogate mother to Julia. This probably explains why Lisa is the most controlled, soft-spoken and serious of the three Roberts siblings. "Lisa's the mother. Julia's the driven one and I'm kind of the problem," Eric once acknowledged.

Until the family moved to the Maner Road home, which was large enough to offer the girls their own bedrooms, Lisa and Julia slept together in the same bed. "Lisa has this celestial thing," Julia would later explain. "I would wait until she was asleep and touch her, to tap into this safe place so I wouldn't be scared at night."

Later, like most teenagers, the two sisters would fight over household chores, such as whose turn it was to load the dishwasher, whose turn it was to clear the table. And Julia used to pull Lisa's long blonde hair with both hands. After hearing a news report of two sisters who had been fighting in the kitchen and stabbed each other, however,

Lisa and Julia moved their arguments to another part of the house. "We never fought in the kitchen again," Julia would laughingly recall.

The two sisters bear only a vague resemblance to each other. Julia is 5-foot, 8-inches tall and, like Eric, bears a striking resemblance to Walter, who was part Cherokee Indian. Lisa, on the other hand, favors Betty's Scandinavian side of the family. Like Betty, she is short, standing only 5-foot, 3-inches tall, and very blond. As a baby, Julia's hair was also blond. As she grew older, however, her natural hair coloring became a dark blond. "Julia's hair is really much blonder than you'd think," Betty once explained, adding that Julia would return to Smyrna from her annual visit to Camp Birchwood as towheaded as everybody else. "Julia's hair has been dyed so much in the past couple of years she's threatening to cut it all off," Betty had then laughed.

Not long afterward, Julia did indeed cut her hair—into a short platinum blonde style, which she was sporting at the 1991 Academy Awards ceremony. In fact, Julia has become famous for her "mood hair," which has covered the spectrum of hair coloring—from coal black to platinum blond to red. "Red hair gets a lot of attention," she once explained. "It's supposed to be this flaming passionate thing. It makes me giddy."

Although Lisa and her mother more closely resemble each other, Julia and her mother share a lot of the same mannerisms, such as a tendency to buy hats and to wave their hands in high animation when they talk, a trait director Garry Marshall once commented on, exclaiming "Look at her hands! It looks like a clone," during Betty's visit to the *Pretty Woman* set. According to Betty, it's an inherited trait, since her mother had the same characteristic. "My father used to kid us both about it," Betty

60

recalled. "He'd say if they ever tied our hands behind our backs, we wouldn't be able to talk."

As soon as Julia had left Fitzhugh Elementary School behind and had enrolled at Griffin Middle School, Betty began commuting to downtown Atlanta to work on *The Georgia Bulletin*, the official newspaper of the Catholic Archdiocese. Then, in the early Eighties, Betty accepted a job closer to home at the Ridgeview Institute, a private, non-profit psychiatric hospital specializing in the treatment of chemical dependence. In the late Eighties, she rejoined the Archdiocese staff, this time working in the Tribunal, the legal wing of the Diocese.

When Julia was eight years old, she had braces put on her teeth by Dr. Ted Aspes, a Smyrna orthodontist, to correct the large space between her upper front teeth. A result of thumbsucking, "The gap was so big between my front teeth you could shove a popsicle stick between them," Julia once confided.

Obviously proud of his work, Aspes has two photographs of Julia hanging in his office. One is of his eight-year-old client before the orthodontia. The other is of a wide-grinning Julia with perfectly aligned teeth in a publicity photo from *Pretty Woman*.

By the time Julia enrolled as a freshman at Campbell High School, she was an attractive teenager, pleasant and friendly to everyone, yet essentially shy and reserved with anyone but her closest friends. In truth, high school was when Julia began to blossom.

"My fondest memories are from high school, when I'd hang around with my best friend, Page," Julia would recall years later. "We'd have tuna sandwiches and Diet Coke, watch soap operas and talk about what we wanted to do with our lives when school was over."

Free-spirited and fun-loving, Julia enjoyed the action

61

of high school. She loved hanging out at the Galleria mall on Fridays and Saturdays, when it was packed with fellow high schoolers, table hopping at Ruby Tuesdays and The Upper Crust, two of the favorite teen haunts. She loved going with the crowd to the nearby Pizza Hut after a football, baseball, or basketball game. Or to the local Dairy Queen on South Cobb Drive, where everyone hung out. Then there was always ice cream at Steve's or Carole and Tommy's after the Friday night Panthers games. And after school there was always Starvin' Marvins for a quick snack.

"Although Jules is always talking about how she was Miss Nobody in high school because she wasn't a cheerleader, that's not really true," said Joan Raley, a classmate of Julia's from the time the two were in sixth grade. Like her older sister, Lisa, Julia was very active in after-school activities. She was a member of the Student Council all four of her years at Campbell High, won the Parliamentary Award her sophomore and junior years, and was elected class treasurer during her junior and senior years, explaining to those who would vote for her, "I see myself as a person who can communicate ideas from students to the administration."

She belonged to the Spanish Club in her sophomore year, and the Allied Medical Club her freshman year. She also had the honor in her senior year of being one of the school's twelve finalists in the "Miss Panthera" beauty contest. And she played on the girl's tennis team her freshman, sophomore, and senior years. "She wouldn't give up when they said her left eye wasn't good enough," recalled Betty. "She made the team. She has too much determination to listen to me."

"In high school, I was like everybody else," Julia would later explain. "I had my girlfriends. I did sports.

I wasn't really great at anything, just middle of the road, a basic kid. I enjoyed school but somehow I never really fit. I was never a cheerleader, none of those really glorious high school things.''

Like acting, what Julia learned in school she admittedly learned mostly on her own. "I started reading more when I started failing algebra class because I stopped going to it—there wasn't any point," she once explained. "So I started going to the library, and one day I came across this huge book called *Leaves of Grass* by Walt Whitman, and I spent the rest of the semester reading that book.

"I started reading more poetry, and then I was lucky enough to have a wonderful English teacher, who had us reading *The Canterbury Tales*. In that same class we watched *Becket*, and I found my first real affection for movies. The school had a handful of really great teachers, it turned out, and I started getting more and more interested in writing, with some encouragement."

Two of Julia's favorite teachers were David Boyd, who taught English, as well as boy's basketball and baseball, and Keith Gossett, who taught English, along with freshman football and wrestling. Julia has visited both of them at Campbell High on several of her infrequent visits home, causing no end of commotion at the high school, where she is now held in high esteem as the school's only truly famous graduate.

David Boyd, who was Julia's tenth grade English teacher, recalled her as "being an A-minus, B-plus student. She was a fairly typical high school student. She enjoyed watching a lot of sports teams. She enjoyed basketball. . . . She enjoyed supporting the teams.

"When we read *Julius Caesar*," Boyd continued, "I remember she was a very emotional Brutus. She really put a lot into it. In a sense, I guess, her success doesn't surprise me because she was the type of individual who was unafraid of risk, who could leave Smyrna and go for it.''

Keith Gossett also has favorite memories of Julia. "In my composition class, I'd say we were going to do something different, and a lot of times, the students would be very negative. But Julia was always open to different things. It was like she was always watching and thinking about things. She was a very conscientious student.''

When Julia and Lisa attended school, Campbell did not have a drama department. Now the school not only has a drama department but also a Julia Roberts drama award, which is given to the most promising drama student of the year.

"Most of us really thought she was going to be a writer because she always said she wanted to write and she always *was* writing," recalled Joan Raley. "She wrote wonderful poetry. I still have a poem she wrote for me about a guy I was going out with.''

Julia has kept journals and written poetry most of her life. It is something she still does. She takes her personal journal, which she has titled "All The Makings of Insanity," with her wherever she goes. It's filled with her secret thoughts, thoughts which she once confided "could crucify me" if seen by anyone else. But mostly the notebook is filled with her prose and poetry "about moments in my life that have had an effect on me.''

"Actually," she once said, "it's mostly fucking hearts and flowers poetry.''

"If she publishes anything now, she says she'll do it under a different name, so it can be judged on its own merit," confided Betty.

Although as a high school student Julia was basically a low profile kind of gal, it's almost impossible to meet anyone in Smyrna in her age bracket that doesn't have some recollection of her.

"She used to dress real preppie and always had nice clothes," recalled a Campbell graduate from Julia's class of 1985. "The only guy she seemed to hang around with was Maddox Kilgore, although I heard she dated Joe Thompson, the school's star basketball player for awhile. She was a little heavier than she is now. She's really thinned down."

"Julia was real quiet, not much of an outgoing personality," added another former classmate. "She seemed like a nice person. She wasn't a cheerleader, didn't run with the most popular crowd. She was sweet, quiet, and, from the way she dressed, seemed to have a little bit of money."

"She was always well-groomed," said a classmate. "Her hair was feathered back and she wore her hair more shoulder-length. I remember her laughing a lot. I remember it echoing down the halls. It was a loud laugh. Other than that she blended in. She never stood out."

Maddox Kilgore, one of Julia's closest friends then, remembers her laugh, too. He calls it "hyena-like."

"We took a SAT preparation course our senior year and she sat behind me," Kilgore recalled, "and I'd say something that tickled her and she'd break into this howling laugh. The whole class would stop to let her get it out of her system."

Joan Raley also remembers Julia's dramatic abilities at a very young age. "When we got bored in class, Jules could be real creative," Raley recalled with a laugh. "She could muster up tears in a second to get out of homeroom and, of course, I'd have to follow her out to help her."

Another classmate, Kelly Jones, recalled Julia as being "very nice, very outgoing at school and at parties. She always had a lot of girlfriends. She always wanted to have fun. Julia was easy going and I have really fond memories of her. She always said my hair was perfect," Jones laughingly added, "and she'd run her hands through it, saying 'Oh, I feel so much better now.' She was always joking."

Despite her inheritance, which was invested mostly in certificates of deposits and growing rapidly, thanks to those years of high interest rates, Julia worked part-time at a variety of jobs throughout high school to earn her own spending money and buy her own clothes. She waitressed at the Pizza Inn on South Cobb Drive, where everyone went after the Friday night football games, during the winter of 1983. Then she worked part-time at a clothing store in the Cumberland Mall, and at one point even reportedly worked as a cashier at a Piggly Wiggly grocery store not far from her home.

The summer of 1984 Julia worked as a concessionist at the Galleria Mall Cineplex, making popcorn and ringing up candy sales, while wearing the theater's basic uniform of black trousers, white blouse, red vest, and bow tie, for a minimum wage of $3.35 an hour. Of course there *were* certain perks to the job—Julia got free popcorn, free soft drinks, and free movies any night of the week, except on weekends.

"She wasn't shy," recalled Jeff Feasal, who was the theater's assistant manager, "but I don't recall her being loud or boisterous. She seemed to fit in with the rest of the kids, but she was not someone who would stand out. I was surprised when I saw her in *Mystic Pizza*. She'd slimmed down and had lost her girlish look."

The fact that, at 5-foot-eight, Julia was taller than most

of her girlfriends and was much heavier then, especially through her hips, has been a topic of conversation among many of her former classmates, who recall her as having been "a big-boned person with wide hips." Julia, too, has even addressed her size, explaining "My body went through a drastic change at eighteen or nineteen. I was kind of not getting taller but still growing, starting not to be a girl anymore, but a woman."

Like most teenagers in most small towns, Julia spent many happy hours in Smyrna's two shopping malls. Not only did she work in them, she shopped and hung out in them. "I heard she was pretty wild, you know, nutty, crazy in the malls, laughing, joking, playing practical jokes," recalled a former high school classmate, adding "She was always nice to everyone, though. She'd always say 'Hey!' and smile."

So, whenever she returns to Smyrna, Julia still tends to pay a visit to either the Galleria or Cumberland malls. In April 1990, for instance, Julia winged into Smyrna to visit her mother on her way to do post-production work in New York. It was a whirlwind twenty-four-hour stop-over, during which Julia went to the Cumberland Mall sans makeup and wearing a dress three sizes too large for her. Nevertheless, she was instantly recognized.

"We walked into the Gap and, sure enough, someone immediately knew who she was and came right up to us," Betty recalled, adding "It's gotten to the point where she can't move around, where we can't roam around the mall the way we used to, and that's hard. Julia loves to act, loves to perform, and she gives it her all. Then she just wishes everyone would forget about her until her next performance, and that she could be allowed to have a private life."

Unfortunately, by the very nature of having risen to

the exalted position of international celebrity, Julia's wish for privacy is one that will never be granted. Even Greta Garbo found it impossible to be alone when she left the privacy of her New York apartment. It's the high price one pays for fame and fortune, whether they're residing Los Angeles, California, or Klein, Texas.

Chapter Four

In March, 1991, on the heels of her success in *Pretty Woman*, *The National Enquirer* published an article portraying Julia as having been a promiscuous and notoriously boy-crazy teenager, especially when it came to the school's male athletes, during her last two years at Campbell High.

"When baseball season came around, we had batting practice and Julia was always hanging around," a former school athlete supposedly claimed. "It was the same in football and basketball seasons. Julia always chased the sports stars. It made her the butt of locker room jokes, where the guys nicknamed her 'Hot Pants Roberts.' "

Although this portrait of a man-hungry, promiscuous teenager was later denied by many of her former classmates, the story was devastating to Julia. She publicly shrugged it off, but later confessed "I've been really hurt by the press. I've had some really terrible things said about me. But I've learned to laugh, ignore it, and forget it."

Besides, her high school classmates remember her quite differently. According to them she was the antithesis of promiscuous and throughout four years of high school was only seriously interested in one boy.

"Nearly all the other girls were having sex with the football team," recalled Jeff Hardigree, a former Campbell High football star. "But not Julia. She'd go so far, but never all the way. She used to love talking about sex. She was very interested in it, but she seemed to have a problem when it came to doing it. I'm pretty sure she was still a virgin when she left school."

Another Campbell High School classmate, Tom Acres, agreed. "She wasn't that spectacular to look at in those days. There were prettier girls around. Everyone liked her, and she was great fun at parties, but she wasn't popular as a date. Guys loved to talk to Julia but, when the lights dimmed and the music slowed, they'd drift off and she'd be on her own.

"I don't really believe she was interested in anyone other than Joe Thompson," Acres recalled, adding "even when he made it obvious he wasn't interested, she couldn't let go."

"Julia," recalled Cal Boyd, who was Thompson's best friend and a teammate, "had a massive crush on him and connived to get a date with him. But they only dated a few times before Joe dropped her."

In what would become a pattern of behavior, especially after suffering rejection, Julia became obsessed with Joe Thompson. "She chased him relentlessly for months and she thought about him day and night," recalled Holly Aguirre, a former classmate and friend of Julia's. But it

70

was to no avail. Joe Thompson, Campbell High School's star basketball player, simply was not interested in Julia Roberts.

The son of a Georgia state senator and the grandson of Bobby Dodd, the legendary football coach at Georgia Tech, Joe was a year older than Julia. He had received an appointment to West Point and so, within months of his graduation, he had departed Smyrna. When he returned a year later, Julia was already on her way to New York.

"I had convinced myself that I had three choices," Julia would later explain of her quick exit from Smyrna. "I could get married, I could go to college, or I could move to New York. Nobody was asking to get married and I didn't want to go away to school, so I moved."

It came as no surprise that both Lisa and Julia would eventually leave Smyrna almost immediately after their high school graduations. They desperately wanted to remove themselves from the Motes household, where turmoil had begun reigning supreme by the early Eighties.

Betty and Michael Motes were again having a flurry of severe financial difficulties and, as a result, the fighting between the two had significantly increased.

On August 5, 1980, Betty was sued by the credit union of one of her former employers, Penick & Ford, Ltd., a Cedar Rapids-based manufacturing company, for the unpaid balance of a $500 loan she had made seven years before when working in their Atlanta office. Four days after being served with the suit, Betty sat down and wrote them a letter. "I felt we were square," she explained, pointing out that when she'd resigned the company had owed her two weeks of vacation time and the balance of the loan had been "about the same amount."

"I do not feel I owe this money," she added. "How-

71

ever, I am willing to make some sort of settlement since I have neither the financial means or the time to go through any sort of court proceedings.''

Three weeks later, on August 26, Michael Motes was sued by a medical collection agency, and two months after that he was sued for several hundred dollars by an Atlanta photographer. The following year, 1981, Michael Motes was sued by the Haverty Furniture company for a blue print sofa and loveseat and coffee table the couple had purchased in May, 1979, to furnish their Maner Road house. Betty was served with the papers on December 7, 1981.

Apparently having had enough financial and emotional angst, Betty filed for divorce from Motes on February 28, 1983, claiming the couple had separated in October, 1982, and had lived in a continuous state of separation since then. Michael Motes was served with a copy of Betty's divorce complaint on March 15, 1983. And then life took an interesting twist.

Only one day after Motes was handed a copy of the divorce petition, Betty filed another petition, this one with the probate court of Cobb County, in which she sought to replace C.R. Vaughn as the guardian of Lisa and Julia's property. Apparently believing being married, even to a husband she listed as "unemployed," would enhance her chances of assuming the girls' guardianship, Betty failed to mention she had filed for divorce only the week before. Or perhaps she had changed her mind about the divorce entirely because a short while later Betty reunited with Michael Motes and her initial divorce action was put on hold.

In May, 1983, C.R. Vaughn resigned as Lisa and Julia's guardian, a position to which Betty acceded a few weeks later, after convincing The Continental Insurance

Company to issue the required $53,000 bond equal to the sum of her daughters' trust fund.

Why Betty wanted to become the girls' guardian four years after the fact, and only shortly before Lisa and, then Julia, would turn eighteen, is a mystery only Betty herself can solve. But she did take over the reins of the trust fund, doling out money to the girls between 1983 and November, 1985, until she resigned the position shortly after Julia's eighteenth birthday.

Only a month after Betty replaced C.R. Vaughn as her guardian, Lisa graduated from Campbell High School and promptly moved to New York, leaving Julia and their seven year old half-sister, Nancy, still at home.

Although Lisa moved to New York in 1983, she reportedly is still struggling to find her place in the spotlight, while supporting herself in several different behind-the-scenes production jobs in New York. She has been a serious acting student and has appeared in several off-Broadway productions, but nothing much in the way of a break has come her way. "She's taken a lot of acting classes, appeared in showcases, and has done stage work," Betty would explain, adding "but Lisa has her own pacing. She doesn't want to use Eric or Julia. Lisa does her own thing."

Maybe so but, so far Lisa's only screen role has been a tiny part as a reporter in the TV movie, *To Heal a Nation,* in which Eric starred as Jan Scruggs, the Vietnam veteran who fought to have the war memorial constructed in Washington, D.C.

After arriving in New York, Lisa barely had a chance to unpack her bags in Eric's apartment, where she was temporarily residing, before Michael Motes filed a countersuit to Betty's divorce action. In his July 6, 1983, petition Motes claimed Betty had perpetuated a fraud upon him by voluntarily resuming cohabitation with him, while telling him she had dismissed her March divorce complaint. According to Motes the couple had separated, not in 1982 as Betty had stated, but on June 15, 1983.

"You know," Betty once laughingly told a reporter, "my brother, who is eleven years older than I and still lives in Minnesota looks at me askance because I'm the only person in our family who ever got divorced—and I managed to do it not once, but twice."

But the divorce was no laughing matter. It was a long, bitter, protracted fight carried on through both civil and divorce court for two miserable years before finally coming to a halt only weeks before Julia departed for New York.

In court records dated October, 1982, Betty sought custody and support of the couple's only child, Nancy, who had been born May 19, 1976, and title to the Maner Road residence. She also sought to have the couple's personal property equitably divided and to have Michael Motes solely responsible for an outstanding bill he had incurred at Rich's department store.

Betty had hired James J. Macie, an Atlanta attorney, to represent her in the divorce action, much to the consternation of Michael Motes who, through his attorney, the late James C. Strayhorn, asked the court to have Macie disqualified as Betty's attorney. Motes had every reason to be upset, as it turned out, because prior to entering the field of law, Macie had been a priest, more specifically he had been Michael Motes' priest and, as such, had been privy to Motes' confessions for several years prior to the divorce action.

Despite Strayhorn's insistence that he withdraw from

the case, however, Macie was loathe to do so. As a result, according to an observer, "The attorneys almost had a fist fight in the courtroom. They actually squared off right before the judge."

After Motes filed a petition asking that he be granted the divorce and that the family home be sold and the profits equitably divided, Betty went ballistic. In a series of amendments to the original petition, she accused Motes of having stripped the Maner Road residence of almost all of its artwork, furnishings, and personal effects, which she demanded he replace.

Betty then followed this with a September, 1983, court order demanding Motes produce copies of all income tax returns filed from 1979 through 1983, all bank records from those years, all records of his income, and just about everything else, from car payments to credit card statements, she could think of within the realm of finances.

Motes was subsequently ordered to pay $200 per week child support while the attorneys and the court attempted to resolve the couple's differences. In an order much like that issued in conjunction with Betty's divorce from Walter Roberts, the couple was "restrained from doing, or attempting to do, or threatening to do, any act of injuring, maltreating, vilifying, molesting, or harrassing the adverse party of any of the children of the parties."

The divorce dragged on for several months until, after numerous charges and counter-charges, hearings and motions, the couple finally reached a temporary agreement on October 18, 1983, regarding the division of property and child support and visitation rights.

Under the agreement, Nancy Motes was to remain with Betty, Michael was to pay seventy-five dollars a week for her support, Betty was to receive the couple's 1977

Ford Pinto and remain in the Maner Road house and to assume all mortgage and utility payments.

In an intriguing stipulation, the court also ordered that neither Michael nor Betty could take Nancy to any Narcotics Anonymous meetings, a subject not mentioned in the couple's final divorce decree of the following year. In that decree, dated March 8, 1984, the amount of child support was reduced to twenty-five dollars a week, probably because at that point Motes was already in arrears on his support payments from the temporary agreement.

Motes received the couple's 1975 Plymouth and all of the household furniture, furnishings, objects of art, and silverware in his possession, with the exception of "one Adam commode and all the genealogical files for the Bredemus and Billingsley families," which were to be returned to Betty.

It was then ordered that Michael Motes could go to the Maner Road house to pick up his personal possessions, which were itemized in the divorce papers and included everything from an antique iron bedstead to one small metal bookcase, two government upright headstones to a set of salmon-colored bed sheets and pillow cases.

"It was," recalled a knowledgeable source, "an extremely bitter divorce. They fought about everything, right down to the pots and pans. It was, in my opinion, a very dysfunctional family."

Fearing an altercation with Betty, whom his attorney described as being "pretty volatile" and having a "violent temper," Motes insisted on having someone accompany him to the Maner Road house when he went to pick up the rest of his possessions. As a result, Strayhorn hired an off-duty member of the Marietta police force, Bobby Spann, to stand guard as his client carried his belongings from the home.

"All I did was to make sure there was no trouble," Spann recalled, adding "there were no other people in the house other than Mrs. Motes. I handed her the court order and Mr. Motes went in and moved his stuff out. I knew what was to be taken and I checked it off as he brought it out."

In May, 1984, Betty issued a check in the amount of $37,210.27 to Lisa as her share of Eileen's inheritance. She would send Julia a check the following year for $28,857.07 after she, too, turned eighteen. In the meantime, Julia spent several thousand dollars from her trust fund on travel during the two years her mother and stepfather were engaged in their life and death struggle over faded issues of DAR magazines and antique commodes. Who could blame her for wanting to get away at every available moment?

So, as she and Lisa had always done, Julia spent part of June at Camp Birchwood, visiting with her Uncle John and his family in Minnesota. Then, since both Eric and Lisa were living in New York by then, she divided her time between them and enjoyed Manhattan. When she returned to Smyrna for her final year at Campbell High, there was no doubt in her mind that she would move to New York immediately after her high school graduation. She returned to the Big Apple in November for Thanksgiving and returned again during Easter vacation in April, 1985. At that point she was counting the days until her June graduation.

Three long months later, Julia marched down the aisle in hat and gown and with diploma in hand. She returned to the Maner Road home to begin packing for her move to New York City. Three days later, her car packed solidly with clothes, books, and records, she bid Smyrna *adieu* forever and headed eastward.

"It wasn't exactly some heroic move on my part," Julia would later explain. "I wasn't up in Manhattan braving the elements alone. I moved in with my sister Lisa, and it was the same as being at home—except Mom wasn't there and, if we started wrestling, we didn't get yelled at."

Even as a child Julia had found New York an exciting place to be. In fact, one of her fondest memories was of the New York trip to visit Eric she and Lisa had made with their father not long before his death. She never forgot the sights and sounds, the sightseeing and adventures they had shared, and how excited Eric was that his family had been, even temporarily, reunited. No one could have guessed that, tragically, it would be the last time the foursome would ever be together again.

Perhaps it was that long ago sweet memory of a family reunited that had kept Julia returning to New York throughout her school years. Or perhaps it was simply the lure of excitement New York offered an adventuresome teenager. Whatever the reason, Julia spent most of her school vacations visiting Eric and then Lisa, who moved there within weeks of her 1983 high school graduation.

"I started going up at thirteen," Julia once explained, adding "everybody else would go to Ft. Lauderdale for spring break and come back with this great tan. I'd come back pale, having been in New York where it was freezing. So I was always a little different from everybody else. It was also funny because I would come back from New York and I would have met somebody and nobody would believe me. I felt kinda stupid talking about it because they're all talking about these great parties, talking about people we all knew, and I would sit there and say, 'Well, Robin Williams said to me that, uh . . .' "

Years later, after she'd become a major movie star, Julia's high school friends would admit it *had* been difficult for them to juxtapose small town life in Smyrna with Julia's tales of life amidst celebrities in New York. "Julie would say 'I was in New York this weekend and I hung out with Billy Idol or Carrie Fisher and . . .' I'm not saying we didn't believe her," explained Maddox Kilgore, "but it *was* pretty unbelievable."

It had also been awesome for her friends when Julia had flown to Australia in spring, 1984, to visit her famous brother, Eric, who was on location down under, starring in *The Coca Cola Kid*, So imagine her classmates' response when Julia returned to Smyrna with a shiny new car Eric had given her. Interestingly, Julia's out-of-town exploits appear to have created a lot of buzz, rather than envy, among her classmates, few of whom, if any, realized the underlying anxieties of her home life and her need to escape them.

In an interesting and ironic twist of fate, despite Betty's treatment of Walter in regard to the girls, Julia and her mother are extremely close, more like sisters than like mother and daughter. As a result, Julia consults her mother on virtually every aspect of her life, from her movie roles to her romances to cooking a Thanksgiving dinner.

"My kids are the kind of kids who want everything the same every Thanksgiving and every Christmas," Betty laughingly recollected. "Well, in November, I believe it was 1989, Julie only had one day off so she invited friends over for dinner and then kept calling me from Los Angeles while she was cooking the turkey. I kept thinking it would be cheaper to look it up in a cookbook.

"At one point, I drove Nancy's godmother home and got back to find the phone ringing and Julia shouting, 'Where have you BEEN? I needed you!' I told her, 'Well, gee, I didn't know I wasn't supposed to leave the house until your dinner was finished!'"

In addition to Julia's phone calls, Betty also has gotten used to the sight of Federal Express envelopes arriving at all hours of the day and night. "Julia," she once laughingly explained, "sends everything Federal Express, scripts, other things."

Julia has also made sure that Betty and Nancy have been on virtually every one of her movie sets. They drove over to Louisiana when she was making *Steel Magnolias* and spent a week. They flew out to Los Angeles when she was making *Pretty Woman*. And they were in North Carolina when she was filming *Sleeping With the Enemy*.

"Actually one of the things that's been the most fun about watching Julia rise," she added, "has been the fact that she has really gone to a great effort to make me a part of her life. She has sent me scripts she's considering and she calls me with her joys and sorrows."

As one acquaintance of Betty's recently observed, "I kinda get the impression Betty is living her dreams through her kids. She's very proud of them but does not push them. I think she looks at Julia and sees what might have been."

Part of the reason for her close involvement in Julia's career is that Betty has always been the strongest common denominator in an equation that has somehow led four out of her four children into wanting to be actors. And while her first husband, Walter, was obviously the guiding force in Eric's decision to become an actor, Julia's and Lisa's decisions to become actresses seem to be more closely linked to Betty.

80

"We always refer to acting as the family disease and for sure, all the children were exposed to it very early," Betty once recalled, adding that, as little children, Lisa and Eric had told their parents that they wanted to act. "They said it from the moment they first began talking about 'what I'm going to be when I grow up,' " Betty said. "It was certainly not that either their father or I encouraged them because we both felt you couldn't find a more difficult field than acting."

Betty also claims to have tried to dissuade Julia from also entering the profession. "I told her 'Honey, you don't know what you're doing—show business is so rough.' But she wouldn't listen to me," Betty had laughed. "So here I am eating my words."

And yet, just last year, Betty told an Atlanta reporter that Nancy Motes was studying drama and was also determined to become an actress. So, while Betty may not be *pushing* her offspring on to the stage, something is certainly nudging them in that direction. And that something is most probably Betty who, according to several acquaintances, "is one of these Ginger Rogers types. You know, showbiz is in my blood, born in a trunk, that kind of thing."

Nevertheless, Betty claims to have a hands-off parental attitude when it comes to her children. "My philosophy on my kids is that once they leave home and start their own lives, I would not presume to tell them what to do," she explained when being queried about Julia's ill-fated engagement to Kiefer Sutherland. "I also married when I was very young. Everyone has to make their own mistakes. That's how they . . . well, perhaps mistakes is not the right word. They have to make their own decisions."

Since becoming a wealthy movie queen, Julia has been generous to her mother, buying her a white Mustang

81

convertible with a bright red interior as a birthday present in August, 1989, and then offering to buy Betty and Nancy Motes a house.

"At first I said oh, no, no, no . . . ," Betty said, referring to the convertible. "I mean it's difficult when you've brought kids up to have them suddenly giving you things like this. But Julia said, 'Look, I'm going to do this.' And Nancy, of course, was delighted. She kept looking at it and thinking about when she was going to get her learner's permit the next year."

As for the house, Betty refused the offer. "I told her I'd already HAD a house. I didn't want a house. Nancy and I love the townhouse we found . . . and I don't have to worry about reselling when Nancy graduates from high school."

So, although Eric has been thrust outside the clan, Lisa and Julia, their half-sister, Nancy, and matriarch Betty remain closer than ever. Julia has been as generous to Nancy Motes as she has to her mother, flying her to Los Angeles during a recent spring break and taking her to Disneyland, even paying for Nancy's orthodontia.

"The girls *are* very close to each other," Betty has admitted. "They both keep in close touch with Nancy, who says she has three mothers, which is sort of true. To tell you the truth, we still have a lot of fun together, the girls and I, when I go to visit in New York or California.

"Julia is really a very well-balanced person," Betty continued, adding "I said to her not long ago 'I'm proud of what you've done, but I'm even more proud of what you've become as a person' because Julia is basically a very, very sweet girl with her feet on the ground."

Thus, asked not long ago if she had any regrets about her own life, Betty responded, "Not really. We all make our choices. And I made mine. I think if I didn't have the kids I might have regrets. But whatever mistakes I may have made, the children made it all worthwhile. Julia is really doing something I dreamed of doing as a teenager. I get an enormous amount of joy from watching this child.''

On October 29, 1985, the day after Julia's eighteenth birthday and only four months after Julia had moved to New York, Betty was again back in court, this time citing ex-husband Michael for contempt of court for being $300 in arrears on his child support payments, $500 behind on an outstanding Rich's department store account, and for not having returned the Adam commode and the genealogical files belonging to Betty.

After her ex-husband agreed to adhere to the divorce agreement, Betty had the contempt citation dismissed in early December, and life on Maner Road returned to a calm it had never known. But not for too long.

Less than a year after Julia's departure, Betty and Nancy Motes were no longer residing in the Maner Road house. Instead, by spring, 1986, they were living in a two-story townhouse only a few miles away. In 1988, after having stood vacant for almost two years, the Maner Road house was picked up as an abandoned property by Engineered Structures, Inc., a general contracting firm which subsequently remodeled the house inside and out and turned it into their company headquarters.

By that time Betty had worn deep ruts in Atlanta Road, the path leading from her home to the Marietta square, where the Cobb County courthouse is situated. In fact, only months after *Pretty Woman* had been released and Julia had become an international movie star, Betty made one last pilgrimage to downtown Marietta in her on-going court battles with Michael Motes who, by August, 1990, was $1950 behind in his daughter's child support.

It's no small wonder that Lisa, and then Julia, left home as quickly as their car wheels would carry them. By most accounts, the Motes household had been an unpleasant place to live for years. Yet neither Julia nor Betty seem to remember their lives that way.

Betty would feel compelled to tell inquiring reporters in July, 1991, less than a year after having dragged her ex-husband back into court, that she had absolutely no idea where Mr. Motes was living, when in fact he was living less than a mile away from her, directly across the street from Campbell High School.

And Julia seems equally selective about her family memories. When asked by an interviewer why one of the five earrings she was wearing resembled a ban-the-bomb symbol, Julia straightfacedly replied, "I come from a family that believes in peace and love, and I still believe in them."

Chapter Five

New York was the land of promise to Julia. The vast city, with its bright lights, twenty-four-hour-a-day action, and impersonal sea of faces was an exciting symbol of freedom for the free-spirited seventeen-year-old who, as far back as she could remember, had longed to throw off the shackles of small town Smyrna, where the humidity was not the only smothering facet of her existence.

Years later, after she'd become a major star, Julia would recall how she used to feel "a restlessness without focus, an urgency, an anxiety, like something's going to break," when she was a teenager. "I still feel that sometimes," she admitted, "but for different reasons than I did when I was seventeen and wanted to leave Georgia."

Although Eric was then living in a penthouse apartment at 45 West Seventy-third Street, only a block from Central

Park on the Upper Westside, Julia moved in with Lisa and together they shared a tiny Chelsea apartment at 306 West Eighteenth Street, not far from Greenwich Village, where Lisa was attending acting classes at The Neighborhood Playhouse.

"Lisa really cushioned a lot of things for me," Julia once admitted. "I always considered her fearless. When we were kids I always thought she would protect me if I was scared. And at seventeen, in New York, it was the same thing."

Julia had ostensibly moved to the East Coast with plans of enrolling as a journalism major at Wesleyan University in Middletown, Connecticut, where, according to Betty, she'd already been accepted. To this end, Betty had withdrawn $4,500 from her trust fund, earmarking it "college tuition and living expenses."

However, it's doubtful Julia ever seriously planned to attend Wesleyan, or any other university. "The minute I got out of Smyrna and stopped hot-rolling my hair, all of these ideas of what I wanted to do were dropping in the street like wet sponges," Julia once explained. "I knew if I stayed in Smyrna I'd have to go to the University of Georgia or get married. And I gotta tell you, higher education wasn't for me. I couldn't see bolting out of bed at eight A.M. to be ten minutes late for some fucking class with some fucking guy who's just gonna stick it to me again."

Betty was neither surprised nor saddened that Julia decided upon an acting career, rather than going to college. She had always suspected Julia was interested in pursuing a film career. "She was just reluctant to say so," she explained, "because she was uncomfortable about it." Julia, too, would ultimately admit she had, indeed, fantasized about being an actress, but had kept the dream to herself. "I didn't want it to seem like I was doing it just because the others (Eric and Lisa) were," she explained. "There comes a time, though, when you have to own up to what's pulling you."

The truth is that, from the moment she left home, there is no indication Julia was ever "pulled" toward, or seriously pursued, anything other than acting . . . and men. Whatever the truth about Julia's sexual mores during her high school years, shortly after she arrived in New York she stopped talking about sex and started doing it.

"I don't know how she is now," said a former acquaintance, "but in those days Julia was very outgoing, very much a party girl, and had a lot of friends, especially boyfriends. She was very flirtatious, even with guys who didn't really interest her. She had a lot of flings, at least four that I personally know of in New York. From what I've heard, she didn't change her life style on movie sets, either. She operated the same way."

According to another acquaintance, Julia also liked to drink, especially tequila and beer, which "she drank straight out of the bottle. She was wild, very free-spirited, always up for a good time, a real party girl."

"It's been interesting to read about her different romances over the last few years," the friend added, "because when I knew Julia, whoever she was involved with ran her life. They dominated her. At least that's the impression I got. But they only dominated her briefly because she always got rid of them."

"Yeah, I guess you could say she was boy-crazy," Bob McGowan, her former manager confirmed, "but in a cute way. Like the time she called me up from the Empire Diner—this was right after *Satisfaction* and right before *Mystic Pizza* she said, 'Bob, the cutest guy is waiting on me. His name is Charlie Walsh. I'm going to tell him you are interested in meeting him because you were in here eating one night and saw him. And that you sent me down here to have him call you because you didn't know how to reach him. Okay? And when he calls you you make an appointment and I'll just happen to be in your office.'

"So he called and came down and Julia happened to be there." But, as McGowan is quick to point out, it was a satisfactory relationship for all three—Julia, Walsh, and himself.

"Charlie, who changed his name to Dylan, is now one of my biggest clients. And he and Julia dated for awhile, off and on, and I believe they're still friends, even though I don't think she's maintained any of her other friendships from those days. So, I guess you could say it all worked out."

According to those who knew Julia during her mid-Eighties sojourn in New York, she didn't dress any differently than she does now. "She was sort of ahead of her time, fashion-wise," said a former friend, recalling how Julia even then was wearing oversized jackets with the sleeves rolled up and torn jeans with holes in the knees long before they were in style.

"She wore no make-up yet she was beautiful," recalled a former admirer, who remembers Julia as being "a fun-loving kid, living at a lot of different places, short of money a lot of the time but always busy, always running around doing something."

In those days, although she was living with Lisa in Chelsea, Julia's favorite hangouts—the Empire Grill and the Columbus Restaurant, an inexpensive Sardi's, where a lot of producers, directors, and actors, like Tom Cruise, Oliver Stone, and Robert De Niro, regularly hung out—

were both near Columbus Circle, not far from where Eric lived.

So it's not surprising that it was while walking along Columbus Avenue one sunny summer afternoon, less than a month after having moved to the Big Apple, that Julia was "discovered" by Mary Sames, a New York talent agent and Glenn Daniels, a casting director.

"Glenn and I were walking down Columbus Avenue and I saw this girl coming towards us," Sames recalled, adding she had turned to Daniels and said, " 'Glenn, look at that beautiful child!' "

Daniels looked in the direction Sames was pointing. What he saw was Julie Roberts, a young woman he'd met only the month before while visiting actress Dana Wheeler-Nicholson and her boyfriend, Eric Roberts. Wheeler-Nicholson, in fact, had asked Daniels if he would meet with Julia to see if he thought she had any potential as an actress.

"I met with her—she was Julie then, not Julia—and, frankly, I was underwhelmed," Daniels said. "I really don't remember too much about the interview, except that she had a very strong Southern drawl and I told her she had to do something about her accent."

It was shortly thereafter that Daniels and Sames had encountered Julia walking toward them in blue jean shorts and a tank top on Columbus Avenue. After being introduced by Daniels, Sames gave Julia her card and asked her to call, which she did the following week.

"When she came into the office a couple of days later," Sames recalled, "she had the thickest Southern accent I've ever heard—and I'm from Texas myself. She sat in a chair across from my desk with her legs crossed, her arms folded and, truthfully, she was breathtakingly beautiful."

When Julia met with Mary Sames, she had no publicity photos, which is curious since less than a year before Betty had spent $850 of Julia's trust fund for "modeling school tuition and photos." Nor did she appear to have much confidence in her abilities as either a model or an actress. And yet, like all who have met Julia, she impressed Mary Sames as having a unique charm and an intriguing blend of many interesting qualities.

"She seemed so innocent, so completely without guile, and yet at the same time so guarded, so wary, that I was fascinated by what I perceived to be a unique personality," Sames could still recall almost eight years later. "I mean, here was this free spirit, this breathtakingly beautiful young girl who was nevertheless shy and awkward and gave off the vibes of a fragile, wounded bird."

It was because of Julia's obvious need for nurturing and special attention, Sames explained, that she decided to refer Julia to a young personal manager she knew—Bob McGowan.

"Don't think I haven't taken a lot of teasing about having turned her down over the last six years," Sames laughed. "But I just didn't know whether I'd have the time, the energy, to work with her. I was very stressed out, the office was in total chaos, and I realized instantly that this demure, shy, waif-like girl sitting across from me needed somebody special and kind-hearted to take care of her, that she was going to need twenty-four-hour-a-day nurturing; and, frankly, I just didn't have it in me at the time."

So Mary Sames picked up the phone, and dialed Bob McGowan.

"Mary said, 'I have someone I think you should be interested in. She's too new for me, but I know you're developing young people,' '' McGowan recalled, adding his response had been, '' 'Great, have her call me.' '' A short while later he received a call from Julia and a few days later she appeared in his office.

"As soon as she walked in she lit up the room," McGowan said. "I mean, there were a bunch of adults in there and she came in and kind of took over the whole conversation. She was only seventeen but she had a presence even then. She was seventeen going on forty. She looked like a kid but mentally she was much older."

This same description of Julia's "presence" has been echoed repeatedly by virtually everyone who has come in contact with Julia during the intervening years. Mary Jo Slater, a casting agent, remembers seeing Julia in New York not long after she moved there: "You'd just turn around and look at her," Slater recalled, adding "You put her in a room with a thousand actresses and she'd be the one you'd point to because the star quality is there. She was born with it. She glows. She's unique. She's her own person."

"She's got an indefinable, elusive, magical quality of being able to draw people in yet at the same time remain enigmatic. And that's the mark of many great stars," Jeff Katzenberg, chairman of Walt Disney Studios, would explain shortly after *Pretty Woman* became Touchstone's highest grossing film in the company's history.

"She reminds you of no one else, and yet you feel you know her right away," admitted Joel Schumacher five years later, after directing Julia in both *Dying Young* and *Flatliners*.

"She has a direct, nonverbal communication with the audience that is the mark of all legendary actors," added Joe Roth, one of Julia's most powerful mentors.

"Men think Julia is extraordinarily beautiful and women think they went to school with her, that they can call her up and be her best friend," explained Sally Field.

Bob McGowan's response to Julia, however, was somewhat different. Even though he admits, "She had that spark from the beginning," what McGowan saw was "This young raggedy thing with a thick Southern accent. I thought I'd give her a chance," he once explained, "because I felt sorry for her. She didn't have a dime."

Julia, of course, did have a lot of dimes—approximately $28,857.07 worth, all of which she received shortly after her eighteenth birthday that following October. Yet McGowan claims that throughout their four-year relationship, Julia was constantly in need of money.

"I never got involved in her personal life and we never talked about her childhood, so I don't know about any inheritance," McGowan said. "But I can tell you she was broke when she was around nineteen or twenty because she was always borrowing money from me, always a couple hundred there, a couple hundred here. . . . I remember, one day she called me up and said she needed $3,000 right away. I said, 'Okay, I'll give you a check.' And she said, 'No, it has to be cash.'

"But one thing about Julia," McGowan laughed, "she was always fair and honest with me. She always paid me back. She was very good that way. I always got my commissions. There was never any problem."

An equally odd wrinkle in McGowan's four-year relationship with Julia was that, although he concedes he "paid her rent several times," he never knew where she lived. "I was never at her apartment, and never asked her," he explained with a laugh. "Besides, she was always moving around . . . with her sister then not with her sister then back with her sister . . . who could keep track?''

At one point, Julia set up a meeting with Bob McGowan, hoping that he would agree to manage Lisa, too. But it didn't work out. "It's not a good idea to manage sisters," McGowan explained, adding "Lisa was very nice, very bright, and she'd done a lot of theater, so I sent her to a couple of agents, but I don't think anything much came of it."

According to McGowan the sisters have noticeably different personalities. "Lisa is kind of authoritative, more direct, and businesslike, whereas Julia's much more relaxed. She would come into the office and lie on the couch or the floor. She was just a free spirit," McGowan laughed. "I think Julia looked out for her sister a lot, but Lisa also looked out for Julia, too, letting her live with her and everything, but I know Julia paid the rent a lot of time."

After agreeing to manage Julia, McGowan made two suggestions: go take some acting lessons and try and get rid of that southern accent. Although Julia took his advice, she only attended two or three classes with acting coach, Sally Johnson, before dropping out.

"I went to acting classes a few times, but it never seemed very conducive to what I wanted to do, somehow," Julia would explain six years later. At the time, she was sitting in her dressing room on the set of *Hook*, taking a break from the rigors of portraying Tinker Bell for which she was earning a reported five million dollars.

"I never really decided, I'll go to school, I won't go to school," she continued. "Things just sort of happened. Basically, I've learned on the job. It's an instinctive thing with me. Sometimes people seem kind of disappointed by that because they want to hear about all these grueling years. But I'd never done it before. So I thought what I did must be pretty much what everyone does."

Despite her nonchalant approach to acting, however, Julia did put a committed effort into losing her accent. She worked hard over a period of months with a New York speech coach, Sam Chwat, who, she would later laugh, had her repeatedly saying "cat," "dog," and "I'm going to a restaurant."

"I couldn't hear my accent," she would later confide. "I used to go to these auditions and say, 'Hello, I'm Julia Roberts.' And I never understood why the first thing out of their mouths was 'Where are you from?' After awhile I began replying 'Connecticut,' but it didn't work."

Despite McGowan's best efforts and Julia's ambition, however, no one showed any interest in hiring her, not as a model and not as an actress. "The first couple of years she didn't work at all," McGowan admitted. "I couldn't even get agents to respond to her, you know. She tried to do commercials. She went on a lot of commercial calls, but she couldn't get anything. I sent her over to the Click Modeling Agency, but they turned her down. She's a lot thinner now. Back then they said she was too heavy."

So, like most struggling young actresses, Julia worked at a variety of odd jobs, everything from salesclerk at Athlete's Foot, the shoe chain, to soda jerk at an ice cream parlor. But, like the acting lessons, Julia's forays into the work-a-day world were brief.

When she wasn't working, which was most of the time, Julia would spend her time hanging around McGowan's office, making phone calls, talking to his other clients, trying to keep abreast of what was happening in the world of auditions.

"She was extremely ambitious," McGowan explained. "She had a burning ambition to make it. She would even go on calls and auditions that were other clients' callbacks. She would bug me, or my secretary, to find out where the auditions were and then she would just show up. She's a pip, that one," he chuckled. "She can do anything she makes her mind up to do.

"You see, when I first started, none of my clients had agents," he continued. "So I would get (audition) break downs and do the work myself. I had a bunch of clients the same age and I'd submit them myself and a lot of times if I couldn't get Julia an appointment, she'd go with someone who had the appointment and crash it. She did a lot of auditions for someone who didn't have an agent," he laughed.

Years later, after she'd become an international star, thanks to *Pretty Woman,* Julia would admit she *was* ambitious. "I wouldn't be in this business if I wasn't," she conceded, even though she said she felt the word "ambition" had a negative connotation.

"People don't understand all the hues," she explained. "It's not just money, greed, fame. My ambitions are to seek out challenges, to discover new things about myself—maybe some things I haven't wanted to deal with. I also want to be part of a group I respect, from whom I can get an influx of ideas and creativity." One can only wonder what the response to this bit of contrived and sophomoric rhetoric was from those who had known Julia when she'd been blithely crashing their auditions. Chances are it provided her colleagues from those days with a hearty chuckle.

"Julia always seemed to be very honest and to the point. She was never a liar, never dealt in bullshit. She may have told a few fibs here and there, like everyone else, but she was never a liar, which is why it's beyond me that Julia buys and sells all that Hollywood bullshit now," confided a former acquaintance.

Julia was in New York for more than a year, going to auditions, whether invited or not, table-hopping at the Empire Grill and the Columbus Restaurant, trying every way she knew how to break into the business. But nothing was happening career-wise.

"I auditioned for commercials, TV, anything, but I don't think I really impressed anyone. I didn't get called back a lot, just enough to keep going," she would recall years later. "I really didn't know what else I could do. I'd go to all these auditions and I remember getting so excited about getting a call back or just meeting the director. Now I'm asking—is the director going to be there? If not, I'm not going."

Years later, after she'd become a star, Betty would confess, "I've always admired Julia because she always finds something positive in the experience—if somebody said just one nice thing to her, that's what she'd latch onto."

Then, after a year of no progress, at least career-wise, Julia landed a small role in a forgettable film titled *Blood Red*. According to Betty, Julia got the role when Eric's manager, Bill Trevsch, had a meeting with the producers and the director of *Blood Red*, a low-budget film in which Eric was preparing to star.

"They were discussing the tiny role of Eric's sister in the film," Betty loved to explain later, "because they were having trouble finding an actress who looked enough like Eric to play his sister. So the manager laughed, pulled out a photo of Julia, and said 'How about this girl?' The producers and the director looked at the picture and said, 'My God, she does look like Eric!' And Julia got the role!''

However, Eddie Bunker, a screenwriter and close friend of Eric's, debunks Betty's version of Julia's first step toward fame. Bunker claims it was Eric, not his manager, who personally went to bat for Julia on *Blood Red*.

"It was Eric," says Bunker, "who went to the director and said 'I've got this sister. Is it okay if she plays my sister?' It was Eric who introduced her to contacts in New York and who kicked open doors for her in Los Angeles. How else do you get into Hollywood? There's a thousand girls out here as pretty as she is, and she was not even a trained actress. The hardest thing was getting through the door. Julia always played the game. Before she did anything, she charmed everyone in this town."

Judging from what Julia herself has said about the people she'd met through Eric, he must have been a great help to her either personally or through his manager. Julia has admitted that Eric had been responsible for her first film role. Several years later, once she'd arrived at the top of the Hollywood heap, however, she seemed to suffer from convenient memory loss, telling the press that having a famous, often infamous, brother had never actually done much for her career.

"For as many people I meet who love Eric Roberts, I meet just as many who think he's a jerk," she had explained, adding "It doesn't help, it doesn't hurt.

"Eric has given me advice and, of course, my first movie role," she confessed as an afterthought, adding, "but the biggest help has just been watching him, how wonderful he is, and the choices he's made."

Julia would admit later, however, that due to their

vastly different approaches to the craft of acting, the last thing she wanted was Eric's assistance. "The one time Eric directly helped me with an audition, he nearly drove me crazy," she laughed. "He'd taken me out to dinner and we'd talked about this audition I had for *Spencer: For Hire*, and then we'd read this scene over and over. He wouldn't give up. And I got bored because I just wanted to have dinner. I'm not much on just rehearsing and rehearsing, anyway."

"It probably *was* Eric who got her the role," McGowan said, "because I remember getting a phone call from the producer and *then* sending them a photo of Julia. I think this all happened sometime during the summer in 1986."

Indeed, it did. Julia's future film debut was recorded for all to read in a Wednesday, August 17, 1986, "People" column in The New York *Daily News* beneath a headline, touting "Julie Roberts is Playing Sister of Eric." Curiously, despite Julia's later admission that Eric was responsible for her first small step toward fame, Julia is quoted in the column as saying Eric knew nothing about her good fortune.

"He (Eric) didn't even know I tried out for the part and that I got it," Julia had breathlessly confided. "When he got back from Cannes a couple of days ago, I told him and he really flipped. It's my first role and I'm only eighteen. I'm planning to go to college, but that's off for now. I want to ride this lucky break to the fullest."

A photograph of a youthful, radiant Julia smiling her by-now-familiar wide grin accompanied the story. It would turn out to be the first of thousands of similar photographs of Julia to be published around the world within five years. Back then, however, Julia only had her aspirations and an extraordinary amount of self-confidence to support her dreams of stardom.

"She was sure of herself. She was extremely confident," McGowan recalled. "I remember one time she said to me about publicity—and this was when she couldn't get arrested—'I'm going to wait until I'm a starlet first before I start doing all this.'

"I remember when that story ran in The *Daily News*, too," McGowan laughed. "Julia called me up and she was all excited about it, but she said, 'When I said I wanted publicity, I didn't say I wanted big publicity!

"Where did this sense of self come from?" McGowan reiterated, "I don't know. Maybe from her mother. They're very close. But I believe you either have it or you don't."

At that time, of course, no one could have predicted just how far, or at what breakneck speed, Julia's "lucky break" would take her. Even Bob McGowan confesses he had no idea then that Julia would become an international superstar, blazing a trail across the Hollywood skies with the speed of a high-powered rocket.

"I thought she was going to be a working actress and very successful," McGowan said. "But I never thought she'd be a superstar like this. I mean, something like this happens maybe every twenty years."

Blood Red was a troubled project from beginning to end. In fact, by the time the film finally went into production in fall, 1986, it had been knocking about Hollywood, in search of financing, for ten years. The results was a much-revised script, which even an intriguing cast of players like Eric, Dennis Hopper, Burt Young, Aldo Ray, Susan Anspach, Charles Dierkop, and Horton Foote, Jr. could not salvage.

"*Blood Red* was a real interesting thing for Eric and I," Julia told a *Rolling Stone* reporter in a January, 1989, interview, "because we realized that even though we're related, even though we may look alike and be in the same profession, we don't go about the process of acting in the same way at all. We're really different. He went to the Royal Academy of Dramatic Arts in London. I'm a kamikaze actress."

The saga of oppressed Sicilian winegrowers in northern California fighting a ruthless railroad magnate, *Blood Red* had as much difficulty finding a distributor once it was completed as it had had in finding investors. As a result, the film was not theatrically released until four years later, and then on a very limited scale. It essentially went directly into video stores in early 1990.

The reason for its travails, according to a *Daily Variety* review, was that the film suffered from "a predictable script, flat direction, and miscasting." Julia's review of the film was much more succinct. She described *Blood Red* as a film in which Dennis Hopper had her father killed and she had to wear a corset for the whole picture.

"Eric Roberts," penned a reviewer, "is more subdued than usual. (But) his scenes with real-life sister Julia are intriguing because of the visual match. She doesn't get much chance to emote, but that nascent star quality already is evident." Thus, despite its flaws, *Blood Red* will probably become a film classic in the future *only* because it marks the true film debut of Julia Roberts.

Blood Red completed filming around Thanksgiving time, 1986, and a month later, shortly after Christmas, Julia found herself in Las Vegas, appearing in an episode of the NBC series, *Crime Story*, which, titled "The Survivor," was telecast the night of February 13, 1987.

When she returned to Smyrna to spend the 1987 Christmas holidays, Julia had her first exposure to stardom. "My friend Paige was home from Iowa and we were walking around and I realized people were staring at me," Julia later recalled. "At first I thought it was just my imagination. But Paige noticed it, too. 'Why are people looking at you?' she said. Then a couple of people came up because they recognized me from that small role in *Crime Story*. But it was weird," Julia laughed, "because they didn't really know who I was. They'd just kinda go, 'Are you . . . ?' And I'd say, 'Nah, you're in Cumberland Mall.' "

Eight months later, Bonnie Timmerman, the casting director McGowan had cajoled into hiring Julia for *Crime Story*, cast Julia in an episode of another Michael Mann series, *Miami Vice*, the popular Don Johnson police saga noted for its violence and his fashion flair. Titled "Mirror Image," the *Miami Vice* episode was telecast on October 25, 1988. By that time, however, Julia was well up the ladder of success.

Taking advantage of Julia's role in *Blood Red*, Bob McGowan continued sending out photos and pitching her to various casting agents with whom he had a solid relationship. One of those was Joanna Ray, a Los Angeles-based casting director, whom McGowan discovered was looking for young actresses to star in a low-budget film about the comic misadventures of an all-girl rock band.

Figuring Julia might be right for any one of the roles, McGowan telephoned Ray, trying to at least get her an audition. "I told her, 'Listen, Joanna, I've got the perfect girl for this.' And she says, 'Does she play an instrument?' So I said "I'm not sure. Let me ask her and I'll get back to you.'' So I asked Julia, 'Do you know anyone who plays the drums?' She said 'Yes.' So I called Joanna back and told her, 'Yeah. She plays the drums.'

With Joanna Ray headed to New York, and interested in meeting his drum-playing client, McGowan promptly enrolled Julia in a crash course of drum lessons. "I picked the drums because I figured it was the easiest instrument to learn," McGowan laughed, noting that Julia ultimately *did* land a role in the film—not as a drummer but as a bass guitar player.

Once Julia had landed the role of Daryle, the bass player with boy problems, she was forced to become a member of the Screen Actors Guild and was dismayed to discover she would not be able to register under the name "Julie" Roberts because there was already a SAG actress by that name. So she decided she could either reinstate her real name, Julia, or use her middle name, Fiona.

Unsure about which choice to make, Julia called Betty in Smyrna, explained the situation and said, "So, what's it going to be—Julia or Fiona?" The two decided using her middle name would be too confusing, so "Julia" Roberts, who'd been called "Julie" by family and friends as far back as she could remember, was born again.

Upon landing the role in *Satisfaction*, Julia also needed a talent agent to represent her since, as her manager, Bob McGowan was not legally authorized to negotiate contracts on her behalf. Since McGowan was friendly with Risa Shapiro, a William Morris agent whom he'd been regularly calling regarding representation of Julia, he decided to give it one last try.

"I used to call Risa up all the time, asking her to try and get Julia and audition for this film, that film," McGowan explained. "But she'd always tell me the same thing, which was 'Bob, I just can't do that.' Every now and then, though, they'd send her on something idiotic, like an industrial or some bullshit like that. This time I told her, 'Look, this is what's happening. Julia's probably going to get something like $50,000 and you guys can do the deal.''

According to McGowan, however, the agency still wasn't interested in handling Julia. It wasn't until he pointed out that Aaron Spelling was involved with the film, and that Julia's contract contained an option for her services should the film lead to a television series, that the agency decided to add Julia to their client roster. Thus it was economics, not foresight, that led Julia into the William Morris fold and her enduring friendship with Risa Shapiro and Elaine Goldsmith.

"I had to practically beg Risa to take her," McGowan recalled. "I told her 'Look, put this on a personal level. Take a shot with her for one year. I'm throwing you the deal.' And they did. The Morris agency signed her. But no one wanted to handle her,'' McGowan said, ''so she was assigned to two up-and-coming agents—Risa and then, later, Elaine Goldsmith.

"And Elaine Goldsmith, whom I'd never met, didn't want her. Neither one of them wanted her. Funny, huh? But that's exactly what happened.''

Julia spent the four weeks prior to the start of principal photography studying the guitar, which she found to be slow, gruelling work. "There's nothing more frustrating than having this great instrument and a great song and not being able to put the two together,'' she later explained. But she kept at it, with private lessons in the morning and a group rehearsal with the rest of her fellow players every afternoon. As a result, by the time the movie began to roll, Julia had become a fairly decent guitar player in a relatively brief amount of time.

"We all knew the quicker we learned, the quicker it would be fun," she explained, "and that's what happened. We got it up fast and we had a good time." Little could Julia have known that, within three years, she'd be jamming with Richard Gere and Garry Marshall at a wrap party for *Pretty Woman,* a film that would bring her more fame and fortune than she ever imagined, even in her wildest dreams.

Chapter Six

Satisfaction, which was originally titled "Sweet Little Rock 'n' Rollers," was a tiny-budgeted film shot on an unbelievably tight thirty-five day schedule between May 13 and June 24, 1987, on location in Charleston, South Carolina, and Baltimore, Maryland. It had no stars and, as it turned out, no real future in the movie houses of America.

A year after its completion, the film would open and close with the speed of a blinking eye. Not even it's cover song, "Mystery Dance" by Elvis Costello, one of Julia's favorites, could save it from being consigned to everlasting shelf life in the nation's video stores.

As a film offering, *Satisfaction* would unfortunately prove to be memorable only to movie buffs interested in obscure trivia, such as the fact that the film marked the motion picture debut of TV actress Justine Bateman; contained a rare, albeit miniscule, appearance by singer Deborah Harry, who portrayed the sometime-girlfriend of a burned-out Sixties songwriter; and marked Julia's first publicized on-set romance, thereby establishing her pattern of falling in love with several of her future male co-stars, a situation Julia does not deny but to which she has angrily taken offense.

"My relationships happened over three years of my life, not some wild, outrageous weekend," she has explained with obvious irritation. "I think what keeps me from getting *really* annoyed is the security I feel in what I know. Yes, movies sometimes promote a fantasy that can be confusing, but that also comes from someone whose life is already confused. I've been in that situation. But, at this point, my life is very clear."

In the case of *Satisfaction,* Julia's romantic involvement was with Liam Neeson, a thirty-four-year-old Irish-born actor with a ruggedly handsome face, piercing blue eyes, and an abundance of charm. Although Neeson portrayed Deborah Harry's boyfriend in the film, by the end of the thirty-five-day shoot, Julia and Liam had become a cozy twosome.

Fourteen years older than Julia, Liam was born in 1953 in Ballymena, a tiny northern Ireland town, where he was raised in a staunch Catholic family headed by a school janitor and a strict Catholic mother, who worked as a cook, in a Protestant neighborhood. A rather gentle demeanor and principled politeness, however, don't reflect Neeson's working-class origins and former employment as a forklift operator, as well as what has been described, as "a decidedly filthy mouth." Considering Julia's penchant for profanity, the two must have had some lively discussions during the year they lived together.

Having grown up surrounded by sisters, both older and

younger, the six-foot, four-inch actor has never hidden his admiration for members of the opposite sex. "I love women! Every shape, size, and color created," he once proclaimed. "They are the better sex. Men have a lot of ground to make up as regards to emotions and their place in society." In fact, Neeson had his first taste of acting at age sixteen when he tried out for (and won) a part in a school play because he "fancied the girl who would be playing my sister."

Although Julia and Liam were living together when *Satisfaction* was released with little fanfare in February, 1988, Liam was so embarrassed by the film he refused to either attend a screening or pay money to see it.

"I have no intention of ever seeing it," he told an interviewer, explaining he had only accepted the role because "I was doing *Suspect* and feeling a wee bit depressed and really ugly and awkward and the script had pretty girls running around and I thought, 'This sounds great.'"

However, Julia saw the film twice—first at a screening, then again with Eric a few weeks later at a Westwood theater, not far from Venice Beach, where she and Liam were then cohabiting. And, although she was less vitriolic about the film than Liam, she also found it an embarrassing representation of her work.

"Eric laughed but, when it was over, we talked and he made it seem not so bad. But the film taught me a lot about what I hope to never do again in a movie," Julia had laughed, adding, "There's only one scene I was embarrassed about that I was supposedly in. But I had the day off, so it was actually kind of funny.

"In the film there's a scene where I'm supposedly in the van with my boyfriend, and the van is rocking, and a grand amount of time passes, as if we've been going at it for quite long? Well, actually, it was an empty van and there were a couple of grips behind it pushing it back and forth. I was at the beach all day.''

Although *Blood Red* had been Julia's first film, *Satisfaction* was actually her first major movie break. Not only did the film link her with the powerful William Morris agency, it introduced her to producer Alan Greisman and his wife, actress Sally Field, who quickly became one of Julia's early, and staunchest, Hollywood supporters. It was this friendship which ultimately would jumpstart Julia's career into full speed.

Immediately after having wrapped *Satisfaction* Julia appeared in a small role in *Baja Oklahoma*, an HBO movie in which she played the free-spirited daughter of Lesley Ann Warren. And, as has been her pattern throughout all of her films, with the notable exception of *Hook*, Julia spent a great deal of her time bonding with the crew, telling jokes, and playing ping pong between camera set-ups and scenes.

''Julia was one of the nicest people I've ever met on a set,'' recalled a *Baja* crew member. ''There was no attitude from her. She didn't have the barracuda mentality that often affects actors. She wasn't obsessed with acting. She was very natural. She had an interesting mix of being very real, very focused. She knew what she wanted and where she wanted to go in terms of her career and she felt confident it was going to happen at her pace.''

Julia, of course, had no reason *not* to feel confident. By the time she'd begun working on *Baja*, she had landed two movie roles and two television parts in less than a year. She'd also landed a handsome Irish lover with whom she would be living beside the beach in sunny California as soon as she completed *Baja*.

Yes, Julia had every reason to be ecstatic during the

summer of 1987. Despite her year of disappointment, she had become a working actress in a comparatively brief span of time with relative ease, no pun intended.

Within days of having completed *Baja Oklahoma*, Julia was back in New York, preparing to audition for another low-budget movie, *Mystic Pizza*, was to be filmed on location in Mystic, Connecticut. It was a film which Julia, as well as a hundred or so other actresses, was determined to add to her resume. And she didn't care which of the three female leads she landed.

"They'd sent me a script and I read it, but I actually didn't know what part I was up for," Julia would later confide with a laugh. "I just assumed that I was Jojo, who was described as cute, earthy, and unable to commit to marriage to her boyfriend, because Kat was too young, and Daisy was too voluptuous or something."

But, to her surprise, it was decided by the producers, and the casting director, Jane Jenkins, that Julia would read for the role of Daisy, instead. "It went fine," Julia would later recall, "but the casting director told me I just didn't look very Portugese." Nevertheless, Dan Petrie, the director, and Mark Levinson, the producer, asked Julia to return for a second audition the following day.

"Bob, when I see this guy, I'm gonna blow him away," Julia excitedly told McGowan, as she rummaged through his closet, looking for just the right suit to borrow for her second read-through. "That's when she started wearing men's suits," McGowan laughed. "I thought it was quite sexy, to tell you the truth. She'd wear the trousers and the jacket, nothing else. I thought it looked hot."

Having chosen what she considered to be just the right

look, Julia stopped by a drug store on her way home that night and bought a can of black hairspray. When the hairspray failed to sufficiently darken her hair to the coal black she'd envisioned, Julia took black shoe polish, mixed it with mousse and spent hours transforming herself into her vision of an ethnic-looking Daisy with jet black hair. It was, she would later laugh, "grotesque." Since she had so much hair, the project took most of the night. But Julia didn't care. She was too excited to have slept anyway.

The following morning, at the appointed hour, Julia walked through the door of the casting office and discovered a lobby filled with other would-be-Daisys, all of whom looked "attractive" to her. She was wearing McGowan's suit, sans blouse, with the jacket sleeves rolled up and long black tresses of curly hair cascading wildly over her shoulders. She was a picture of ethnic beauty as she sat there, a tall, lean Portuguese, listening to her Walkman repeatedly play Jimi Hendrix's "Wild Thing" in an effort to psych herself up for the reading.

A devout fan of rock 'n' roll, especially the rock music of Elvis Costello, Julia would frequently listen to a particular tape in the morning to achieve the proper mental attitude for whatever the day was supposed to yield. In those days, Costello and The Police were among her favorite performers. Of course, that was *before* Lyle Lovett became the focus of her affection.

"I remember thinking, 'What is going to give me the edge over these girls?,' " Julia later recalled. "I had my Walkman on. I was listening to Jimi Hendrix live at Monterey, singing 'Wild Thing.' I played it over and over again, and the more I played it, the more cocky I got. And the more attention I got from the women in the room. And the more they stopped reading their pages and started watching me, the more sure I got that I was going to get the role."

Julia was right. She won the role of Daisy, but not before suffering an embarrassing snafu when during the audition the actor playing opposite her ran his hand through her hair with a great deal of passion, only to discover it completely blackened by the shoe polish when it re-emerged from Julia's long tresses. At that point everyone, including Julia, broke into uncontrollable fits of laughter.

It wouldn't be until much later that the film's producer, Mark Levinson, would confess that he and the director, Daniel Petrie, had still been in the process of fine-tuning Daisy's character when they'd begun auditions for the role, and that it had been Julia's interpretation of the character that had ultimately brought Daisy into sharp focus for them.

"Julia walked in and she was very much like a light at the end of the tunnel," Levinson explained. "There was no doubt that she would be Daisy the minute she walked in the room. She made it a lot clearer for us on how to get to that character."

"Julia was real smart to put that rinse in her hair and make it jet black, like the color of the Portuguese-descent character she played in the film," added Petrie. "It worked. It made her look exotic and perfect for the part. She was exactly what I needed for the role . . . unpredictable, and willing to take chances, fiery, spirited, and yet very real."

Despite its low-budget and its cast of newcomers, *Mystic Pizza,* proved to be a charming, poignant rites-of-female-passage film about three working-class women, all waitresses at a pizza shop in the seaside resort of Mystic, Connecticut. Shot in fall, 1987, the movie starred

Lili Taylor, Annabeth Gish, William R. Moses, Adam Storke, Vincent Phillip D'Onofrio, and, of course, Julia in the role of the twenty-two-year-old voluptuous Portuguese firecracker, Daisy Araujo, who falls in love with a wealthy young man and shares a summer of romantic adventure and craziness with her two best friends.

Since the script described Daisy as having "all the right curves and all the right moves to drive men crazy," and "the kind of girl men would kill for," Julia was forced to not only gain weight in all the right places for the role, but to endure endless good-natured jibes from the crew the moment she stepped onto the set. "I would walk around the set and the crew would kid me. They'd say, 'There's that girl men are going to kill for today.' Now, how the fuck can you live up to that?," she'd later laugh.

Despite her protestations, Julia loved the role of Daisy. Not only did she get to swear a blue streak, she got to trash her yuppie boyfriend's expensive Porsche. "Daisy," she would later admit, "was somebody I might have been if I had been different, if that makes any sense. I could relate to her in a lot of ways, but at the same time she had a lot of gusto, a lot of chutzpah that I never had," Julia told her hometown newspaper shortly before the film debuted in October, 1988. "It was a little scary being Daisy, though, because she's kind of like ten feet tall and I'm happy being five-foot-eight," she'd added.

Again, following her pattern of creating a family atmosphere on the set, Julia spent most of her time with the crew, swapping jokes and telling stories. "She really interacts with the crew. She's not the kind of star who hangs out in her trailer and never talks to anybody. She really makes you feel she's part of the team," recalled a crew member.

Thus, on the very first day of filming *Mystic Pizza*, the

sound of raucous laughter filled the air, so loud that the sound man was picking it up during a scene. When Petrie sent a crew member outside to see what was going on, what he found was Julia, sitting on the steps of the house where they were shooting, with about fifteen crew members around her. "She had them eating out of her hand," he recalled. "They were just cracking up."

The morning of October 28, 1987, began like every other morning on the *Pizza* set, only this particular day marked Julia's twentieth birthday, something she hadn't confided to her fellow crew members because, she would later explain, she hadn't wanted to look like an egomaniac by drawing attention to it.

Nevertheless, as the day slowly progressed, she began to feel a little melancholy. She missed Liam, her mom, her family, and friends. By late afternoon she had truly begun to sink into a depression when, suddenly, to her astonishment, a huge cake decorated in the form of a pizza, materialized on the set. It was a present from the cast and crew, who had somehow discovered her birthdate and had been secretly planning a surprise party for days. Julia, who blushes easily when embarrassed, turned bright red and fled the set, only to return minutes later after she'd regained her composure.

"I'm shy and I'm an extrovert," she explained. "So everyone seems to get a kick out of the fact that I blush very easily. But I do. Certain things kind of make me go, 'Well, I've got to run, see you later . . .' "

Despite her easy manner and the fact that *Mystic Pizza* was only her third film, Julia was totally dedicated to giving the role her very best. She was as focused on *playing* Daisy as she had been in *auditioning* for Daisy.

"She has a certain amount of savvy that she can throw out as strength in a situation. She gets what she wants," admits one of her *Mystic* co-stars. "When she needed time for a scene, she got it. She'd just go rehearse if she needed to. At her age, she had the balls, so to speak, to demand it. But she never held up filming for it, though."

According to the film's director, Daniel Petrie, however, he would have preferred for Julia to *not* have rehearsed her scenes. "She has a wonderful spontaneity on screen that really makes her light up," Petrie explained. "Most actors have that in their eyes. But Julia has it in her eyes, her face, everywhere. She's the kind of actress you want to shoot without a rehearsal because she's so quirky you never know what you'll get!"

Although *Mystic Pizza* featured a cast of unknowns and, therefore, had no real box-office pull, and received only mixed reviews, the $3.5 million film did a respectable $14 million worth of business after making its debut in October, 1988.

The film served Julia well. She won rave reviews for her portrayal of Daisy, which Michael Wilmington, film critic of *The Los Angeles Times*, termed "a minor triumph." He lauded Julia for "generating her own smoky tension: the livid fire of a small-town belle, blazing up high against the possibility of inevitable small town entropy or eclipse."

In addition to laudatory reviews, *Mystic Pizza* also earned Julia a modicum of fame. "Every day for a week," Julia laughingly recalled, "people came up to me and said 'I thought you were six feet tall' because Daisy looked about six-and-a-half feet tall on the screen. Then I walked into this room and there were a bunch of guys sitting on a sofa, and one them said to me, 'So where's the fox from *Mystic Pizza?*''

Not long afterward, during a newspaper interview, the writer mentioned that in person Julia appeared much more "diminutive" than she did on screen as Daisy. "I know, that's what everyone says," Julia responded, adding "I feel like such a disappointment. For months after *Mystic Pizza* I had at least twenty different people say, 'Gee, we thought you were six feet tall.' "

More than a year later, Julia had an unusual brush with fame while visiting her mother in Smyrna. The two had gone to the movies and Julia was in the ladies room, when she suddenly heard a woman's voice say, "Uh, excuse me? The girl in stall number one? Were you in *Mystic Pizza?*"

"I said 'Yeah.' And she says, 'Can I have your autograph?' And she slides a piece of paper under the stall door," Julia recalled, shaking her head in disbelief. "Well, I just told her, 'I don't think right now is the time.' "

Determined to get the mileage out of Julia's triumphant reviews, Risa Shapiro sent out 100 copies of an *Esquire* magazine photo spread of Roberts in a skin-tight mini-dress doused in water, timed to the film's release. As a result, studio executives became aware of Julia almost overnight and began telephoning. "Next time she's in Los Angeles," they told Shapiro and Goldsmith, "give us a call."

Within a month of having completed *Mystic Pizza* Julia moved from New York to Los Angeles. The reasons were two-fold. She was convinced that a westward move would enhance her career, if for no other reason than she needed the contacts and exposure being in the hub of movie-making would bring her. And, secondly, Liam lived in Los Angeles. He had moved there the year before, in January, 1987, for the same reason, and his acting career had begun to flourish.

Thus, by March, 1988, Julia was living with Liam in a funky apartment in a three-story ivy covered stucco building on Twenty-sixth Avenue, only a block from the beach in Venice, California. Julia loved the beach and so did Liam. Most of all they loved the climate. The sun and the warm days were a relief from the New York winters Julia had endured; and they were certainly far removed from the bone-chilling cold and rain of an Irish winter.

It was probably Julia's love of the ocean that almost led to her demise in late spring, 1988, when she came down with a severe case of spinal meningitis. Although it could never be proven, she always suspected she'd contacted the deadly virus while swimming in the waters off Miami Beach during the filming of *Miami Vice* eight months before. However, considering just how polluted the southern California beaches have become, it's more than likely she caught it while splashing in the Pacific Ocean near her Venice Beach home.

At first believing she merely had the flu and was run-down from the rigors of having made three back-to-back films, Julia was reluctant to go to the doctor. It wasn't until she'd gotten sicker, instead of better, and several weeks had passed, that Liam and her mother, Betty, finally convinced her to see a physician. When a series of blood tests identified the meningitis, Julia was promptly taken to the hospital. And not a moment too soon. By the time she was checked in, she was desperately ill, running a high fever and half delirious.

Realizing just how ill Julia was, Betty flew in from Atlanta to join Liam at her bedside and then, when Julia was released weeks later, stayed on to be at her side during the month she spent recuperating at home. In fact, Julia's illness was so serious that the entire Roberts clan, even Eric, ended up visiting her at the apartment. Since it was the first time in sixteen years the family had been in one place at the same time, Mark Flanigan, the young actor whom Lisa was then dating, decided he would record the summit meeting for posterity.

"Hey, I'll never catch you all in one room again. Let's take a picture," he told the group, snapping a Polaroid of the gathering. Julia later had the photograph blown up and framed as a poster.

Several years later, when recalling her life and death bout with the deadly virus, Julia confessed "I thought I was going to die, and so did everyone else. So I was forced to face it and found that I wasn't scared to die, that it wasn't a scary thing. Not that I want to die," she'd added. "I want to live forever. It's just that having been there I found out it wasn't such a bad thing."

By mid-June, 1988, Julia was well enough to begin considering auditioning for film roles. So, when Meg Ryan decided to bow out of a movie titled *Steel Magnolias* to star opposite Billy Crystal in *When Harry Met Sally,* Risa decided the role of Shelby Eatenton-Lacherie, the sweet, doomed diabetic daughter of Sally Field, would be a perfect vehicle for Julia and immediately attempted to set up an audition for her.

Despite her best sales pitch, however, Shapiro met with resistance from Herb Ross, the film's director. "Herb Ross did not even want to look at the tape of *Mystic Pizza*," Bob McGowan recalled. "What happened was there was someone else in *Mystic Pizza* who was after the role, and their agent talked them into looking at it."

What the casting people and Ross saw in the film, of course, was Julia wise-cracking and swearing her way through life as Daisy, a role far removed from the hushed tones of Shelby Eatenton-Lacherie, the epitome of Southern womanhood.

Since the part of Shelby was considered to be one of a handful of plumb dramatic roles, the competition to replace Meg Ryan was intense. Every agent in Hollywood with an actress in that age bracket was trying to get their client a read-through. So it was only begrudgingly, and as a favor to Sally Field, that Ross added the name Julia Roberts to the list of the seventy-five other young actresses he was personally auditioning.

"When I got the call to audition for the movie I asked who was in it," Julia would later recall. "And I was told Sally Field, Shirley MacLaine, Dolly Parton, Olympia Dukakis, and Daryl Hannah. I felt like, 'Yeah, right.' I went to audition with the intention not getting it—it was too perfect. I would go do the reading and do the best I could to try to impress somebody for a future role."

But Julia's nonchalance about the audition belies the aggressive spirit with which she sought the role. No one, least of all a true "steel magnolia" such as Julia, would undergo five consecutive days of stressful auditions were they not determined in their efforts to ultimately succeed. Besides, as Elaine Goldsmith conceded several years later, "When Julia wants something, she goes after it. Julia's got passion. She's very focused."

After psyching herself up and making it through three auditions, Julia was called back twice more, both times to read with Sally Field. Having met Julia through her husband, Alan, during the filming of *Satisfaction,* Sally had decided Julia, and only Julia, was perfect to portray Shelby, her screen daughter.

118

Thus, three hours after her fifth and final reading, Julia was notified she had been tapped for the coveted role of the ill-fated Shelby. She was surprised, delighted and, she would later admit, a bit overwhelmed at the thought of joining such a star-studded cast of players. She also was concerned about working with Herb Ross, whom she found to be irritatingly bombastic and, as such, intimidating.

Apparently one of the few men *not* to have succumbed to Julia's charms, Ross ordered her to lose weight, lighten her hair, and even change the shape of her eyebrows before she arrived to begin filming. It was a tall order, since rehearsals were scheduled to begin in little more than a week from the day she was hired.

Despite Ross's irascible temperament, Julia was in a partying mood that night. So she, Bob McGowan, Dylan Walsh, who by then had moved to the West Coast to pursue his acting career, and Risa Shapiro did a "totally Hollywood thing to celebrate." They went to the famous Polo Lounge at the Beverly Hills Hotel and toasted Julia with all the champagne she could drink.

A couple of days later Julia, who was the last cast member hired, was on a plane, winging her way south to Natchitoches, Louisiana, where rehearsals where scheduled to begin almost immediately.

"Sally knew Julia and liked her, and really worked with her," Betty Motes explained. "She really wanted Julia to get the part. She's that kind of person and that kind of actress. I can't imagine her not being gracious or helpful with anyone she works with."

It's true that it was due to Sally's persistence, and the fact that he had been unable to find anyone else who measured up to his personal vision of Shelby, that Herb Ross finally, reluctantly agreed to hire Julia. But there's

119

another truth involved, as well. And that is, throughout her career Julia has shown an instinctive ability to charm the right people at the right time. The fact that she had beguiled Sally Field upon their first meeting certainly contributed in no small measure to her good fortune when push came to shove in the *Steel Magnolias* auditioning process.

"The minute I met her I wanted to wrap my arms around her," Field later explained, reflecting upon their immediate bonding and, in doing so, attesting once again to Julia's waif-like presence, her vulnerability, her need for love and nurturing that Mary Sames had responded to several years before.

"Yes, Julia's manipulative in that if she wanted something and she thought somebody could help her get it, she would zero in on them," conceded a friend from her past. "Anybody who could help her she'd work on and make them like her."

The question, therefore, is not *whether* Julia is a manipulative personality, but whether she's *aware* of this trait which has served her so well, both personally and professionally, but too frequently at the emotional detriment of others.

Whatever the answer, the intriguing truth is that Julia is a first-rate actress, instinctively able to play whatever role necessary in a world she evidently considers, whether consciously or unconsciously, to be nothing more than one vast stage filled with mostly supporting players.

In the films that would follow *Satisfaction* and *Mystic Pizza*, Julia's ability to turn her movie sets into one big happy family would become legendary. Curiously, though, no one apparently has ever stopped to wonder *why* Julia would pour so much energy into creating a family that would disband as soon as the film was completed in two or three months.

Evidently crew members were so relieved to discover they would not have to deal with a temperamental star, they simply accepted Julia's off-screen persona at face value and bought into her home-movie-within-a-movie re-creation of a family at work and at play. The fact that they were fulfilling a deep-seated psychological need never entered their minds. Why should it? No one could have known, least of all from Julia, how necessary a family, even a temporary family, was to her sense of well-being.

Having swallowed Julia's carefully conceived mythical childhood of warmth, caring, and nurturing, her co-workers could not possibly have realized she was creating, rather than re-creating, an environment she'd never truly experienced in real life.

In becoming a movie actress, Julia chose exactly the right profession in which to fulfill virtually all of her fantasies. In what other career could she have possibly sustained her on-going role of Julia Roberts? Certainly not in the small, intense world of the stage, where everyone knows everyone else and ultimately everyone's secrets and quirks. Definitely not in a long-lasting television series, where one is forced to interact with the same people for years.

No, with its transient lifestyle, its emphasis on the more shallow aspects of life, and few reality checks, the film industry was absolutely the perfect choice. As a movie star, you don't have to be stable to be loved and admired, you simply have to be *box office*.

Chapter Seven

Steel Magnolias was, quite simply, the biggest thing to happen in Natchitoches, a sleepy little haven of 17,000 Southern souls, since John Wayne had ridden into town as one of *The Horse Soldiers* thirty years before. So having Dolly Parton, Shirley MacLaine, and Sally Field all in their midst at one time wasn't just news, it was *big* news to the townspeople, as well as their neighbors. As a result, the various locations utilized as sets were usually surrounded by sightseers from near and far.

Not wanting to miss a star in their fold, the local citizenry began rising earlier than normal to catch at least an hour or so of the day's filming before *they* had to go to work. They also began dining out at the town's only two restaurants, hoping to catch a glimpse of the celebrities temporarily residing among them. Local landowners took to dropping by their houses, which they'd rented out to the stars, just to make sure everything was running smoothly, while still other, more industrious local citizens spent their days hawking *Steel Magnolias* tee shirts to curious visitors from other nearby communities. In short, none of the stars could make a move without encountering well-meaning members of the populace.

"Everybody knows every move you make," Dolly Parton complained, adding that filming there was "a little closed-in." To keep from getting claustrophobic, Dolly invited her family—11 brothers and sisters—to visit as often as they could, and retreated to her rented home, where she spent most of her off hours in the kitchen, whipping up two of her favorite childhood dishes, home fries and corn bread.

Daryl Hannah rented a farm on the outskirts of town and, whenever she wasn't on the set, she could be seen either horseback riding through the countryside or jumping on the trampoline she'd set up in the backyard. Although she usually rode alone, Daryl would sometimes invite Julia to ride with her and, together, the two would go galloping through the rolling farmland. Since they were close in age, Daryl and Julia became close friends during the shoot. A devoted horsewoman, Daryl also went to the local racetrack with actor Sam Shepard and screenwriter Robert Harling to place a bet or two on Chickie Double, a horse from her rented farm.

"One minute Daryl can be this big-eyed puppy and then the next she can get wild and silly, pinning clothespins to everyone's shirts just for kicks," Julia laughed.

Sally Field had her two-year-old son, Sam, from her second marriage to producer Alan Greisman with her throughout the filming, and could usually be seen carrying him strategically placed on her hip between takes and during lunch. "People were worried I wouldn't look old enough to be Shelby's mother," Sally later laughed, "but there was no problem because I was so tired I aged drastically. Every morning I was totally wrung out, so it was a perfect time to shoot the film."

Off the set, Sally divided her time by being a full-time mother to her son, and part-time mother to Julia, giving her such advice as: "The only way you learn is by making mistakes."

"Something about her makes you care for her, watch her," Sally explained about her maternal feelings toward Julia. "And it goes beyond her looks. The part of Shelby didn't call for a great beauty, which was fortunate because no one, including Julia, agreed with me that she was one. She grew up as kind of an ugly duckling, not a 'pretty woman,' and the impression we form of ourselves in early adolescence always remains."

With her maternal instinct obviously tweaked, Sally protected and encouraged Julia with the furor of a lioness guarding its cub. Sometimes sensing Julia was nervous about the next day's lines, for instance, Sally would invite her over to her house to rehearse and invariably would end up cooking dinner for Julia. She'd send it home with her, admonishing her to, "Bring the plate back." Another time, Field halted shooting for ten minutes so that she could prep Julia for a crucial scene.

"Sally's inexhaustible support staggered me," Julia later confided. "It got so I didn't call my real mother for three months! I would call Sally and say, 'Momma,' and she would just answer me back."

In fact, one of Betty Motes' favorite anecdotes is about the time she and Julia and Sally were together in an elevator when Julia said, "Mom . . ." and both women responded, "Yes?"

"I spent some time there, especially towards the beginning of the movie, because Julia was feeling a little over-whelmed," Betty explained. "And it was really amazing. I've never seen such harmony."

A needlepoint cnthusiast, Sally encouraged the other actresses to take up the hobby and ordered kits for each of them. Soon the hobby became such a craze that Ross outlawed all needlepointing on the set. As a result, Julia never finished hers. "Without Sally to encourage me," she later admitted, "I just didn't get around to it."

Although the relationship began on a rather tenuous note, mostly due to Julia's insecurities, Julia and Shirley MacLaine also became good friends and wound up spending time together.

"The first time we met I felt she was looking right through me," Julia later confessed. "It was my most tense moment, which is very funny to me now. I went over to her house one day and we got into this intense conversation in which I talked nonstop for an hour and a half about feelings and families and ideas and goals.

"And when I finished," Julia recalled, a note of awe in her voice, "this amazing woman dissected everything I'd said, starting from the beginning. I was absolutely blown away by her extraordinary gift of really listening to a person."

Shirley threw barbecues at her rented lakefront house next door to Julia's rented home, which she shared with her four-month-old bassett hound puppy, Gatsby, but she tended to be more reclusive than did the other actresses. Shirley and Dolly Parton hit it off in a big way, however, laughing about silly things and telling each other dirty jokes.

"It was an extraordinary experience," MacLaine would later recall. "It was sort of like the environment itself dictated the necessity of keeping everyone's fearful side in check, and that's what everybody did. So there was never an ounce or a moment of fear—and that's what governs all those mechanisms of temperament."

Since all of the cast members were settled into Natchitoches life two weeks prior to the July 12, 1988, start of production, one of their first get-togethers was a Fourth of July picnic with everyone playing kid's games. Later, throughout filming, there were frequent impromptu hoedowns at the Bodacious Club, one of Dolly's favorite local haunts, which she once described as "just a lil' ol' beer joint out on the edge of town." Despite her self-professed "closed-in" feeling, Dolly even turned up a time or two, with several members of her family in tow, to sing with the local "Bodacious" band.

Not to be outdone by the others, Olympia Dukakis gave a dinner party which, to the surprise of her guests, was comprised solely of leftovers. "I've been busy with my cousin," Olympia explained to her laughing, good-natured co-stars. Her cousin, of course, was Michael Dukakis, who was then neck-deep in politics as the Democratic Presidential hopeful.

"We were really pals," Olympia would later confide, referring especially to Shirley MacLaine. "We talked a lot and went out to dinner. I spent a lot of time with Daryl, too. We went shopping a lot."

"Usually in the first week of shooting, I get very nervous and insecure," confessed Daryl, adding, "but they rallied around me. We all bonded immediately."

Julia, too, felt the group's support. "It's one thing to watch them act," she said, "but it's another thing to work with them and see firsthand that they're not just really great actors but also really great people."

Despite all of the good times shared between the actresses on their days off, however, the actual filming of

Steel Magnolias was extremely stressful for Julia, who found herself frequently at on-set odds with Herb Ross about how Shelby should be played. "Herbert has his ideas of action and result, and I have mine, and they didn't always receive each other perfectly," Julia later admitted. "But," she added, "you have that relationship and that's one you deal with every day and you do what you have to do to get the result you feel is most true."

At that point, Herb Ross was focusing as much of his energies on his relationship with Lee Radziwill, sister of Jackie Onassis, as he was on the film. Radziwill had accompanied Ross to Atlanta to scout locations for the film in May and, when rehearsals started in Natchitoches the following month, she began flying in every weekend to be by Herb's side. In fact, only a month after *Steel Magnolias* wrapped, the two were married in Lee's Upper East Side New York apartment.

Having played peacemaker between Julia and Ross throughout the making of the film, Sally Field later admitted, "Herb is a good director, but in some ways he was extremely hard on Julia. We all felt it was uncalled for, but she's a warrior."

"I *am* a taskmaster," Ross admitted. "I never spoke privately to anyone. If I had criticism or advice, I would say it in front of the other women. But," he added, proffering a note of praise for a job ultimately well-done, "Julia worked hard. She stayed in bed for the coma scenes eight, twelve hours a day, until she was ill and dizzy."

Several years later Julia brushed off her on-set confrontations with Herb Ross by explaining that working with directors such as Garry Marshall and Joel Schumacher had been "so good for me it's hard to remember any others."

But her confrontations with Ross only served to heighten Julia's anxiety at the time. One of Julia's major concerns was that the role of Shelby, her first truly dramatic film effort, called for a depth of on-screen emoting she had never before had to summon up. "It was a really difficult part. In terms of the friends I made on the set, it was tremendous. In terms of the things I've received from the outcome of it, it was tremendous," she explained a year later, shortly before the film was to open. "But it was not an easy road to travel. Challenge-wise it was difficult, like taking the SATs every day."

In the weeks preceding the filming, Julia had become close to Robert Harling, the playwright who had based *Steel Magnolias* on the real-life tragedy of his sister, Susan, who had died from the effects of diabetes in 1985 in Natchitoches, the family's hometown. "Julia became like a member of my family," Harling confided. "She'd come over and we'd have hamburgers and look through albums and talk to Mom and Dad. They got very close. She's very important to my family."

Having established this relationship with the family, Julia felt an enormous affinity for Susan, so much so that whenever she visited them during the filming, she would always refuse to look at snapshots of Susan. "I thought if I ever looked into her eyes I would lose control," Julia later explained, adding, "When I finally did see them, I was a mess. I was just a puddle."

Feeling as she did about Susan and the Harling family, Julia became thoroughly immersed in the dead woman's life. One night she and Harling were having dinner in one of the several houses being utilized as a set. "We were talking about Susan," Julie later recalled, "and Bobby said, 'You know, Susan used to babysit in this house.' Suddenly I had a feeling she'd been sitting in the chair I was sitting in. It was very odd and uncomfortable.''

With those kinds of strong feelings about the character, and the strong bond she formed with the Harling family, it's not surprising that Julia created a tremendous responsibility within herself toward bringing Susan back to life, even if only on celluloid.

"I had a lot of conversations with Robert Harling, and I felt an obligation to a truth, to explain to the people who would see this movie, 'This is true; this is what happened.' I felt I had a mission to be just to the woman that she was; yet, at the same time, understand that I was not her, that I didn't look like her, that my clothes weren't the clothes she wore, that this wasn't a documentary, that I was playing Shelby Eatenton, not Susan Harling.''

As luck would have it, the first day's shooting schedule involved one of Julia's most difficult scenes in the film—the scene in which Shelby has a diabetic fit in the beauty salon. It was, she would later confess, one of the most difficult she'd ever been asked to do. She was terrified prior to shooting the scene, terrified during the scene and thoroughly exhausted afterwards.

"I was concentrating so hard on what it would be like inside myself—the way my heart looked, the rate it was pumping, all the blood racing through my veins—I got so far down inside my body that as we were coming to the end of the scene a panic went through me,'' Julia recalled with a shudder. "I had gotten stuck down there and didn't want anybody to know. I thought 'I'm never going to get out of here!' I finally did, but I sobbed hysterically after it was over. It was the first day and things got too close to what had really happened. Bobby (Harling) flipped out—he had to leave.''

Harling *was* on the set that day, and *did* have to leave.

He was, he later admitted, too moved by Julia's acting and by the memories it rekindled to remain a spectator. "She would take herself so far down it was scary," Harlings recalled of Julia's performance. "She had this magnificent control. She came as close to death as you can while you're still alive. After every take they'd have to pick her up and help her back to her trailer. I had been through those sort of things with my sister and I just wanted to go over and hug her and tell Herbert, 'Okay, stop it. Let's not do this anymore.' "

Weeks later during Shelby's death scene, when she was hooked up to tubes, lying unconscious in the hospital, Julia's intensity was so great it even spooked the crew. "She wouldn't sit up and talk or have a coke. She'd just stay there," recalled a crew member, "and that created an eerie feeling. You really felt there was a life hovering in the balance, even though you knew it was just a set built in a gymnasium. There was an incredible power in her stillness."

Since appearing in *Steel Magnolias*, Julia has become legendary for the emotion she pours into her roles. "To do that, you have to get a little crazy," explained one of her former producers. "Julia has the guts to really dive in. That's one of the primary reasons why she's accelerated the way she has. She's not shrewd, she's not smart and thinking ahead. She's intelligent and willing to go with her instincts."

Joseph Ruben, who would enter her life several years later as the director of *Sleeping with the Enemy*, also was amazed by Julia's ability to immerse herself in a role. "In real life she doesn't hold anything back emotionally," Ruben would later observe. "You always know how Julia's feeling. It's her body language, her face. She's so expressive as a person, forget as an actor, that

I think it carries over in her acting. An audience sees her and knows what she's feeling."

Julia's explanation for her seemingly unlimited depth of emotion, however, is quite different. "I'll swim out as far as I can until I feel like I'm going to drown, and at that point, I'll swim back but," she explained, "first I have to figure out just where that point is." Although she was speaking of her professional life, Julia could have just as easily been discussing the emotional perimeters of her off-screen life, especially her tumultuous romance with Kiefer Sutherland.

Although Julia and her *Steel Magnolias* co-stars from all outward appearances got along well, not all of the crew considered Julia to be a loving member of the family. According to several sources involved with the production, Julia's nasty, demanding demeanor within the confines of the hair and make-up trailers finally led those crew members to nickname her "The Troll."

"She was a monster," claims a source. "She couldn't sit still. She was always late getting to the set, which meant everyone had to hurry to get her ready so that shooting wouldn't be held up, and she was never happy with her hair or her make-up. She was always in a bad mood, throwing fits, throwing brushes and combs at people. It was absolutely horrendous."

"Julia was a wild, fun party girl. She'd stay out all night," said another crew member, "that's why she was always late for her call. Dolly Parton wasn't kidding when she said later that Julia was 'a sleepyhead.' "

Julia's vision of her time on the set, however, was quite different. "It was kind of like being in a race and they (her co-stars) were all people on my team," she told a newspaper reporter not long after she'd wrapped *Magnolias*.

"They would start running faster and they'd be like, 'C'mon, just run a little faster. You can do it!' So I'd start running faster. They were great support, and they left it so if I did feel lost, got dizzy, didn't know what was happening, then I could just go up and say, 'What's happening? Could somebody tell me?' They would definitely clue me in."

So, despite Julia's late night partying and resulting early morning brouhahas with the hair and make-up people, and her travails with Herb Ross, of course, the overall atmosphere on the *Magnolias* set was apparently pleasant.

"I think we were a good combination," Sally Field said of the on-screen/off-screen mother–daughter relationship between her and Julia. "I became the mother role for her and I think she felt she was able to lean on my steadiness and my experience, while I was able to use my delight and affection for her.

"Julia," Sally continued, "is much more independent than I ever was. She's a real free spirit and that's one thing I've never been or ever will be. I've often wished I was, but I'm always sort of grounded, which is why I think I get a kick out of the Julias of the world. I'm delighted by them."

With her down-to-earth sense of humor, Dolly Parton probably had the most astute observation of the reasons behind the good fellowship of the five female stars. "I think the reason we all became such good friends," Dolly Parton would later laughingly observe, "is because we all had the same exact Winnebagos, we didn't have beautiful clothes to fight over, and there were no available men in the cast."

Well, not exactly. Dylan McDermott was available . . . but only briefly.

When Julia had flown off to Louisiana to co-star in *Steel Magnolias,* she and Liam Neeson had then been an "item" for more than a year. Once Julia was situated in Natchitoches, however, it didn't take long before sparks began to ignite between Julia and Dylan McDermott, the handsome twenty-five-year-old actor portraying her screen husband. Thus, faster than you could yell "Fire," their on-screen romance became an after-hours duet of love as well. And Liam Neeson was suddenly completely out of Julia's life.

Like Julia's other lovers, Neeson has consistently refused to discuss Julia, the circumstances surrounding their break-up remains a matter of speculation to all but their closest friends. However, those who knew Julia and Liam as a couple concede the Irish-born actor "was crazy about Julia."

"He was one of the nicest people you'll ever meet in your life," a friend recalled. "When Julia was in the hospital with spinal meningitis he called the hospital all the time. He was very worried about her, very concerned." And most likely very confused when he discovered that, within a matter of weeks, he was suddenly out and Dylan was very much in Julia's life.

Whatever Liam's initial response to the breakup, Julia Roberts is no longer a subject near and dear to his heart. In a recent interview, Neeson was asked about his relationships with both Julia and Barbra Streisand, a more recent flame. "Is this what it's going to say on my tombstone? 'He dated Julia Roberts and Barbra Streisand,' " Neeson responded with obvious irritation. With that, the interviewer quickly dropped the subject of past romances and moved on, which is obviously what Liam had done four years ago.

Since life moves rapidly in the world of movie-making,

it wasn't long after *Steel Magnolias* wrapped in mid-September, 1988, that Julia and Dylan became engaged. As tight-lipped as his precedessor Neeson, the only comment McDermott has ever made regarding the beginning of his relationship with Julia on *Steel Magnolias* was that "We all hung out together. It was the kind of movie where everyone really hung out."

But if Julia's assessment of Natchitoches is correct, there were very few places to hang out in. "It's a small town, like—whoof!—it's got like two restaurants and all the traffic lights blink at 9:30 P.M.," Julia explained of the tiny town of which she is now a solid part, literally carved in granite. "They did this thing called the Walk of Honor on the sidewalk outside the biggest bank in town," she would later recall. "They had these plaques, and each of us had one. We all had a fleur-de-lis and our name. JULIA ROBERTS—ACTRESS. It was really neat. They had one there for John Wayne and John Ford, who made *The Horse Soldiers,* and one for the painter, Clementine Hunter. So now it's in granite. I guess I'll never be a doctor."

Within a month of having left Natchitoches behind, Julia was out on the road again, this time promoting *Mystic Pizza,* which was scheduled to be released in October.

With her sister, Lisa, by her side she traveled to Atlanta for a semi-vacation during which she divided her time between visiting with her mother and her half-sister, Nancy, for whom she purchased braces as a thirteenth birthday present, and doing a round of local interviews. She was, she told a local reporter, very excited about attending a Friday night screening of *Mystic* with her family at the Galleria, the theater complex where, only a few years before, she had been popping corn and selling tickets.

"It's nice," she confessed, "to be able to come back home with a triumph to lay at your mama's feet. That's a really neat feeling. I think there's something to be said for the humility of coming from a small place," she said of Smyrna, "remembering where you came from and what it was like to have your feet stained with clay all summer long. I think coming back semi-frequently is a good, consistent grounding thing for me."

At the time she was delivering this down-home assessment to a reporter from *The Atlanta Constitution*, Julia was lazily stretched across a large couch in a luxurious suite at the Ritz Carlton hotel in the upscale Buckhead district of Atlanta. The interview ended on an amusing note, with Julia confessing she didn't think appearing in films would create much of a public clamor in Atlanta, or anywhere else, for that matter.

"I don't think people will put two and two together in a million years where I'm concerned," she said of her accruing stardom. "I don't think anyone's really gonna care. 'Jules is back in town!' So what?"

Shortly before departing for Atlanta, Julia and Bob McGowan had met at his office in New York. Since her managerial contract with him was about to expire, McGowan had asked if she wanted to continue working with him.

"I said 'Julia, what's going on with you? Are we going to work together or not?' And, I'll never forget this, she came over and hugged me and said 'Bob, you started all this. I want you in my life forever.' "

135

Forever, however, turned out to be less than ten days. A week after this heartfelt conversation with Julia, McGowan received a telephone call from Elaine Goldsmith, whom he had never met. "She got into the picture after *Steel Magnolias*," he explained, adding all his business dealings had been with Risa Shapiro.

With what has now become legendary bluntness, Goldsmith got right to the point. "Julia doesn't want you as her manager anymore," she told a stunned McGowan.

Several months later, in January 1989, Julia was back in New York, setting up housekeeping in a Greenwich Village apartment, described as a cozy, sunny top floor of a brownstone, complete with fireplace, skylight, and old wide-plank floors. But Bob McGowan never heard from her. In fact, he has never heard from her since the day she hugged him in what turned out to be a goodbye "forever."

"When Julia is through with someone, she is through," explained a one-time friend, adding, "She puts the same kind of determination into that as she does if she wants something. She has that killer instinct, and she'll zero in on whatever she wants."

Julia, however, doesn't see those traits in herself. Nor does she see the dishonesty in following what is obviously a path of least resistance, a trail which ultimately leads someone else into dealing with any unpleasantness that might crop up in Julia's life, professional and otherwise.

"That was the first completely difficult decision I had to make in my life," Julia would explain, regarding her severed ties with McGowan. "Bob had gone to bat for me, but I felt I had to be honest. We'd outgrown each other. There were too many people around me making decisions and I wanted a clearer line between me and the work."

The "clearer line" would prove to be Goldsmith and Shapiro. It was to them Julia handed the power over her life, both professionally and, when necessary, personally. "I'm the show," she explained not long ago. "Elaine and Risa are the business. They take care of the stuff I'm not meant to deal with. If it concerns me, they let me know."

"Julia didn't like confronting things, even with me," McGowan explained. "Plus I think we *did* sort of out-grow each other. It's like the boyfriend/girlfriend thing. After a couple of years of me telling her what to do and how to do it, someone else comes along and tells her the same thing, and it's all new and exciting. I have no hard feelings about it. Julia did a lot for my career. She helped put me on the map (as a manager).

"The only thing that bothered me," he confided, "was the closeness and the way it was done . . ."

Returning to Los Angeles from her promotional tour on behalf of *Mystic Pizza,* Julia would spend the ensuing eight months looking for a role far removed from that of Shelby. As she would later explain, she didn't want to be forever cast into the role of a sweet-girl-next-door role. She was determined to avoid the stereotyping for which Hollywood is so noted.

As a result, she turned down several film projects, one of which was a far cry from any role she has ever played, and probably ever *will* play. It was that of a World War II concentration camp victim caught up in the events surrounding Willem DaFoe in *Triumph of the Spirit.*

"I was really vacillating," Julia later admitted. "It was a very good script, and Willem's a great actor, but they wanted me to shave my head. It may seem superficial to say I can't shave my head, but it would have been five years before I looked like myself again. And that's a long time. Willem said it would give me the opportunity to kill the stereotype I have as a glamour girl," she laughed, "but I told him I'm not tired of it yet."

At one point, Julia verbally agreed to star opposite William Baldwin in a project called "Beyond a Reasonable Doubt," the story of a young woman involved in a jury trial who falls in love with the accused. The film was to have been produced by Phyllis Caryle and financed by the Trans World Entertainment banner.

But TWE supposedly rejected the Roberts/Baldwin coupling because they were both unknowns at the time. "They didn't believe Julia Roberts could carry a film and they had no interest in Billy Baldwin," Carlyle would later recall. "It's not unusual. In this business, a studio only gets behind someone once they're established. By the time things came together, the ship had sailed."

Indeed. By the time the company changed its mind and wanted Julia as its "Reasonable" star, her star had risen and it was too late. As Carlyle later confirmed, "It was a case of Julia's career taking on a momentum that couldn't be contained."

Acting on Julia's behalf, Elaine Goldsmith decided her client would be better off starring in another bigger, more Hollywood film. "I turned down more movies that year than I ever thought I'd turn down in my whole life," Julia later admitted. But she knew she would recognize the right script when it came along. And she did. The film was called "3000." By the time it was released, however, it had been retitled and would forever be known to movie-goers throughout the world as *Pretty Woman*.

Chapter Eight

As originally authored by screenwriter J.F. Lawton, the "3000" script was a bleak tale of a wealthy businessman who hires a drug-addicted prostitute for a week, introduces her to the finer things the world has to offer, then drops her off on the same Hollywood Boulevard corner where he'd encountered her seven days before. The plot was a rather grim portrait of the twosome's week-long relationship based on the idea, Lawton would later explain, that "men would rather buy women than respect them." The title, therefore, referred to the sum exchanged between the businessman and the prostitute for services rendered.

The script initially had been purchased by Steve Reuther, head of production for the now-defunct Vestron Pictures, who had retitled it, "Off the Boulevard." It was during the brief time Vestron had the film project under its roof that Julia had become involved. Before the company could even begin pre-production, however, Vestron fell on difficult financial times, ultimately disbanding, and Reuther, as one of his final acts before departing, sold the film to Disney. And Julia suddenly found herself uninvolved.

Like Julia, actor Hector Elizondo, had also been attached to the film during its residency with Vestron. And, like Julia, he, too, had suddenly found himself out of a job when it was sold. Upon being rehired by Marshall, Elizondo was amazed at the transformation the script had undergone in the transition from Vestron to Disney.

"In the beginning it was a dark uncompromising script," recalled Elizondo, who portrayed the kindly hotel manager who taught Vivian to eat without slurping. "It was not a fantasy. She was a real prostitute in a real world. He was a real bottom-line corporate raider and in the end, she went back to the streets. It was Al Pacino and Michelle Pfeiffer, that's who they were trying to get."

Sting, Sean Connery, as well as Pacino, had all been approached to play the male lead. And they had each turned it down. Richard Gere had also initially passed on the role. "It just was not the kind of movie that I do," he later explained. "In this film the wild exotic flower was the girl. Usually," he added with a laugh, "*I'm* the wild exotic flower."

Disney's decision to hire Garry Marshall as the director of their newly acquired project was a strange choice, since Marshall is noted for his deft touch with light comedy and Lawton's script was the antithesis of comedy, light or otherwise. In the end, of course, it turned out to be a brilliant move.

Once Marshall had come on board as the director, much to the iritation of Lawton, the script had been almost totally rewritten. "The script changed a lot. It was not a happy or funny story in the beginning," Julia would later recall. "Then they took it on this journey and turned it into a delightful, funny, extremely different story."

Retaining only the characters and the barest thread of the original plot, it had been transformed into a contemporary Pygmalion-like fairy tale. And it continued to undergo a metamorphasis, with constant daily rewrites being performed throughout the filming. "We had this writer on the set, his name was Marty," Julia would later laugh, "and Garry would always say, 'Marty, come up with something funny for this.' And this poor guy would be running around with eight different lines."

Once the project had been sold to Disney, Julia had to convince both the Disney execs and Marshall that she was the right actress for the new role of Vivian. Despite several meetings with Marshall, however, Julia was making little headway in her bid to portray the Hollywood hooker. She found Marshall to be "witty and clever" and totally noncommittal whenever she brought up the subject of playing Vivian.

"Garry told me later," Julia recalled, "that half the people at Disney were concerned that you couldn't dress me up—that I could have on jeans and look sort of dirty or whatever but you couldn't dress me up—and the other half were saying the opposite. So Garry was saying, 'So I don't know—' Meaning I absolutely wasn't right (for the role) no matter what I was gonna do."

Although Marshall ultimately decided Julia would be perfect in the role, the studio brass was still insisting that he hire a big name with box-office power, rather than an unknown. And, at that point, Julia was an unknown.

None of the Disney executives had seen *Mystic Pizza* and *Steel Magnolias* had not yet been released. So, in desperation Elaine Goldsmith convinced Ray Stark to screen a print of *Magnolias* for David Hoberman, president of Disney's Touchstone Pictures, and Michael Eisner, chairman of the Walt Disney Company. She also convinced Sally Field to telephone Eisner to tout Julia's acting skills.

Despite the efforts of Goldsmith and Field, however, Julia still had to read for the role several times before the Disney execs agreed to offer her a screen test. "No one had seen *Steel Magnolias* so no one really cared that I was in it. I could've been Waitress No. 3," she recalled years later, adding that she had wanted the role so much she had "chased it down like a dog."

"She was not an automatic," Goldsmith conceded. "Disney tested her for the part—and she had to wait until the eleventh hour before she got it. The studio was reticent about casting her until they'd cast the male lead. Finally, we told them she would take another movie, so they finally agreed and signed her."

The "eleventh hour" deal gave Disney three weeks to pick up Julia's option, which they did—on the day it expired. "Elaine was a like a dog tugging at your cuff who wouldn't let go," Hoberman would later laugh. "She was dogged in her pursuit of the role, getting us to believe Julia was right for it."

Upon hearing Disney had picked up her option, and that she had the role of Vivian, Julia couldn't wait to telephone her mother in Smyrna to let her know that, after a year of not working, she'd finally found a film role she considered to be a perfect vehicle to show off her talents. Suddenly, just as her mother picked up the phone, Julia realized that, despite being a comedy, the role was that of a prostitute.

"My mom works for the Catholic Archdiocese of Atlanta," she laughingly explained to a group of reporters. "I mean, my mom's boss baptized me. So I called her at work, and it was like 'Hi, mom. I got a job.' She said 'You did? What'd you get?' And I said, 'Oh, it's a Disney movie! I gotta go, I'll talk to you later.' "

Once Julia had been signed, Marshall began casting about for a proper male lead and became convinced that Richard Gere was his man. Later Marshall would explain that he had been determined to hire Gere to star opposite Julia because he wanted "two one hundred percent beautiful people" who could act. But, despite "a lot of pleading" from his agent, Gere was not interested in the role, although he did soften his stance a bit after meeting with Marshall in Los Angeles.

"We got along great," Gere later said of his initial meeting with Marshall, "but we didn't talk about comedy at all. Somehow it was about the Dalai Lama and Dostoyevski."

Regardless of the pleasantries exchanged and Marshall's enthusiasm for the project, however, Gere returned to New York still unconvinced the role of Edward was right for him. Nevertheless he followed Marshall's advice and rented a tape of *Mystic Pizza* so that he could see this bright, beautiful young actress Marshall was touting. "I hadn't seen her work before," he admitted. "She was terrific."

Leaving nothing to chance, Marshall flew to New York a short while later to again discuss the project with Gere.

This time he also took Julia with him. "We sat around my office and read the script, which was not very well written at the time and didn't take advantage of possibilities," Gere recalled. "So we very carefully talked about a lot of ideas. My character, for instance, was very underwritten while Julia's character, Vivian, had all the energy. That was one of my problems."

Marshall agreed with Gere's assessment of the script and his role of Edward. "We did a little rewriting to make it more substantial," Marshall would later admit. Script problems aside, however, Marshall believes it was Julia who convinced Gere to get involved with the film. "I think he saw she wasn't just some crazy girl, some starlet. She could act and that impressed him." It also didn't hurt that, like Julia, Gere admittedly suffers from "deep insecurity and shyness."

Whatever the reasons behind Gere's change of heart, within weeks of his meeting with Julia and Marshall, he signed on the dotted line. He *would* be Edward to Julia's Vivian. Marshall was ecstatic. So was Julia, who was intrigued by the controlled, quiet, depth of emotion and intellect Gere exuded. She found this blend of qualities very attractive. She also was instinctively aware that, like herself, Gere suffered from his own insecurities.

With the two leading actors of his choice under contract, Marshall began focusing his energies on getting the script to match his expectations. And Julia concentrated on researching the role of Vivian. Sex in terms of lust and emotion she understood. Sex in return for money was something else and she was determined to find out what. So she spent hours talking to various Los Angeles prostitutes, trying to find out who they were and why they were what they were, but it wasn't an easy task, at least in the beginning.

"A couple came on kind of strong and tough at first," Julia would later recall, "but once I sprang for lunch and took them to Del Taco, they seemed to be nice and talkative. I met enough of them to get a sense that a hooker is not what the average person imagines one to be. She could be the girl you're sitting next to on the bus.

"It's real sad," she continued, "because these are girls, not unlike me. They look like your average girl, talk like your average girl, and they have wonderful hopes for the future. But they're in this situation, and they don't really acknowledge it that much. They cry a lot, but their common goal is a real focus for the future. One girl wanted to be a makeup artist for Jane Seymour; she was very specific. One girl wanted to be a psychologist. That was amazing to me."

At one point Julia even ventured into a Hollywood strip joint. "It was sad, too," she later confided, "because you realized that the girl who took off the most clothes on stage got the most money. They have a view of men— and life—that no one should have to live with." She had no way of knowing at that point just how vast an impact this particular profession would have on her personal life less than two years later.

After spending several days and nights with the women as they worked their way along Hollywood Boulevard, Julia met with Garry to discuss the role of Vivian. She was delighted when he had the writers incorporate some of her perceptions into the script. "It made me feel I was part of bringing this person to life," she confided to friends.

With his self-confidence, his New York brand of humor, his warmth and paternal understanding, Garry Marshall was exactly what Julia needed in a director. This was especially true after the humiliating on-set brow beatings she had taken from Herb Ross, her director on *Steel Magnolias*. With love, Julia bloomed. With tension, she withered. It was a deep-seated holdover from her traumatic childhood

Perhaps it's simply the sign of a good director, but Marshall instinctively knew how to handle Julia as both a human being and an actress. "Julia," he explained, "needs a lot of holding and hugging, particularly in scenes where there's meanness. She performs well when loved, which is why Richard Gere and I took great pains to try and make her feel comfortable, make her feel loved and make it a pleasant experience—not because we're such nice people, but because we felt that was the best thing for the project."

Thus on July 24, 1989, with Richard Gere playing Edward Lewis, a cutthroat corporate raider with a heart of pure cold, Laura San Giacomo as Julia's feisty sister of the streets and Hector Elizondo as the understanding hotel manager who teaches the novice streetwalker proper table manners, *Pretty Woman* began filming on location throughout Los Angeles. At that point the story bore little resemblance to the original saga of Edward and Vivian that Julia had so wholeheartedly once embraced. Gone, along with the title, were the harsh reality, the sad ending. In their place was a contemporary mix of *My Fair Lady* and *Cinderella,* except in this story Cinderella happened to be a beautiful young hooker-with-a-heart-of-gold.

As *Pretty Woman* fans will recall, much of the film's action supposedly took place in the $4,000-a-night Presidential Suite at The Regent Beverly Wilshire, an upscale Beverly Hills hotel on the corner of Wilshire Boulevard and Rodeo Drive.

However, the truth is that Edward and Vivian actually were relegated to a penthouse set constructed within the confines of the once-famous now-abandoned Ambassador Hotel several miles away in a less-than-posh Wilshire Boulevard neighborhood, not far from downtown Los Angeles. And those swimming pool sequences? Well, they were filmed at the Westwood Marquis hotel. In fact, the only scenes shot at The Regent Beverly Wilshire were of its lobby.

Of course, the Hollywood Boulevard scenes, where Vivian prowled in her short leather skirt, tight top, and high heels, were actually filmed on that famous boulevard of broken dreams. "I took so much shit for that outfit," Julia later laughed. "In fact, at one point there were so many catcalls directed at me I went back to my trailer. I felt hideous and just wanted to hide. I know how to deal with any kind of attention somebody's going to give Julia Roberts," she continued, "but the attention that Julia got as Vivian, standing on Hollywood Boulevard in that outfit, was not the kind of attention I'm used to or prepared to deal with. Vivian's clothes were a thousand times more provocative than anything I'd have in my closet. Vivian, of course, would simply say, 'Fuck you! Blow it out your ass!' But I turn red and get hives."

Even though Julia was surrounded by a family of well-meaning cast and crew members, it had become clear to Marshall that certain scenes were going to be very difficult for her to comfortably enact. This was especially true of those scenes involving nudity. "We went slowly and Richard was very, very helpful. She blushed when we first did the screen test. She wasn't used to being that scantily clad," Marshall explained.

Julia, in fact, actually *had* broken out in hives the first time the script called for her to appear in her bra during a scene. "I'm really against nudity in movies," she later explained, adding, "When you act with your clothes on, it's a performance. When you act with your clothes off, it's a documentary. I don't do documentaries.''

Knowing how Julia felt, Marshall devised a devilish plan to relax her when the time came to shoot the first scene involving semi-nudity. So, just prior to filming the scene (where Vivian lounges in a bubble bath while negotiating with Edward over her fee and then, when the deal is struck, enthusiastically submerges herself in the bath water), Marshall went to Julia and bluntly told her: ''Now you're gonna take off your clothes, and there are men here with tattoos.''

With great reticence Julia got into the over-sized bathtub filled to the brim with bubbles and did the scene. However, when she re-surfaced from the bubbles, and swept the water out of her eyes, she discovered the camera was running but no one was left on the set. ''She was startled and then she laughed and got the idea we were going to do this lightly,'' Marshall recalled, adding his prank had been an icebreaker and also ''kinda fun.''

The bathtub scene was not the only surprise Marshall pulled on Julia in an attempt to not only relax her, but also bring out the best in her performance. During the first few takes of the scene in which Edward presents Vivian with a jewelry box filled with diamonds and rubies, Marshall felt the results were ''nice but not special.'' So he pulled Gere aside and told him, ''Snap the lid of the box on her fingers to surprise her when she reaches for the necklace.''

Following Marshall's advice, Gere snapped the jewelry box lid on her fingers just as she reached into the container; and Julia, instead of being angry or annoyed as numerous other actresses might have been, broke into her famous high-pitched laugh.

''A girl who looks like that, with a man like that, who

can still laugh that bottomless laugh—well, that is a girl you can love," Marshall once said, after regaling listeners with several of his Julia-on-the-set anecdotes.

"We try to shoot each performer differently," Marshall explained to a reporter after *Pretty Woman* had wrapped. "And the approach for Julia, quite honestly, was that we shot her like Bambi. She moves around, Julia. She never quite stands still. You just kinda, sorta see her, and that's the way we shot here. She's there, she's beautiful—bam, she's gone. We kidded about it: 'All right, we're doing Bambi in the penthouse today.' "

According to Marshall it wasn't just the moments of nudity in the film that called for tender understanding of Julia's fragile emotions, either. "The dramatic moments where she was going to be very vulnerable were very hard for her, too," he said. "You're with Richard Gere for six or seven weeks, and suddenly you do this scene where he screams in your face and yells at you. It hurt her. He's used to that, but she was devastated by that scene. After each take she was crying, and we'd have to hold her a moment to make sure she was all right.

"In the scenes where she got verbally beaten up by Edward's lawyer and Edward screamed at her, she was playing the vulnerability off-camera so she could play against it on camera," Marshall added. "So off camera, I had a sobbing mess on my hands. But on camera she fought against it, and I think that worked."

Julia found Richard Gere to be a very charming, very warm person, and also a very encouraging presence on the set. "There were days when we were on a stage for a long time," she once explained, "and when that happens you get a bit cagey and there comes a point when your judgment clouds. You don't really know what you're doing, you're just doing it. Well, on a lot of those days, I would come home to a message on my machine from Richard that said 'You did good work and I'll see you tomorrow.' ''

Julia and Richard became close friends, although not as close as Julia reportedly would have preferred. But Richard Gere was in a committed long-term relationship with model Cindy Crawford and, unlike Julia's previous male co-stars, was not interested in having an off-screen liaison with his on-screen girlfriend. Nevertheless, it was due to the wide-spread gossip of Julia's on-set flirtation with Gere that allegedly led to her break-up with Dylan McDermott.

The six-foot blue-eyed McDermott was making a film, a low-budget horror flick, in Morocco when he heard reports about his fiancée and Richard Gere becoming very much together on the *Pretty Woman* set, apparently too close for comfort as far as Dylan was concerned. So he telephoned Julia, who assured him there was absolutely no truth to the rumors about she and Gere. When the stories continued, however, McDermott decided to fly to Hollywood to check things out for himself.

''Julia was supposed to come visit him while he was making *Hardware*, but she didn't, which is when he knew something was up,'' a friend recalled. ''Then he began getting gossip from Hollywood about the sexy bed scenes between Julia and Richard Gere, and he got really upset. He was getting so frustrated, he finally got the film's producers to change his shooting schedule so that he could take a week off. He flew to Los Angeles, went to the set, and he saw the chemistry between Julia and Gere, and he didn't like the look of it.''

It was during his brief visit to Los Angeles that Dylan

A poor but aspiring actress, Betty Bredemus (in her 1952 high school graduation photo) enlisted in the Armed Services in 1953, where she met Walter Roberts. They married in July. (*Archival Photo/Guy D'Alema*)

Walter Roberts bought this bungalow in February, 1971, only three months before Betty filed for divorce. It was auctioned off for back taxes on the courthouse steps several years later. (*Courtesy of Guy D'Alema*)

Julia was seven years old when she posed for this 1974 school photo. Years later she would laugh about the gap in her front teeth, which she said was wide enough to stick a popsicle stick through. (*Archival Photo/Guy D'Alema*)

Campbell High School had no drama department until its most famous graduate hit it big in Hollywood. Now the school has not only a drama department, but also a "Julia Roberts Drama Award." (*Courtesy of Guy D'Alema*)

Julia (standing, second from left) exhibited the same determination in high school that she has in pursuing movie roles. Told her eyes weren't strong enough to play tennis, she joined the girls' tennis team anyway. (*Archival Photo/Guy D'Alema*)

Although she was well-liked by high school classmates, Julia (second row, far left) remained apart from the crowd, even in this 1983 photo of the Campbell High School Spanish Club. (*Archival Photo/Guy D'Alema*)

No one could have known from looking at this sophomore class photo that Julia's home life was filled with the tension and potential violence that led her mother to begin divorce proceedings against Michael Motes in 1983. (*Archival Photo/Guy D'Alema*)

Like Julia, Lisa Roberts (seen in her 1983 high school graduation photo), left small-town Smyrna, Ga., within days of her high school graduation and moved to New York, where Julia joined her two years later. (*Archival Photo/Guy D'Alema*)

After living in several shabby houses, Betty and Michael Motes bought this Smyrna home in 1977. Julia lived here until moving to New York in 1985. Three years later the house was picked up by an engineering firm as abandoned property. Remodeled, it is now the company headquarters. (*Courtesy of Guy D'Alema*)

Walter Roberts was obsessed with regaining custody of Julia and Lisa after Betty married Michael Motes in 1972. He fought—and lost—two court battles and ended up having Julia and Lisa for only two summer weeks and Christmas Day. (*Archival Photo/Guy D'Alema*)

After years of poverty and unhappiness, Walter took a job as a vacuum cleaner rep and then married Eileen Sellars in 1974. The couple adored each other, but the union ended in tragedy. (*Archival Photo/Guy D'Alema*)

In profile, Eric Roberts bears a striking resemblance to his father (seen here with his second wife, Eileen, enjoying Christmas dinner the year before their deaths). It was Eric who handled the funeral arrangements for both Walter and Eileen before leaving Atlanta forever. (*Archival Photo/Guy D'Alema*)

Eric was a long-haired teenager when this 1975 photo of him and his stepmother was taken at her 26th birthday celebration. Two years later Eileen drowned in a tragic boating accident, despite Eric's attempts to save her. (*Archival Photo/Guy D'Alema*)

An early publicity photo of the actress, before she was forced to change back to her given name, Julia, by the Screen Actors Guild, whose roster already included another Julie Roberts. (*Archival Photo/Guy D'Alema*)

JULIE ROBERTS

Bob McGowan met Julia shortly after she arrived in New York. As her manager, McGowan helped launch her career, getting her roles in "Satisfaction" and "Mystic Pizza." (*Courtesy of Bob McGowan*)

These early publicity photographs were taken in New York, when 17-year-old Julia was still thinking of becoming a model. "None of the agencies were interested," says a friend. "They told her she was too heavy." (*Archival Photo/Guy D'Alema*)

Julia's first movie role was in the 1986 film, "Blood Red." She played Eric's sister, marking the first time in film history that a brother and sister in real life played the same in "reel" life. Eric was Julia's biggest fan then. Now the two of them rarely speak. (*Courtesy of Globe Photos, Inc.*)

Julia (with Annabeth Gish in a scene from "Mystic Pizza") resorted to subterfuge to land her role of Daisy, claiming to play a musical instrument, then dyeing her hair jet black with shoe polish and mousse. (*Courtesy of Paul Slaughter/Globe Photos, Inc.*)

Julia's first big break came when she landed a role in "Satisfaction" with Justine Bateman (standing, left) Trini Alvarado, Britta Phillips and Scott Coffee. The film was forgettable, but Julia was not. (*Courtesy of John Seakwood/Globe Photos, Inc.*)

Liam Neeson was her co-star in "Satisfaction" and the first of several leading men to become her off-screen lovers. The two lived together for about a year. Then Julia landed the role in "Steel Magnolias;" Liam was out and Dylan McDermott was in. (*Courtesy of Mitchell Gerher/Globo Photos, Inc.*)

Julia was all smiles as she clasped a Golden Globe for her performance in "Steel Magnolias." (*Courtesy of Ralph Dominguez/Globe Photos, Inc.*)

Julia brought out the maternal instincts in Sally Field, who campaigned for Julia to portray her daughter in "Steel Magnolias" and later developed "Dying Young" specifically for Julia. (*Courtesy of Christine Loss/Globe Photos. Inc.*)

Despite an all-star cast, Julia was the only one nominated for an Academy Award for her performance in "Steel Magnolias." (Left to right) Olympia Dukakis, Shirley MacLaine, Darryl Hannah, Sally Field, Dolly Parton, and Julia. (*Courtesy of J. Watson/Globe Photos, Inc.*)

Julia had ended her engagement to Dylan McDermott shortly before flying to Chicago in late 1989 to play opposite Kiefer Sutherland in "Flatliners." Within months the two were in love. By Spring, 1990, they were living together. (*Courtesy of Globe Photos, Inc.*)

Julia, seen here with Richard Gere on the set of "Pretty Woman," was so nervous about doing her first love scene with him she thought she was going to throw up. She'd already broken out in hives at having to appear in a semi-nude scene. (*Courtesy of Shooting Star*)

Garry Marshall, her director on "Pretty Woman," became one in a long list of father figures for Julia who, he once confided, "needs a lot of hugging and holding." (*Courtesy of Ron Batzdorff/Globe Photos, Inc.*)

Joel Schumacher, seen here with Julia on the set of "Dying Young," fell in fatherly love with her during their first meeting to discuss "Flatliners." He became one of her most ardent admirers, explaining "She's just mesmerizing." (*Courtesy of Christine Loss/Globe Photos, Inc.*)

Julia, with Kiefer during happier days, turned up a platinum blonde for the 1991 Academy Awards ceremony. She refers to her various hair colorings, which have ranged from black to orange to platinum as "mood hair." (*Courtesy of Dan Golden/ Shooting Star*)

Julia and Jason Patric became romantically entangled during a "bonding" weekend at a posh Arizona spa only five days prior to her widely-publicized, but ill-fated wedding to Kiefer. (*Courtesy of Ron Davis/Shooting Star*)

Despite her emotional travails and exhaustion, Julia completed her role of Tinker Bell in "Hook" in August, 1991, before disappearing in a cloud of pixie dust for a two-year, self-imposed sabbatical. (*Courtesy of Globe Photos, Inc.*)

Julia and her mother, Betty Motes, attended the Los Angeles movie premiere of "Benny and Joon." Despite the emotional turmoil caused by her mother's second marriage, the two remain extremely close. (*Courtesy of Alan Berliner/ Gamma Liason*)

Julia and Susan Sarandon, seen here at a Manhattan fashion show given by Richard Tyler, Julia's favorite dressmaker, became best friends during Julia's two-year hiatus from Hollywood and films. It was through Sarandon's brother that Julia met hubby Lyle Lovett. (*Courtesy of John Barrett/Globe Photos, Inc.*)

Rumors of a romance between Julia and Daniel Day-Lewis began to surface in October, 1992. When Julia—not so quietly—bid Jason Patric *adieu* in mid-January, columnists both here and in Great Britain published stories of the transatlantic affair, which supposedly ended only a month prior to her June marriage to Lovett. (*Courtesy of Sylvia Norris/Globe Photos, Inc.*)

Julia and co-star Patrick Bergin, who portrayed her psychotic, abusive husband in "Sleeping with the Enemy," started out as friends but, as their on-screen relationship deteriorated, so did the friendship. (*Courtesy of Shooting Star*)

Although the rest of the world considers her beautiful, Julia is self-conscious about her looks. She rarely wears makeup because she doesn't like to call attention to her mouth, especially her lips. (*Courtesy of Stephen Trupp/Globe Photos, Inc.*)

In an attempt not to be outdone by competitors' coverage of Julia's marriage to Lyle Lovett, *The Globe* took this "Steel Magnolias" wedding photo of Julia and Dylan McDermott, superimposed Lovett's head over McDermott's, then published it as their cover shot of the nuptials. (*Courtesy of Globe Photos, Inc.*)

Julia became Mrs. Lyle Lovett in a June 27, 1993, wedding that shocked everyone but the couple's closest friends. Only days after the nuptials it was discovered the two had been dating less than a month. (*Courtesy of Sygma Photos*)

discovered, as had Liam before him, that he was out, no matter if no one else was in. "She dumped him," said a friend, "and he was devastated, terribly upset. She broke his heart."

Returning to the set of *Hardware,* Dylan told his commiserating co-workers, "It's over. I'm going to have to get over it." But it apparently was a difficult chore. According to friends, Dylan lost twelve pounds in the month following the breakup. The following year, however, after *Pretty Woman* had been released and Julia had won a Golden Globe, Dylan called her during a stopover in Los Angeles. "He thought perhaps they could, at least, be friends," confided a friend. Apparently Julia wanted to see him because she invited him over for a visit.

In describing his visit later to friends, McDermott told how he'd walked in to Julia's only to discover a house in disarray. "There was dog shit on the carpet and the bedroom door was open, and the sheets had rolled off the bed onto the floor," the friend recalled. "The Golden Globe was sitting on the dressing room table surrounded by clutter."

A notoriously fastidious "herbal tea man," who doesn't drink alcoholic beverages or smoke, Dylan apparently was disgusted by what he'd seen during his brief, very brief, visit with Julia. "I felt like a toilet seat," he later confided to friends.

A short while later, Liz Smith, the syndicated columnist, wrote of the twosome's uncoupling. "They started having a wild affair and seemed to be very, very much in love," Smith penned. "Julia was very sweet to him, very into him. Then all of a sudden she dumped him. Her time limit seems to be twelve to eighteen months. As soon as the romance gets serious she can't handle it. She can't seem to handle the reality of committment." Little did Smith realize at the time just how astute this observation about Julia's emotional instability in affairs of the heart would turn out to be.

As one would suspect, especially with all that love floating around, Julia preferred to hang around on the *Pretty Woman* set, talking and trading jokes with the crew, rather than remain in her trailer between calls. "She tells a good joke," recalled a crew member. "She likes to hear a good story and after that she turns them into her own. She's very creative that way."

Other times she and Gere, along with one of the prop men, would play music on the set, often bringing in tapes for each other to hear. Halfway through the filming, Julia found a little dog, which she immediately adopted and brought to the set every day. Sometimes they had to stop filming to feed the dog, but nobody complained. When the dog ruined a couple of takes because of its barking, Marshall simply yelled "Cut!" and told the cameraman to reload.

Hector Elizondo was another of Julia's favorites among the cast members, and the two spent a great deal of time discussing everything from acting to poetry. "I was impressed by the fact there were actual books in her trailer, and by her interest in literature. She had poetry, a book of essays, and she was reading a novel. And they were well thumbed."

Elizondo also was impressed by Julia's ability to "concentrate and really listen. She had a sense of privacy—a sense of being self-contained and belonging to herself as opposed to wishing to please other people all the time. I had a feeling she was serious about her work but not solemn about the way she did it. I liked her a lot."

"The set of *Pretty Woman* was really a happy place," Julia's mother would recall. "It was a happy movie to make. I was out there when they had to re-shoot a scene and I watched Julia and Garry Marshall and he was really like Big Daddy. He's one of those very, very nice people and obviously was a real father figure for Julia.

"It was a very close group, even the crew," explained Betty who, along with daughter Nancy, has visited Julia on every one of her movie sets. "When it came time to film the love scene, the crew was shaking like a leaf because they knew how she felt."

And how she felt, Julia confided to a *Playboy* magazine writer, was "so scared and nervous" about doing her first love scene with Richard Gere that she thought she was going to throw up. "I felt like I was twelve years old and had never been kissed," she confessed. "Then I called my mom, and then I did throw up; and then I called my mom again. But it went very smoothly."

Having no idea just how amusing his quip actually was, Garry Marshall later laughingly confessed: "I kidded Julia's mother that I'm the one who made your daughter take off all her clothes."

It was while she was in the middle of filming *Pretty Woman* that *Harper's* magazine had named Julia "a contemporary beauty" in their annual glimpse of "The Ten Most Beautiful Woman in America." Hence, a few days later, Garry Marshall walked onto the set and, seeing Julia, kiddingly announced in a loud voice: "Well, I see we have a contemporary beauty in our midst."

"I was happy (about being chosen)," Julia joked, "because the library in my high school gets this magazine and all the teachers who flunked me will see it."

Not long afterward *Playboy* magazine dubbed her to have the finest "Lips of the Nineties," just as they had deemed Kim Basinger to have had the most exquisite "Mouth of the Eighties." "They've never gotten in the way," Julia responded. "When they're your own lips, you don't really think about them. But there was a time in high school when I felt a little grief because I had an unusual mouth, unlike the other girls who had perfect mouths with little heart-top lips. But I never have done anything to accentuate my mouth. It's crooked and I have a couple of little scars. I never wear lipstick because I don't like to call a lot of attention to my mouth. In fact, I'm really bad at putting it on. Every time I've put it on, I've taken it off before I've gone out."

Interestingly, in the *Pretty Woman* press kit, the film's chief make-up artist, Bob Mills, discusses the great pains that were taken to accomplish Julia's "no make-up look" which, he wrote, "encompassed various corrective techniques."

"The hollows in Ms. Roberts cheeks were filled with highlights as were the eyesockets. The jawline was also highlighted to broaden it. Shadows were added to slim the nose and contour the forehead. The cheekbone line was lowered to produce a fuller effect. Hidden liners to thicken the lashes were applied, the lips were corrected to soften the very generous quality of her own."

And, although there is no mention of this in the press materials, a body double was substituted for the movie's opening scene where you see Vivian donning the mini dress, the bracelets and the long boots, while the camera follows each movement, caressing her bust and legs. Whether film-goers realized it or not, however, the face of the owner of these various body parts is not revealed. And that's because they did not belong to Julia. Nor did the slim, sleek body featured in the classic *Pretty Woman* poster shot of Vivian in a mini skirt, tight-fitting top and above-the-knee black shiny boots. It was Julia's face superimposed on the body of Shelley Michelle, a Hollywood body double, who has earned a generous living by having various parts of her well-constructed, finely toned anatomy distributed to numerous well-known Hollywood actresses. It was Shelley's legs, for instance, not Kim Basinger's legs, that were immortalized in the 1988 film, *My Stepmother is an Alien*.

At the end of filming, Marshall, who called Julia his schlumpy girl, came to her trailer to deliver a card addressed to "My schlumpy girl," then added a necklace with a diamond heart and told her, "Wear this wherever you go and know there's someone who loves you."

"I was a puddle," Julia would later confess.

"Even when Julia is being schlumpy," Garry Marshall later commented, "she's schlumpy with elegance."

A few nights later at the wrap party, Marshall, who once played drums in a Catskills dance band and Gere, an accomplished pianist, along with two crew members who played guitar, formed a quartet to entertain the revelers. "Then," Marshall laughed, "we heard that Julia played bass and we thought: Perfect!" The quintet jammed to everything from blues to jazz, country, and a little rock tossed in for eclectic good measure.

"I've worked with actresses who have been really difficult," Gere would later admit, "and Julia's not one of them. She's a very real, very decent person, and she's not caught up in the actress thing."

Three weeks after completing *Pretty Woman*, Julia flew to Atlanta for the Southern premiere of "Steel Magnolias," which was a $150 per ticket fundraiser for the Juvenile Diabetes Fund. Although Dolly Parton was forced to bow out of the premiere at the last minute due to a family illness, Shirley, Olympia, Sally, and Daryl all flew to Atlanta to join Julia for the Monday evening extravaganza.

A black tie gala, the event began with a 6:30 P.M. champagne reception in the lobby of the Phipps Plaza Cineplex, followed by a 7:30 P.M. screening of the film and a 9:30 P.M. banquet and dance at the Ritz Carlton Hotel in the exclusive Buckhead area of the city.

Red carpets were rolled out and searchlights beamed through the night sky as more than 1,000 Atlantans arrived to view the film and swap niceties with its stars. Not since *Gone with the Wind* had premiered there in 1939 had Atlanta seen such a glittering gathering of notables which, in addition to the film's female stars, also included Tom Skerritt, Robert Harling, producer Ray Stark, Dawn Steel, who was then president of Columbia Pictures, and fellow Georgian, Kenny Rogers. Julia, it was reported, strolled into the reception on the arm of her half-sister, Nancy Motes.

After the screening, the black tie tuxedoed crowd boarded buses to go to the Ritz Carlton, where a ballroom banquet and dance awaited them. Ironically, the ballroom entrance was adorned with a white gingerbread trellis, not unlike the one that would be constructed two years later on the Twentieth Century Fox lot in anticipation of Julia's wedding to Kiefer Sutherland.

A month after its Atlanta premiere, *Steel Magnolias* opened across the country to mixed reviews. "Herbert Ross's *Steel Magnolias* runs 118 minutes, but seems even longer than *Intolerance*, penned Vincent Canby, the esteemed *New York Times* film critic, adding that Julia "plays a beautiful young woman, who happens to be diabetic, with the kind of mega-intensity the camera cannot always absorb.''

Despite Vincent Canby's acerbic observations, Julia received a Golden Globe nomination, and a short while after that an Oscar nomination, for her portrayal of the doomed Shelby. "My girlfriend said it's like a wine bottle filled with beads and you shake it, and none of the beads come out," Julia said of her sudden fame and good fortune after receiving the Best Supporting Actress Oscar nomination. "But you know that if two little beads would move, they'd all come out. I feel a bit like that. It's starting, but it's not too fast."

Although Julia had been the only unknown among the stellar cast of female stars, she was the only member of the group to have received recognition from the film industry for her efforts. Perhaps that's why, in an interview not long after she'd won the Golden Globe, Julia graciously conceded: "I've worked with some really great actors and I hear them talking about structure, and I listen. But mostly I watch. I learned so much from those five tremendous women in *Steel Magnolias,* by watching them do what they do perfectly. I owe them a lot more than I could ever articulate."

At that point Julia could afford to be gracious. Not only had she won a Golden Globe and earned an Oscar nomination for her performance in *Steel Magnolias,* she also had been the subject of a *Gentleman's Quarterly* article, "Answered Prayers" in which she had confessed, "My butt has changed a lot in the last year." She was alluding to her loss of fifteen pounds, presumably all from that area of her body, and most likely due to the *Steel* dictim of Herb Ross.

"I was staggered to be one of the ten," Julia told *GQ*

writer, Alan Richman, referring to her inclusion in the *Harper's* article. "I don't care what they call me. I didn't open up the magazine and say, 'I want to be the fucking 'hot beauty.' "

Richman was apparently charmed to new poetic heights by Julia whom, he wrote, was comprised of "fascinating features sometimes in harmony and sometimes not." He alluded to her "wide-screen eyebrows. The florid Senior Wences mouth. That nose she calls 'the apparatus.'

"She's a kaleidoscope of body parts," Richman had concluded. To which Julia responded, upon reading the article, "My God, I've got to call my mom, and tell her that genetically I'm great for conversation!"

Chapter Nine

Shortly before beginning work on *Pretty Woman* Julia had contacted director Joel Schumacher, hoping to land the female lead in a film he was tentatively scheduled to begin in fall, 1989, called *Flatliners*. Julia had seen a copy of the script the previous summer, but had turned it down because she had already signed to star in *Steel Magnolias*.

Already intrigued by Julia, whom he had first spied in *Satisfaction*, Schumacher had agreed to meet with her at his home on a Sunday afternoon. "Even though she was just one of the girls," Schumacher explained, referring to *Satisfaction*, "there was just something about her that was so sexy and infectious, I decided to keep an eye on her. Then, when I saw her again in *Mystic Pizza*, well, that was it. That's all I had to see. When I decided to do *Flatliners* she was my first choice."

Nevertheless, Schumacher, whose directorial credits then included such films as *Cousins*, *St. Elmo's Fire*, and *The Lost Boys*, a contemporary vampire chiller starring Kiefer and an unknown young actor named Jason Patric, was totally unprepared for meeting Julia in the flesh. It was an experience, he has since said, he will never forget.

When the doorbell rang at the appointed hour, Schumacher threw open the door to discover a long-legged Julia standing in front of him, wearing short, cutoff jeans and a man's tee shirt. She was barefoot, wearing no makeup and her long, curly hair was piled high atop her head. "I watched her for two hours, while she told me why she had to do this film," Schumacher later recalled, "and I was just mesmerized by her. I kept thinking, 'Where has she been?' "

The two worked out a deal based on a creative meeting of their respective minds. What this meant, Schumacher would later explain, was that "if either of us hated the other, the deal was off." As it turned out the two wound up being instant good friends. Realizing how smitten Schumacher was with her client, and how much he wanted Julia in *Flatliners*, Goldsmith negotiated Julia's salary upward to $550,000, almost double what she had just earned on *Pretty Woman*.

"Elaine was smart, very smart," said an industry insider. "Not only did she almost double Julia's client's fee, but the film was an ensemble piece, which meant it was a no-lose situation for Julia. If it failed, she was one of ten people. If it worked, it was because she was in it. In that way, it was a bullet-proof idea."

Thus, only five days after completing *Pretty Woman*, Julia was in Chicago, preparing to film *Flatliners*, an off-beat story about a group of medical students whose experiments with death lead to revelation and revulsion, co-starring Kiefer Sutherland and Kevin Bacon.

As it turned out, the film also would lead to an "experiment" with love that would ultimately turn into "revelation and revulsion," not to mention world-wide headlines. But, at the time she flew to Chicago, Julia didn't know Kiefer Sutherland and had absolutely no idea what strange twist her life was about to take.

"We'd just started shooting, and I didn't know anybody," Julia would later recall. "We were shooting at night, and it was real cold. I had this one easy thing to do, just run up these stairs, looking for the character played by Kiefer. I started talking to Joel, and I'm asking him, 'How did I get here, did I take the bus?' 'No,' he said, 'you ran.' I thought about how long it would have taken to run there, and all of a sudden, I realized how panicked a situation this was. I'm running and I have to get there for about ten reasons, the biggest of which is to save Kiefer's life, and the least is to tell him it's all right and he's my friend.

"So I get into this place in my mind where I'm breathing really hard," she continued, in her unique, rambling fashion, "and I say to Joel, 'Is Kiefer here?' 'Yeah, he's in his trailer.' So I say I really need to see him, and Kiefer comes out, he doesn't know what I'm doing, he doesn't even know who I am. He came out and I just flailed my preparation at him, tugged at his shirt, and I didn't need him to say anything. I just needed him to be there, to be a person. I remember the three of us standing in the cold, and me feeling this support from Kiefer and Joel.

"That's why you make a movie, for the support, to be like a family," she'd explained. "You can't ask for more than nights like that—amazing nights."

161

Shortly after that, of course, Julia and Kiefer began having many "amazing nights" together, on the set and off. But it was that particular night when what would become a two-year relationship began, not with a bang but with a whimper.

Bonding. Support. Incredible emotional commitment. Love and the perpetual fantasy of a close-knit family. *Those*, not fame and fortune, were the major reasons why Julia had so desperately wanted to become an actress.

Driven by the emotional privation of her childhood, rather than by any intellectual motivation or mercenary stimulus, to Julia stardom was nothing more than an unwanted by-product of her soaring career. Love and adoration were the keys to Julia's lock, not money, which is why she never once stopped to consider what price those accompanying accoutrements would cost her, until it was too late.

Within days of the start of principal photography on October 23, 1989, Julia had once again bonded with the cast and crew, turning the filmmaking project into a surrogate family atmosphere headed by her surrogate father, Joel Schumacher. No wonder, unlike most stars, Julia did not complain when, because *Flatliners* was a low-budget film, Schumacher continued shooting through the Christmas holidays and New Years. She didn't care. She was with her family, surrounded by love and adoration, in a winter wonderland of twinkling lights and magical togetherness.

Since it was the holiday season, most of the married crew members had their kids on the set during those weeks, which turned out to be a delightful treat for Julia. Like many people fearful of true intimacy, Julia has discovered that showering affection on children and animals calls for no particular emotional commitment. It's safe, it's genuine, and it's rewarding because the usual payoff invariably is unconditional love in its purest form.

"She had all the kids in her trailer all the time," Schumacher recalled. "There was always a line of kids in and out of Julia's trailer. She was feeding them, mothering them. And, you know, that's unique. A lot of people in Hollywood aren't nice to the parents, let alone their children!" he'd concluded.

When Julia wasn't engrossed in feeding and mothering stray children, along with her menagerie of stray dogs and cats, she was busy either filming or preparing to film a role which, on a very personal level, had to create a variety of complex feelings, since it dealt with the death of her character's father.

"She does her emotional homework before she comes in," Schumacher once said. "If she has to do a highly emotional scene, she's figured out what she's going to use from her own life and feelings to get there. And she would always let me know, either deliberately or in a more covert way, what the trigger would be from her life. For instance," he explained, "her father's dead in the film, as well as in real life, and my father's dead, and we'd have that to relate to between takes if she came over to me for help staying in the moment."

Although Schumacher refused to elaborate on his conversations with Julia, discussions he admitted had been "poignant and personal," he did recall being "immediately struck by her intelligence and wisdom."

"She was twenty-one years old and I thought I was talking to someone my own age," Schumacher explained, echoing Bob McGowan's assessment of Julia's dazzling maturity for one so young.

"Julia always had a great personality," concedes a former New York friend who's probably known Julia as well as anyone. "She could sit and talk to anybody about almost any topic. And if she didn't know about the topic, the person she was talking to didn't *know* she didn't know about the topic."

Whether or not that was the magic act Julia worked on Joel Schumacher, the fact is that throughout the filming of *Flatliners,* Julia and Joel belonged to a very exclusive mutual admiration society. In fact, neither of them could say enough nice things about each other.

"It's nice to know there's someone like her on the planet. She's brilliant. She's talented. She gets the jokes. She's raunchy. She's the perfect lady," Schumacher confided.

"Joel was just so intense and articulate. When we did small scenes, he would give us something basic and then not say anything, but when he did say something, it was succinct and exactly right," Julia cooed. "And he'll lead you to things so that, in the end, the ideas he has become your ideas as well. He created a really happy set, which makes that eleventh or twelfth hour of work worth it."

"She's quite mesmerizing in person," Schumacher explained, adding, "when the camera hits her, it just gets enhanced to a point where it's dazzling. She's really in a class by herself. I've worked with a lot of other extraordinary women but Julia is just not interchangeable with anyone."

"Some directors, they give you support but they're essentially cool with their flattery because they don't want to give an actor a big head, which I think is poppycock," Julia explained. "Half the time I'm thinking I'm delivering the biggest pile of garbage, and all I need is this one kind word that's going to save me from myself. On *Flatliners* we would do a scene and when it was over Joel would hoot 'I can't wait for dailies!' He would just start screaming and make you feel good.''

Julia, Schumacher ultimately acknowledged, was an intriguing blend of many varying traits. "She can be funny, sexy, even raunchy," he explained, "and she's a master at telling dirty jokes. But she never seems to come off vulgar in any way, shape, or form."

It was because of this earthiness and baudy sense of humor, Schumacher said, that everyone on the set, cast and crew alike, adored Julia. "Like most truly intelligent and enlightened people she has no class system within her," he explained. "People are people and she doesn't treat the high rollers any differently from the blue collar people. It's a very enlightened way to live. She adds a great deal of nurturing and support to the communal situation, which is always welcome."

But the one person on the set who most adored Julia turned out to be her leading man, Kiefer Sutherland. The "chemistry" between Julia and Kiefer apparently had been both immediate and mutual. Although the couple would hide their relationship from the rest of the world for another four months, it became obvious to everyone involved in *Flatliners* that Julia and Kiefer were crazy about each other long before the film wrapped on January 23, 1990.

"I had no reason to like or dislike this person," Sutherland would later recall, referring to Julia. "There was no outside input except for my agent saying, 'Oh, I'm so glad Julia Roberts is doing this film.' And I was going, 'Julia who?' and thinking 'Okay, here's this novice.' Then she comes into rehearsal and she had a really incredible presence just as a person, which made me sit back and take a look.

"Then we started working together and I got really, really excited," he continued, in a stream-of-consciousness dialogue rivaled only by Julia's similar style of semi-coherent musings, "because she was one of the best actors I'd ever worked with. I mean, she was incredibly giving, incredibly open, and she had qualities you can't even articulate when you're watching her work.

"I thought that I had been the only one to see this and that I'd made this great find," he explained, "until friends of mine who had seen *Steel Magnolias* said, 'Everybody knows that, Kiefer. Grow up!' "

Julia was in the midst of filming *Flatliners*, when a *Vogue* magazine article on her hit the newstands. At that time, Julia was deeply into hip "schlumpy," wearing odd hats, five earrings per ear and Jean Paul Sartre eyeglasses, carrying a purse that resembled a steamer trunk, and keeping track of her car and house keys by hanging them on a large eyeball key chain.

Having shown up for the *Vogue* interview wearing her usual garb of ripped blue jeans, cowboy boots, and a nondescript, loose-fitting dingy brown sweater, she was subsequently described by the writer as looking more like "a poetry major than a budding sex symbol." Nevertheless, the magazine reported, Julia had a fashion flair that would no doubt make her comfortable, whether amidst the Beverly Hills crowd or among the scruffy-but-clean patrons of Java, one of her favorite West Hollywood coffeehouses.

"She's a free spirit who likes to roam around barefoot, has memorized the entire Elvis Costello songbook, enjoys her privacy and talks endlessly about 'her boyfriend,' although she never reveals his name," explained the writer, who then quoted Julia as having confessed that

"The most difficult thing in the world is to be simple, to reduce things down to simple terms."

"There are times when Hollywood is very unattractive to me," Julia had explained. "But there was a time in New York when I had nothing but time on my hands. So, when Hollywood has no charm and everyone just wants you, you have to be grateful and remember the times you were sitting in your apartment with nothing to do."

With that, Julia announced that as soon as *Flatliners* was finished and she had wrapped her next film, *Sleeping with the Enemy,* she planned to take a self-imposed vacation from the rigors of then having made six films, if you count *Baja Oklahoma,* the HBO television movie, in three years.

"I just want to go in a field somewhere and pick flowers," she explained.

But the field and the flowers were going to have to wait. Julia's career was just about to take off like a rocket, beginning with her unexpected nomination for a Golden Globe award, quickly followed by an Oscar nomination, for her role of Shelby in *Steel Magnolias,* which had been released to less than thunderous applause in December. Within the ensuing three months, and capped by the March, 1990, release of *Pretty Woman,* Julia would be catapulted virtually overnight into the rarified atmosphere of superstardom, whether she wanted it or not.

Julia was still in Chicago working on *Flatliners* when she learned she had been nominated for a Golden Globe award for her *Steel Magnolias* performance. It was, she admitted, "quite shocking and really a surprise."

"I was on location and the phone in my trailer kept ringing," she later recalled. "I'd had a bad day, and I kept picking it up and hanging it back up. Then I got a bouquet of flowers with a note that said, 'Congratulations on your nomination.' A short time later, my agent called and said I'd been nominated.

"I was really excited and I wanted to tell somebody. It was not embarrassing, but you don't want to be overly bold," she explained. "So I told my director, and he announced, 'We have somebody here who is a Golden Globe nominee.' So they started calling me Miss Golden Globe."

After *Flatliners* wrapped on January 23, 1990, Julia quietly flew to Tucson, Arizona, to spend time with Kiefer and rest up before heading to South Carolina in early April to begin work on *Sleeping with the Enemy*. She was, in fact, happily nesting with Kiefer when Elaine Goldsmith called to tell her she'd also received an Oscar nomination as Best Supporting Actress for her role of Shelby in *Steel Magnolias*.

"The day I got nominated was Valentine's Day and I was with a friend of mine," she told her hometown newspaper. "I got a call about it at five in the morning," she explained, adding "I was too excited to go to sleep and too tired to get excited. So it was about two in the afternoon and we'd known since early in the morning, but it just hadn't registered with me. Then, I'm watching MTV and all of a sudden I started giggling, and I just couldn't stop laughing."

She then likened the Oscar nomination to having been picked as one of the ten finalists in Campbell High School's annual Miss Panthera beauty contest. "It was that kind of feeling of 'Oh, my God. I can't believe they picked me.' It was that feeling on an adult scale. But it's not something that makes me happy all the time. It comes in waves.

"I had pretty much blocked it out of my mind, because you can only find disappointment in an expectant mind, right? And then the call came in and, well, I didn't even make the cheerleading squad at Campbell High, now I'm nominated for an Academy Award? Of course, it scares me and thrills me," she told Steve Dollar, a reporter for *The Atlanta Constitution*.

A few days later, asked how she felt by another reporter, Julia replied, "It feels like it does when you're walking around on a hot summer day and all of a sudden it starts to rain really hard. It's cold, and it feels good, and it makes you want to dance around. Then it stops, and you keep on walking.

"I don't really sit around and constantly think of myself as an Oscar nominee," she added. "I mean, what's the point?"

It was a good mental attitude, considering the Las Vegas oddsmakers had given Julia's chance of winning a three to one shot, behind Brenda Fricker (*My Left Foot*) and Anjelica Huston (*Enemies: A Love Story*). Or maybe it was simply a case of Julia being honored to be honored. Or perhaps Julia was just too personally happy to care about anything other than spending time with Kiefer.

Rumors of a romance between Julia and Kiefer had begun surfacing in late March, 1990, shortly after Julia had been seen in Tucson, Arizona, and Cerillos, New Mexico, where Sutherland had been on location filming *Young Guns II,* a sequel to the semi-successful western of the same title, with his pals Emilio Estevez, Lou Diamond Phillips, and Christian Slater.

It was soon revealed in the press, that her "friend" was Kiefer. It was also discovered that he was such a close friend of Julia's that he had bestowed a diamond "friendship" ring upon her shortly after her arrival in old Tucson. It was not until months later, however, that Julia would admit the ring had, indeed, been a gift from the smitten Sutherland. Later she explained that he had given it to her "without questions and without response," an unusual means of explaining it was *not* an engagement ring.

By the time Julia was seen sporting the ring, Kiefer had presented her with an even more unorthodox present for her twenty-second birthday—a tattoo bearing a red heart inside a black Chinese symbol which, she explained, meant "strength of heart."

"My love for Kiefer will last as long as this tattoo," she gushed to friends who, tactfully, failed to remind her of this sentiment when, two years later, she quietly had the tattoo removed.

Kiefer, however, had not been alone in the arena of major purchases. Julia had done a bit of impulse buying herself. During her brief stay in Los Angeles following the wrap of *Flatliners*, she had purchased a Hollywood Hills love nest for her and Kiefer for a reported $1.4 million.

Although the house was initially reported to be in the posh Benedict Canyon area of Beverly Hills, the three-bedroom home was actually situated off Woodrow Wilson Drive, near the less luxurious but still expensive area of Nichols Canyon.

The only thing visible from the street was the garage. The yard and house are accessed through a gated, enclosed courtyard. With a portico running along the side of the house, it looks very "Tuscan," especially with its small manicured lawn.

A *Los Angeles Times* entertainment writer, Patrick Goldstein, happened to be with Julia the day she visited the house with her business manager, her agent, and several realtors. He recorded the event for posterity, capturing the actress as she peppered the owners with questions, studied the outdoor Jacuzzi with its spot-lighted fountain, prowled the kitchen—stopping to stare at a refrigerator with a see-through door—and stood in the bedroom with its specactular 360-degree view of the surrounding hills and the city below, before sweeping out of the house, sliding behind the wheel of her new BMW convertible and roaring off down the canyon.

"Hey, the furniture's gotta go, but what a great house, huh?" she enthused as she navigated the rain-slick streets. "It's beautiful."

Then, asked if she was going to make an offer, the twenty-two-year-old actress laughed. "Make one? I already did! I'm gonna buy it. They told me if I waited 'til tomorrow, it'd be gone!"

"My boyfriend is gonna die when hears I bought a house," she continued. "He keeps telling me I've got to own things. So first I bought this car. And then he told me I oughta get a house. I remember telling him, 'Why do I need a house?' And he said, 'Well, you gotta have a place to park the car!'"

Months later, Julia would confide: "I'm what you'd call a decision-action person. I make a decision and I act on it. If I decide I'm going to have dinner or buy a house, I do it. But the last few months have been really crazy," she'd added. "I can't have a simple dinner. I don't even have time to read a book. My whole life's mapped out for me. I just try to be grateful that I have so much work that I can be worrying about all this.''

Ironically, it was because of her work that the house turned out to be a $1.4 million garage because, by her own guestimate, Julia didn't spend more than two days there during her first three months of ownership.

Although Julia and Kiefer had been a cozy twosome since sometime in January, in a March 26, 1990, *Newsweek* article Julia hid the fact that she and Sutherland were romantically involved by complaining that, having just returned with the flu after attending the Berlin Film Festival, where *Pretty Woman* had opened, she had not had enough time to buy a dress, or to even find a date for the ceremony.

Thus, when the news leaked out only a few days later that Julia and Kiefer had been seen galloping around New Mexico together, she with a diamond on her finger, he with a sly smile on his face, Julia was furious.

''I have to say I really wasn't happy with that,'' Julia brusquely told a reporter. ''It was speculation. You guys let me down. It's someone's imagination in print. Nobody asked me. I would've told 'em right, anyway.''

She had then changed the subject from her relationship with Kiefer to how much she'd enjoyed her stay in New Mexico. ''I rode out in the desert. Dirty. Havin' a great time. I was in a grocery store,'' she continued, ''and as I was leaving, the checkout lady kept staring at me. She said, 'You know you really look familiar to me. Did you use to work here?' And I said, 'No, I used to work at a Piggly Wiggly.' It's humbling, you know. And then there's part of you that wants to say "Who do you *think* I am?''''

The only reason the two lovebirds had initially kept their romance a secret had been that, when he and Julia

172

had fallen in lust on the *Flatliners* set, Kiefer had still been married to Camelia Kath, a Puerto Rican-born actress thirteen years his senior and the mother of his eighteen-month-old daughter, Sarah. The couple had wed in 1987, the year after *they* had met on the set of another movie, *The Killing Time,* but, in fairness to Julia, rumors of trouble in Kiefer's marriage had been circulating for almost a year before the two found themselves enjoying the Windy City together.

Nevertheless, despite his subsequent claims to the contrary, Kiefer did *not* file for divorce from Camilia until February, 15, 1990, approximately the same time he and Julia were romping around the Sonoran desert on horseback.

The son of actor Donald Sutherland and Shirley Douglas, a Canadian actress, Kiefer and his twin sister, Rachel, were born in London on December 21, 1966. Since his father likes to name his children after directors, Kiefer was named for director Warren Kiefer, who wrote and directed Donald's first film, *Castle of the Living Dead.* He was christened Kiefer William Frederick Dempsey George Rufus Sutherland.

Julia and Kiefer had many things in common. Like the majority of Julia's ex-lovers, Kiefer came from a broken home. He had been four years old when his parents divorced in 1970 and his father moved in with Jane Fonda, his co-star in *Klute.* Like Julia he, too, had discovered that acting in films offered an emotionally gratifying sense of bonding, both on location and on the soundstages of Hollywood.

"I've always thought of location as an island and all you have is one another, so a lot of bonding goes on," Julia once explained. Kiefer once echoed those same sentiments, explaining, "It's soothing and relaxing and you're guaranteed a hundred friends every day. It's a family, a little cocoon.''

Like Julia, Kiefer also loved to party hearty, especially when it came to playing pool and drinking. In fact, by the time Julia and Kiefer met in Chicago, his drinking had become legendary among members of the so-called Hollywood ''Brat Pack.'' Kiefer's favorite drink, tequila, is also Julia's cherished choice of alcoholic beverage. And, despite stories to the contrary, she was a tequila drinker long before she ever set eyes on Kiefer. ''Tequila—and beer, straight out of a bottle, that's all I ever saw Julia drink,'' a friend from her New York party days recalled.

Julia and Kiefer *do* follow separate paths in their drinking, however. Kiefer reportedly is a heavy drinker and, according to friends, ''is not pleasant'' under the influence.

So, with all this commonality, it's hardly surprising that the two were drawn to each other. ''Our relationship evolved well after we left Chicago,'' Kiefer would later explain. ''We had been working together for over a month, and our relationship really didn't take place for two months after that. So my initial attraction to Julia was to her incredible talent as an actor. I adopted a phenomenal, ridiculous respect that evolved into something else.''

Whenever that ''something else'' began, the truth is that by the time Julia stood in front of the Golden Globes audience, she and Kiefer had been cohabiting and were even in the beginning stages of building a romantic getaway on the ranchland Kiefer had purchased several years before in Whitefish, Montana.

By the time Julia departed for the set of *Sleeping with the Enemy*, which was scheduled to begin filming April

2, it was apparent to everyone around her that Julia was very much in love. Yes, she'd had numerous romantic liaisons in New York, on location, and in Los Angeles. Yes, she'd lived with Liam Neeson. Yes, she'd been engaged to Dylan McDermott. But this time it was different. This time someone had truly captured her free-spirited heart.

Although Julia continued to play it cagey about attaching a name to her "boyfriend," it had become common knowledge within Hollywood circles that it was Kiefer Sutherland who had swept Julia off her feet. Thus, by the time Julia faced the cameras wearing a man's Armani suit, and told the world, "I want to thank my beautiful, blue-eyed, green-eyed boy, who supports me through everything and brings so much happiness to my life" during her televised Golden Globe acceptance speech, not a murmur was heard from the crowd of Tinseltown's elite.

"I have to say that the Golden Globes was the most shocking night of my life," Julia later admitted. "I was so unprepared. I heard a recording of my acceptance speech later and I had to laugh. I was such an idiot."

Backstage, however, the media went crazy trying to find out who old blue-green eyes was. They didn't have to wait long. Julia followed the Golden Globes with a Monday, March 26, appearance at the 1990 Academy Awards ceremony, held at the Dorothy Chandler Pavillion in downtown Los Angeles. She and her "Mystery Date," who turned out to be Kiefer, were both wearing Armani suits. "I'm nervous and excited and I just want to sit down," Julia said, as the press swarmed all over her.

Despite her nervous anticipation, however, Julia didn't win the Best Supporting Actress category. Nor did Anjelica Huston, Lena Olin, or Dianne Wiest. The statuette went, instead, to Brenda Fricker for her performance in *My Left Foot*, just as the Vegas oddsmakers had predicted.

"She would have won," lamented Martin Grove of *The Hollywood Reporter*, "had her new hit, *Pretty Woman*, opened during the balloting."

Julia's took the loss of an Oscar in stride, however. Whatever sense of defeat she'd had was tempered by the overwhelming success *Pretty Woman* was enjoying at the box office during its opening weekend. So she was philosophical about the Oscar, telling the press, "It's taken five years of my life, but when I think about the span it takes some people to win an Oscar nomination, that's really a short period of time. And some people never even get a nomination.

"A lady came up to me in the airport and she said, 'I hope you win.' It gives you a boost. It's really nice that people want you to win. That kind of thing is comforting.

"Actors make movies for different reasons, hopefully to entertain people," she continued. "I want people to laugh and have a good time. When I've done that it's great. It's so nice to know somebody appreciates something you spent three months of your life trying to do."

Adding his voice to the crowd, Kiefer admitted, "The thing I'm proudest of is that not only is she beautiful and gifted and talented, but she's a terrifically nice and very down to earth person. *Who* she is accounts for as much as *what* she is."

"Richard Gere is one of my closest friends," Julia told a reporter, "but I guess my favorite actor is Sally Field because she helped me a lot and she's one of my closest women friends. Probably the best time I had was working with Kiefer Sutherland on *Flatliners*, though. He'll always be one of my favorite actors. It's hard to believe he's done so much in his career.''

Julia had not been in the audience when *Pretty Woman* had been unveiled at a preview screening in Hollywood in mid-March, 1990. The word put out by her publicist had been that she was in South Carolina to prep for her upcoming role in *Sleeping with the Enemy*. The truth was, of course, that Julia was ensconsed with Kiefer in the Sonoran desert and was reluctant to leave.

"It's too bad she was unable to attend Monday's West-wood preview," penned Army Archerd, venerable *Daily Variety* columnist. "The pic got repeated applause and the laughter drowncd out much of the dialogue. Young Oscar-nominee Roberts is headed for heavy stardom."

As it turned out, Archerd had been right on target with his assessmcnt of Julia's future. The film opened March 23, 1990, only three days before the Oscar cast, and immediately captured the hearts and dollars of movie-goers around the world. In its first four weeks at the box office the film grossed more than $150 million to ultimately become the highest grossing movie of the year. And Julia, who had received only $300,000 for her role as Vivian, became a *star*.

"The chemistry between the two stars *was* quite beautiful," Marshall conceded, adding that his concern in hiring Julia had not been about her beauty or her acting abilities, but about her comedic skills. "Young pretty girls do not like to do comedy, particularly physical comedy," hc explained. "They usually like to look very lovely and elegant and rarely like to trip."

Marshall then compared Julia to Kay Kendall, the English actress who died in 1959 at the age of thirty-three from leukemia while married to Rex Harrison. "She used to bring dignity and elegance into a scene and also beauty and make you laugh," Marshall recalled, adding "I thought Julia had a quality like that, and a woman who looks like that, who can also make you smile and laugh, is not so easy to come by."

Thus by Monday night, when Julia glided across the Academy Awards stage, it had already become apparent that *Pretty Woman* was having an incredible impact on the viewing public, as well as the nation's movie critics, the majority of whom had singled out Julia for most of their plaudits.

"Roberts has wit and warmth, and she suggests that a new Rosalind Russell or Kay Kendall may be on the way," penned one enthusiastic reviewer.

"Whereas most hookers might steal your wallet," wrote a *Screen International* reviewer, "Robert's character steals the picture."

"Julia Roberts," wrote Janet Maslin, *New York Times* film critic, "is so enchantingly beautiful, so funny, so natural, and such an absolute delight, it's hard to hold anything against the movie. This performance will make her a major star."

And, of course, it did. Julia would go on to win a second Golden Globe, as well as a second Oscar nomination for her performance, and to be forever known as filmdom's most dazzling *Pretty Woman*.

One of the few film critics *not* to be swept off his feet by *Pretty Woman* was Richard Schickel, film historian and *Time* magazine movie critic. "Without taking anything away from Julia Roberts," he penned, "there were doubtless twenty-five other actresses who could have played the role and played it fine. It wasn't exactly a stretch. There was nothing inherent in what she, or Richard Gere, did that pushed the film over the $150 million mark. It took off because the public wanted to plug into the fantasy.'' Julia responded to the reviews with a philosophical shrug. "If you take the good reviews seriously, then you have to take the bad reviews seriously,'' she explained.

At that point, of course, virtually everyone but Schickel was singing Julia's praises.

"A beautiful young girl with talent coming on the scene always attracts a lot of attention and I think Julia personifies the woman of the 90s,'' said Garry Marshall who, having discovered no one knew of Kay Kendall, had then begun likening Julia to a cross between Carole Lombard, Audrey Hepburn, and Lucille Ball.

"She's bright and beautiful and can make you laugh, yet Julia's not fearful,'' Marshall continued. "She knows how to take material and make it her own. She knows when she's not doing it well and she'll try again. She's a smart girl who does her homework and does her job. She made the character of Vivian likeable and charming. I felt watching the dailies that she had a certain magic up there.''

In a *USA Today* interview that ran the same March day that *Pretty Woman* opened around the country, Julia confessed she felt something big was ahead of her but, she had quickly added, she was trying not to think about it. This unexplainable feeling, she confided, reminded her of when she and a childhood girlfriend would have a case of "the mean reds.''

"That's when you're blue but don't know why,'' Julia had explained, without mentioning it was a line delivered on a fire escape to George Peppard by Audrey Hepburn in *Breakfast at Tiffany's*.

Professionally, at least, Julia had no reason to be blue.

Pretty Woman became the largest grossing motion picture in the history of Disney Films. "Walt is somewhere in his grave," laughed Garry Marshall, "saying 'Pinocchio, no . . . a nice duck, no, it has to be a hooker as my highest-grossing picture.' "

Chapter Ten

In what would later become an oft-told industry anecdote, Joe Roth, Twentieth Century Fox studio chieftain, received a personal call from Julia on only his third day as the studio's major powerbroker. She wanted, she told him, the female lead in *Class Action*, the Gene Hackman legal drama which would come and go at the box office the following year with nary a ripple. Although he promised they would work together at some point, Roth declined to hire Julia, and the role subsequently went to Mary Elizabeth Mastrantonio.

"I turned her down because she was too young, and she got mad at me," Roth would later joke, adding "two weeks later I offered her *Sleeping with the Enemy* and we became good friends." It was, Roth admitted, the first and only time a star had ever personally telephoned him in search of a particular role. But Julia's chutzpah paid off.

At the time Julia telephoned Roth, Kim Basinger had already been cast in the lead role of the abused wife running from her psychotically abusive husband in *Sleeping with the Enemy*. However, Basinger had fallen in love with actor Alec Baldwin. Baldwin had signed to star in the Disney comedy, *The Marrying Man*, and he wanted Kim to be the object of his on-screen obsession. So, Basinger had bowed out of *Enemy*, thereby opening the door for Julia to replace her.

"We thought we might be in real trouble when she (Kim) decided not to do it," Leonard Goldberg, the film's producer, would later admit. "Kim was just coming off *Batman* and was on every magazine cover. *Steel Magnolias* was just coming out, and Julia was basically an up-and-coming young actress. We were trading maximum star power to work with a near-unknown. But Julia seemed really right for the role and we figured we'd end up with a better film, if not a more marketable one. Now of course we look like geniuses."

Before Julia was signed to the role, however, she had to meet with the film's director, Joseph Ruben who, like her other directors, was immediately captivated by the young woman sitting across from him.

"I remember this shy, but dazzling smile, and her body language. It was a shyness, but there was something coming out of her smile," he would later recall, adding "That's the part of what makes her so fascinating on screen—all the contradictions, being both very shy, but very much out there at the same time. She's both very sexual and very innocent, too. But she's very vulnerable and there's a private side to Julia.

"There's an incredibly warm aspect to her," he said, "but she can be very cold when she's angry."

Indeed, someone who's known Julia since she was an eager seventeen-year-old aspiring actress, says she is a real life 'steel magnolia,' soft and warm on the outside and pure steel on the inside. "Yes, I'd say she's a steel magnolia. She never got angry with me, at least she never got angry *in front* of me, but I saw her get angry at other people. You can always tell when Julia's really mad because her eyes narrow down and her chin juts out. Believe me, if she's angry, you know it."

Sleeping With the Enemy called for Julia to portray Laura Burney, a young woman married to a handsome and successful businessman. Yet, while the couple appear to be an ideal marital blend, life within the walls of their tidy home has become a nightmare for Laura, who is terrorized and physically abused by her obsessive husband, Martin, played with chilling fervor by Patrick Bergin.

Realizing her life is truly in jeopardy, Laura fakes her own death, and moves to a small Iowa town, where she meets a college professor (Kevin Anderson), assumes a new identity, and begins a new life. She is happily ensconsed in her new world, when it's suddenly shattered by the unwanted arrival of Martin. Once again in her husband's menacing clutches, Laura finds herself in a violent fight for life.

"I thought it was well-written, very suspenseful, and from an actor's point of view, very exciting to try to do because it's very challenging," Julia explained. "The role offered five, ten, fifteen things to play at once, so part of the challenge was that I didn't know if I *could* do it, if I *should* do it, if it was the right decision for me at that moment, and so I did it."

"When I read a script," she explained, "what I look for is a cross between thrill and fear. It's more an instinct and sense of emotion than anything specific. The movies I've done have all been scripts I read and felt something at that moment, a sense of being scared and challenged just enough to feel I don't quite want to do it, but realize I have to deep down inside."

Sleeping with the Enemy met all those requirements, and more. When the movie was finally completed Julia would describe it as "the toughest film I've made yet, partly because of the amount of time I worked.

"It was very intense because of the nature of the material and there were very few scenes I wasn't in," she explained. "So, essentially, I worked nearly every day, six days a week, for over three months. It was very tiring."

One of the major reasons Julia was tired was that the role was a physically exhausting one, filled with violent scenes between she and her screen husband, Patrick Bergin, from beginning to end.

One of the first scenes to be shot, for instance, involved Laura being struck by Martin and falling to the ground. It should have been a simple shot. But it was anything but simple when it came time for a close up of her hitting the marble floor, bursting into tears and then being kicked because she was crying.

Realizing what a difficult time awaited Julia, the crew did everything they could to make her comfortable. They put a furniture pad on the floor to cushion her fall against the marble. They placed a sandbag next to her leg for Bergin to kick. Then, with everything ready, and the actors in place, the director, Joseph Ruben, called "Action!"

Julia fell to the floor directly on cue. But, despite the furniture pad, she flinched when she hit the hard marble, ruining the take. So they did a second take. Only this time, in her zeal to make it look right, she fell so hard her head bounced off the floor.

"I cracked the floor so hard I had a black eye," she recalled, adding, "but that's what made the take really exciting, cracking my head like that. Anyway, I'm in pain, and lying there, when the actor (Bergin) I'm working with comes up to kick the sandbag, misses, and kicks me in the leg. I'm just a blithering idiot at that point. I cannot even see straight.

"When the take was over, the director came up to me and said 'I wanted to call "Cut" when I saw what happened.' And I said 'If you'd called "Cut," I would've wrung your neck. Cause I'm not gonna do that scene again!' "

On her way out the door after another fourteen-hour day of crying and flailing her way through a difficult emotional scene, Julia left the set exhausted and in tears. Realizing the effort she was putting into the role, one of the grips came up to her, took her hand and squeezed it. "It was worth fourteen hours of what I did just for that," she would later say, "because it told me I had done something, you know?"

When Julia first arrived on the set, she and Patrick Bergin, would chat and joke between takes. "There was nothing we weren't able to do, from love scenes to violence," he later said. "It was never a question of mistrust." Being on the receiving end of the violence, however, Julia did not enjoy the same level of trust. Thus, as the couple's onscreen relationship deteriorated, so did the couple's off-screen relationship.

"We weren't necessarily friendly toward each other," Julia would later confide. "I mean, when you come to work and somebody kicks the shit out of you for three hours, you don't really feel like finding out where he is and saying good night."

At one point, in fact, Julia and Patrick had done several improvisational scenes so violent in nature that they actually scared him, director Joseph Ruben later confided. "They knew they were in control, but I didn't," he explained.

"It was an emotionally harrowing experience," Julia would later admit. "There were whole weeks where I'd have to arrive on the set at five A.M., start crying and be the victim in those terrible fights."

The role of Laura had to have been a particularly disturbing experience for someone like Julia who, as Garry Marshall and Joel Schumacher both pointed out, responds to love but shrinks from acrimony. Also, as does any actor, Julia would have to draw on moments from her own life to bring depth and credibility to the emotionally charged role, quite a feat considering the life she'd left behind. "It's as if she has the thinnest skin imaginable," Ruben said at the time, unaware of what secrets rested beneath that skin.

"There's a vulnerability there that knocks you out," he continued. "And there's something that happens photographically with her, that star quality you hear about. She's got this emotional vulnerability that lets you see and feel everything that's going on with her. And the two of them together—bam!"

A classic tale of Julia to emerge from the making of *Enemy* involved an all-night shoot, during which she was soaking wet, freezing, and clad only in an undershirt and panties. Finally tired of being the only uncomfortable person on the set, she turned to the crew and said, ''I think we need a little group support here. So drop your trousers. If you're not going to take your pants off, you can't stay in the house.''

Although half the crew refused to comply and left the set, the other half dropped their drawers and stayed on. Julia still chuckles at the thought of the electricians crouched in a corner in their shorts, and of the crew member who, since he was sans underwear, went through the scene with a towel wrapped around his mid-section. ''It had nothing to do with acting and everything to do with just getting everybody as naked and cold as I was,'' she would later explain, adding with a laugh, ''It was the bonding thing, you know.''

But the half-naked and, by then, freezing crew had their revenge. In fiendish retaliation, they hid in an empty room and lured her in there so they could then mass ''moon'' her. ''She screamed with laughter,'' one of the crew recalled.

Although the film supposedly took place in Cape Cod, Massachusetts, and Cedar Falls, Iowa, it was actually shot on location in Abbeville, South Carolina, a small town look-alike for Cedar Falls, and Cape Fear, North Carolina, a remote spot on the Atlantic which doubled for Cape Cod. It was here, on Shell Island beach, that the production department built Martin and Laura's clapboard house, which was the film's principal set.

Despite her heavy work schedule, Julia invited Betty and Nancy to join her for a visit, which they did, driving to Carolina in the new Mustang convertible Julia had given Betty for her birthday. At one point, even Eric dropped by for a visit. But it was Kiefer's visits that Julia really looked forward to. He traveled to both locations several times to give her the emotional support she needed to make it through the film, which was proving far more physically and emotionally draining than she'd imagined.

"Whenever Kiefer would show up, or come back and spend time, Julia's mood would always get really good," a crew member recalled, adding, "So we were always happy when we heard he was coming back." Although the couple would frequently interact with the cast and crew, Kiefer rarely visited the set. And, when he *did*, it was only because Julia had coaxed him into it.

According to several crew members, Julia and Kiefer spent a lot of time by themselves. "They were playful together. There was a sense of mutual support," said Ruben. "I think they both like to cut through the bullshit factor. I think they make each other laugh. They both know the kind of pressures they're each dealing with, and they both have the same uncompromising attitude about their work, so they can be supportive and respectful of each other."

When Julia wasn't working, which was rarely, she'd spend her day off sleeping, reading, writing poetry in her journal, or riding around town wearing torn jeans and a black leather jacket in a rented jeep, its top off, her thick mane of then-reddish hair blowing in the breeze, tape deck usually blasting out one of her two favorite songs, "Life in the Fast Lane" by The Eagles or "This Year's Girl" by Elvis Costello.

It was during the months of filming *Sleeping with the Enemy* that Julia made the almost instantaneous transition from working actress to movie star. The interest in her from both the public and the media following the March 23 opening of *Pretty Woman* had been so massive it threatened to overwhelm not only Julia but everyone working with her on the film.

"The movie was like an avalanche for her," recalled an industry insider. Elaine Goldsmith echoed those sentiments. "You could definitely say the phone has been ringing," she said. "The reaction we've gotten has been incredibly positive. People really feel she's one of a kind."

As scripts and offers began pouring into Goldsmith's office, the pressures mounted, and Elaine Goldsmith began mentioning that Julia was going to be taking some time off in the near future. "She's going to take a break," Goldsmith explained, adding, "If people want her now, they're going to want her a year from now."

"It was a very emotional and topsy turvy time for her," Ruben would later recall. "Strangers called her name, stopped her, or even grabbed her on the street, while back at the hotel she'd get calls from fans who just wanted to chat."

Julia agreed with Ruben's assessment. "Everything kind of tilted," she said. "But," she'd added, "it's not like I deal with the pace all by myself. My agents, my publicist, the people I've worked with have prepared me for it. And I have my family, my friends. So the support for me is just there. As much as those people help you maintain yourself, they also keep you from going off into some sort of erratic orbit."

Yet, coupled with the savagery she faced almost daily as the abused Laura, Julia's life had suddenly become a living nightmare, both on and off the set. Despite the mounting pressures of a skyrocketing career, however,

Julia managed to focus the entirety of her energies on her role of the abused Laura to the exclusion of almost everything. "She's vulnerable, but she's very strong," Ruben said. "She's very good at getting herself back to center."

But, by the time the film wrapped, after having taken five days just to complete the violent finale in which the terrified Laura is finally forced to confront her psychotic husband, Julia had little stamina left. She was counting the days until she could return home to Los Angeles and especially to Kiefer.

"I've spent the last year and a half making movies and giving, and giving, and giving," she confided to a reporter. "There would be nothing left, but I'd find one more thing, so I'd give that. But there comes a point where you're losing sleep, and it takes a long time to get anything back from all that giving.

"When you have family, friends, and there's love in your life, and you give to that, you can see instant gratification. You can see somebody smile or just pick somebody up or something. It's a lot easier to give that way," she concluded, "than it is to just be giving to this . . . *black machinery* (cameras and sound equipment)."

If Julia throws her entire being into a role it's because she doesn't know her own limitations and, therefore, has no set perimeters, either physically or emotionally. This is true of the phenomenon known as Julia Roberts, both on screen and off, and one of the reasons behind her self-imposed exile from filmmaking only a year after *Sleeping*. No one who has worked closely with Julia, or who knows her on a personal level, will disagree.

"She's incredibly talented," praised Ruben. "There's an ease about her acting, something real and very deep about her acting. Everything comes through her—

through her body, her eyes, her face, her smile. That's very rare and because of it the audience makes a tremendous connection with her. She's one of the most sympathetic actors to come along in a long time. She's the real thing. There's nobody quite like her. She's an original."

And off camera? "Julia is a force of nature. She's so full of life. Most people go through life with a very dim wattage. And they only let out a small part of their light," Ruben said thoughtfully. "But not Julia. She justs blasts it out. You get everything from her—the whole range of what she's feeling. If something pisses her off, she expresses it and goes on. If something hurts her, she expresses it and goes on."

And that is precisely what Julia did when a black compatriot was barred from an Abbeville restaurant in her presence. She vehemently expressed her disapproval, supposedly telling the management in a loud voice, "You shouldn't call this place Michael's, you should call it Bigot's!"

"Julia was very angry on the set the next day," recalled a crew member. "Things affect her and she doesn't just stand by passively. That really did not sit right with her."

But Julia didn't just express herself in the restaurant. A month or two later, she talked about the experience with a reporter from *Rolling Stone* who, having dutifully recorded her thoughts on Abbeville, South Carolina, and the racial bias she had encountered there, published the interview in early August, 1990.

"The people were horribly racist, and I had a really hard time," she reportedly told *Rolling Stone*. "I mean, the town had no restaurants in it. I would go home and sit in this small room with my dog and say, 'So, there's nothing to eat. . . . You wanna go to sleep?' I didn't feel

191

like I was on location anymore. I didn't feel like I had a job. I felt like this hell was where I lived.

"I'm so easily enraged by the flailing ignorance, which is tossed about as if it's God's words," she'd added, "that in Abbeville I felt so assaulted and insulted by these people I just didn't want to be nice anymore."

Horrified, chagrined, and furious that America's "pretty woman" had found their quaint little bastion of Southern hospitality to be something akin to a living hell, the townspeople, in an effort organized by Mike Gallagher, a radio talk show host on WFBC-AM in nearby Greenville, signed a petition and placed a quarter page ad in the *Daily Variety*, with a bold-lettered headline reading, "Pretty Woman? Pretty Low!"

Interviewed by the national press, Joe Savitz, Abbeville's mayor, suggested Julia's criticism stemmed from her naive attempt to take a black friend into "a real redneck type place in Abbeville that does not allow black customers. No self-respecting person would want to go there," Savitz explained.

Realizing what a furor she had caused, Julia quickly softened her stance and her language. She had been referring to only a single incident, she explained, and in no way had meant to imply that the entire region was racist. "I was born in the South so in no way am I trying to create a stereotype," she said in a prepared statement. "I was shocked that this type of treatment still exists in America in the Nineties—in the South or anywhere else."

She also called Mayor Savitz, who reported that, "She said she was 'a little misquoted' in the *Rolling Stone* article. She said she was talking about one person she met, but the magazine made it sound like she was talking about the whole town. I think the residents were a little upset—I think anybody would be upset if somebody said something like that about their hometown—but it was really a big flap over nothing. I think everybody has kind of forgotten about what she said."

Meanwhile, back in Smyrna, Betty Motes defined the *Daily Variety* advertisement to the local press as being "Much ado about nothing."

"Julia has never picked friends by color," she explained. "She always had a lot of black friends in school. What happened is she became friends with a crew member; they went to a place of business; her friend was black; and they were refused service. Julie was shocked. She'd never had that happen around Smyrna or Atlanta. I think she saw enough (racism) that she thought it was condoned," Betty had concluded.

Despite Betty's comments to the contrary, Julia's first encounter with racism had been in Smyrna, a reported hotbed of redneck ideology. It had occurred when, as a sixth grader, she had entered a dance contest paired with a black classmate, only to discover her locker vandalized the following day. Moreover, in a brief campaign of harrassment, some of her classmates had even begun calling her unpleasant names.

When Julia had departed the West Coast to report for work on *Sleeping With the Enemy*, the Hollywood Hills home she had purchased three months before had still been covered in bad mirrored tile and furniture destined for a rummage sale. Returning home more than three months later she discovered to her delight that, during her absence, Kiefer had taken care of everything, from hiring movers to haul her worldly possessions from her Venice Beach apartment, as well as personally organizing Julia's wardrobe in her bedroom closet.

"The house was all ready," a delighted Julia told friends. "Even my clothes were hanging in the closet. Astonishing!" she'd exclaimed. "There had been books and papers scattered all over my apartment, the house needed a paint job, and it was just too much," she would recall. "I had so much in storage that my girlfriends and I joked about a whole town called, Storage, California."

Concerned that their separate careers might take a toll on the relationship, Julia and Kiefer had decided in the early stages of their romance that, unless they were working on the same project, they wouldn't both work at the same time. "When you're on a shoot for three months, you change and even you don't know how," Julia once said, explaining her pact with Kiefer. "That's too much to ask of somebody, to come back and say, 'I'm really different, figure it out.' "

So, after making *Flatliners*, Julia had begun announcing that, after her *next* film, she would be taking a respite from filmmaking. However, despite her yen for a vacation and time with Kiefer, she continued accepting film roles. Ultimately exhausted from the work, and the pace of the work, she finally decided she would take a year off after finishing *Dying Young*.

But then, of course, along came *Hook*, and the opportunity to work with director Steven Spielberg, not to mention the chance to earn a reported $7 million, and suddenly Julia had a work schedule taking her through August, 1991.

"The Julia Roberts phenomenon is indicative of Hollywood's peculiar inability to analyze its own successes," suggested Richard Shickel, noted film critic. "After someone has a whopping success, studios think he or she must have something—and it lays a lot of money over it. In a rational business they'd wait five pictures before deciding if they want to pay her $7 million or, at least tailor a film to her strengths.''

Shickel, of course, was right. But, then, Hollywood has never been a rational business. It's a land of fast deals, quick bucks, overnight stardom and decline, an on-going magic act in which people, not rabbits, are pulled out of a hat and made to dance a rapid rhythm not of their own choosing. This is what was happening to Julia. She'd found herself tap dancing on the Hollywood conveyer belt to the stars, and she couldn't stop it and she couldn't jump off.

"I sometimes lose it a little in the middle of a tough day,'' she confessed shortly after picking up her second Golden Globe trophy. "Winning an award like the Golden Globe made me incredibly giddy and happy, but it was also very humbling. I told myself 'What's there to get so carried away with?' I got honored, but it was my work. I put my heart and soul into it. And I know that I have to move on now and challenge myself to do better. You can't hang on to a Golden Globe forever.''

For several months after completing *Sleeping*, Julia relaxed and enjoyed life with Kiefer, going to shows, dancing at clubs, even sometimes shooting pool. And, when Kiefer had to fly to Kansas City in early October, 1990, to work on the Orion film, *Article 99*, Julia went with him, staying several weeks until she had to return to California to begin work on *Dying Young*.

"Acting is a true love of mine,'' she confided, "but it's not *the* true love. There are times when I get so bogged down by the politics of this business that I just have these great domestic fantasies. Being at home, and being quiet, and reading, and having a garden, and doing all that stuff. Taking care of a family. Those are the most important things. Movies will come and go, but family is a real kind of rich consistency.''

But family, the gardening, and Kiefer were going to have to wait. Julia was busy becoming rich by consistently making movies. Thus, only three months after having completed *Sleeping with the Enemy* Julia arrived in Mendocino, California, where principal photography on her next film, *Dying Young*, was scheduled to begin November 12.

An unabashed tear jerker of the bleakest kind, *Dying Young* starred Julia as Hilary O'Neil, a working-class woman who is hired to nurse Victor Geddes (Campbell Scott), a wealthy young man dying from leukemia, and falls in love with him.

Yet, while the idea may have lent itself to a first-rate novel, the concept did not happily translate to film. In short, *Dying Young* needed Julia's name on the marquee. In fact, the movie needed all the help it could get.

The movie had been developed specifically with Julia in mind by Sally Field, who had optioned the film rights to the Marti Leimbach novel when *Steel Magnolias* had still been in postproduction. Field had pitched the project to Twentieth Century Fox in late 1988. But, since *Steel Magnolias* had not yet been released at that point, no one had been interested in taking a gamble on a young unknown actress by the name of Julia Roberts.

''I told them I had this girl, Julia Roberts, who would

be wonderful,'' Field later laughed, ''but they wanted someone better known.''

Two years later, after *Steel Magnolias* and *Pretty Woman* had been released within three months of each other, Sally returned to Twentieth Century Fox to again pitch Julia, who was anything but unknown at that point.

''By then we had a script,'' Field recalled. ''I went to Fox and said, 'I repeat. There's this girl I know who would be wonderful in this part.' The good thing was I didn't have to say, 'You don't know her yet.' ''

Joe Roth, Julia's recently acquired friend, by then had ascended to the position of Fox production chief, and was more than familiar with Julia. So, not only did he laugh at Sally's joke, he promptly hired Julia to star in the film.

''When you have Julia's name on the marquee, you have the biggest female star in the world, one of less than ten people in the world who can open a picture simply because she's in it,'' Roth explained, shortly after having signed Julia for a reported $3 million salary during a meeting at the Polo Lounge with Elaine Goldsmith, Julia's agent, and Joel Schumacher, who was to direct.

''I was going to do *Phantom of the Opera* with Andrew Lloyd Webber, then he postponed the production because of his divorce,'' Schumacher would later explain. ''A dream had ended and I needed to move on. Emotionally, I couldn't afford to be attached to it any longer. I didn't want to get disappointed again.''

While Schumacher was trying to decide in which direction he should ''move on,'' the telephone rang one day. It was Julia. She wanted him to direct her in *Dying Young*.

''This was the first time a star had ever asked me to direct,'' he confessed, ''and I don't think I would have made that particular movie if Julia hadn't asked me. I'm in love with Julia,'' Schumacher explained. ''She's a combination of many things, which is why she's so fascinating on-screen: sexy but ladylike, guileless yet sophisticated, fragile but strong. She's street smart rather than educated, but extremely well-read.''

Two years later, Schumacher would confide to Jeffrey Lantos, a writer for *Movieline Magazine,* that had it not been for his obsession with Julia, *Dying Young* might have been a better film. "I was blinded by my passion to be around her, and I wasn't thinking clearly," Schumacher conceded, adding, "This is still a disturbing subject for me."

But at the time, Schumacher was unaware of the pitfalls of being blinded by Julia's megawatt personality. Instead he was enthusiastically looking forward to working with her again. In fact, the project reunited Julia and Joel and Sally Field, who were then three close friends.

"Julia and I early on worked out a symbiotic emotional dance," Schumacher explained. "We don't talk a lot. We talk maybe in one sentence what the scene is. She has some preparations she does emotionally, then I have some preparations to help, some things we do that are private. There are ways we talk, not about the scene but something from our past or current lives that is relevant to the emotional fiber of what is going on. Sometimes we don't talk at all, we just look at each other."

Situated four hours north of San Francisco, Mendocino is the perfect replica of a New England town, thanks to its clapboard houses, tiny winding streets and quaint shops, and rugged coastal beauty. It is because of this atmosphere that the popular CBS series, *Murder She Wrote,* has been filming its Cabot Cove exteriors here since the show's inception; and it was here that Julia and Campbell Scott played out *Dying Young*.

After three weeks of exterior shooting in Mendocino, the *Dying* company moved to San Francisco, then to the Napa Valley, where Julia had shot *Blood Red* with Eric only four years before.

By the time the film wrapped on February 8, 1991, Julia had gained the dubious distinction of being able to sleep anywhere in any position. Julia, confessed worried friends, was suffering from on-going fatigue after two years of virtual nonstop work. *Dying Young,* they suggested, just *might* be the death of her.

Returning to Los Angeles after wrapping *Dying Young,* Julia once again announced she would be taking a year-long sabbatical. "People have done a lot of things for me, but I do things for everybody, too," she explained, "and right now it's a lot. I think it's time for me to go away for a little while. I just want to slow down," she said.

But before she could take her much-needed, greatly earned sabbatical, Julia still had to act her way through *Hook,* a big-budget remake of the children's classic which, starring Dustin Hoffman in the title role, Robin Williams as Peter Pan, and Julia as Tinkerbell, was to be directed by Steven Spielberg.

In December, 1990, after having been courted by Creative Artists and a number of other talent agencies, Elaine Goldsmith and Risa Shapiro left the William Morris Agency in tandem and joined International Creative Management (ICM), taking several clients, as well as their biggest revenue producer, Julia, with them.

Obviously Julia really had believed it when she'd once told an interviewer, "I heard 'Your agent is never your friend,' but it's a complete and total fucking piece-of-shit lie. I also heard that 'All producers are scumbags,' which is also untrue of the producers I've worked with. So everybody was wrong. But my brother told me something that *was* true: 'You have to remember that this is show business, not show friendship.' "

Thus, after departing the Morris agency, Julia explained the move by saying, "William Morris is a fine company, but I wasn't so much a company man as a client of Risa and Elaine's. They're smart. They care about me. If they told me they were forming Elaine and Risa Inc., I would have said okay," she'd added.

Less than a year later, however, for reasons known only to the triumverate, Shapiro was out, and Goldsmith was solidly in Julia's life. Since then, Goldsmith has become all things to the actress—babysitting her basset hound, overseeing her investments, always taking care of business, be it professional or personal. The one thing Goldsmith seems *not* to have dealt with is Julia's choice of clothes, which is probably why in early January, 1991, Julia arrived for an interview with Ian Blair, a *Chicago Tribune* entertainment writer, wearing an oversized man's jacket over a white tee shirt, jeans and cowboy boots, her trademark garb since those early days in New York.

Gone were the long curled strands of cascading hair. In their place were shortened strands of platinum blonde hair, which one writer later described as "a platinum blonde helmet." "I just got sick and tired of it, so I had it all cut off," Julia laughingly explained, adding, "and you know what? Everyone freaked out. They all said, 'Don't do it. It'll be awful. You'll regret it.' But Kiefer said 'Aw, go get a crewcut.' "

As a struggling actress, no one had paid much attention to the way Julia dressed. Once she had become a major player in Tinseltown, however, she had received quite a bit of notoriety for her off-beat flair for fashion, and virtually all of it was negative. "In person she looks worse than anything on the street," complained fashion designer Nolan Miller. "She looks like she dresses from the Salvation Army. Who wants reality? I want a movie star."

The infamous Mr. Blackwell apparently agreed with Miller's assessment of Julia's "schlumpy" look. He added her name to his annual New Year's list of Top Ten Worst Dressed celebrities, an honor she later would mockingly confess had "devastated" her.

Why should she care what Mr. Blackwell or anyone else, for that matter, had to say about her? By the time she'd been added to his list, Julia Roberts had become the hottest female movie star on the Hollywood horizon. She had made seven films—*Satisfaction, Mystic Pizza, Steel Magnolias, Pretty Woman, Flatliners, Sleeping with the Enemy,* and *Dying Young*—in four years.

She had earned two Academy Award nominations for her performances in *Steel Magnolias* and *Pretty Woman*. She was the proud owner of two Golden Globe awards, and had been named "The 1990 Performer of the Year" by the nation's theater owners at their annual convention, ShoWest. Furthermore, she had the distinction of being on the January, 1991, cover of *Gentleman's Quarterly*, the only woman ever so honored in the publication's history.

In two years she'd seen her earnings skyrocket from $90,000 for her role in *Magnolias* to $300,000 for *Pretty Woman* to $550,000 for *Flatliners*. With Elaine Goldsmith as her chief negotiator Julia had then leaped to a cool million dollars for *Sleeping with the Enemy* and a hefty $3 million for *Dying Young*.

Julia was twenty-four years old and had the world on a string. Or did she?

Chapter Eleven

From all outward appearances, Julia and Kiefer were a happy and very much *together* couple. They lived together. They slept together. They dined out together. They played and partied together.

"They help each other not take things too seriously," explained Shirley Douglas, Kiefer's mother, in her only interview regarding the romance. "At Julia's age it's remarkable to see someone not dithering," she had added.

The twosome shared a ranch in Montana. They walked Jack, their Border collie, in Laurel Canyon Park, often happily posing for the paparazzi who had learned to stake out the park, the watering hole for star-owned canines. And they traveled together, such as when Kiefer took her to Canada where they held hands as Kiefer showed her all his old haunts and introduced her to his past. Returning to Los Angeles from Montreal, Julia was in such high emotional stride she reportedly burst into tears over homilies in the best-seller *All I Really Need to Know I Learned in Kindergarten*.

In August, 1990, Julia and Kiefer traveled to France, where they met with Joel Schumacher at the Deauville Film Festival, where *Flatliners* was scheduled to be the opening film. Afterwards the couple took a sidetrip to Paris, where they walked both banks of the Seine, hand in hand, happily eating *croque madames*, enjoying the freedom of being just another pair of lovers walking beside the famous river.

"We're just real happy," Julia confided to a magazine reporter not long after the couple returned from France. "I've been lucky to find someone who I not only like and is my best friend but who I so admire and respect and have fallen madly in love with. I've been immensely blessed in the discovery of this person."

They even planned on working together, announcing that, since Mel Gibson had been forced to pull out of the project because of a scheduling conflict, *they* would be co-starring in *Renegades*, a romantic Western set in the late 1800s about a bounty hunter's romance with a part-Native American female bank robber, a role Julia described as "a dream opportunity for me." In return for services rendered, Julia was to receive $7 million and Kiefer a lesser amount of approximately $2.5 million.

Julia then announced that when she wrapped *Hook*, which she would begin working on in mid-May, 1991, she would be taking a year off to recharge her creative juices and, hopefully, to have a baby.

The anonymity Julia and Kiefer had experienced during their Paris sojourn had been both a much-needed respite from the rigors of stardom and a far cry from the screaming, frenzied crowd that had greeted them upon their arrival at Mann's Chinese Theater for the Hollywood premiere of *Flatliners* only a couple of weeks before. It was a scene of mayhem, captured in print a year later by writer Joanna Schneller in a *Gentlemen's Quarterly* article about Julia:

"The crowd outside Mann's is getting louder. The twentysomething men and women have been pressed so tightly against the metal gates lining the sidewalks that their legs are ribbed from the bars. They scream every time a limo pulls up—that is, they scream for the limo, before the person inside actually opens the door. When one particularly long leg hits the red carpet, the spectators lift off. 'Julia! Julia!' they crow. '*I LOVE YOU, JULIA*' an ardent voice insists."

What that ardent voice could not possibly have known is that Julia couldn't have cared less about the crowd's adulation. She is not, and never has been, into mass appeal. What Julia has always cared most about is having a singular love, someone to marry, someone to have children with. Despite the marital woes of her twice-married mother, Betty, or perhaps *because* of them, Julia fervently believes that love and marriage will prove to be stabilizing influences in her life.

So, asked about her goals for the future, Julia's immediate response has been, "Yeah, I have goals, real simple things that are hard to attain. I want to have a family, raise kids, be in love—all those things come way before work."

Despite the rhetoric, however, Julia is a woman in love with the *idea,* not necessarily the daily realities, of being in love, whether she realizes it or not.

* * *

Julia had been at the Montana ranch with Kiefer in mid-February when she'd learned she had been nominated for a second Academy Award, this time as Best Actress for her performance in *Pretty Woman*. She was thrilled and agreed to not only appear as a presenter on the awards show but to also tape a Barbara Walters' interview, one of several segments Walters was editing into a TV special to be telecast the night of March 25, 1991.

Thus, shortly after the conclusion of the Oscar broadcast, Julia appeared, looking relaxed and radiant as ever, sitting on a porch, walking arm-in-arm with Barbara, discussing her life and confiding to Walters and the home audience that "Kiefer and I will be together forever."

Asked by Walters if she *truly* believed she would spend the rest of her life with Kiefer, Julia had replied, "Yeah. Forever love. I believe in that and I believe this is it. We live together and we are happy and we are in love with each other—and isn't that what being married is?"

Before the twice-married Walters could respond, Julia had launched into a heartfelt dissertation on her feelings about Kiefer. "He is the love of my life," she confessed. "He is the person I love and admire and respect the most in the world. Kiefer is probably the most wonderful, understanding person I have ever met."

A short while later the actress seemed to unravel during a rambling, highly emotional conversation about the death of her father. It had been a mesmerizing, yet strangely haunting moment of television because, despite Julia's obvious depth of emotion, it was difficult, if not impossible, to decipher precisely what she was so desperately, so inarticulately, trying to convey.

The juxtaposition of the Walters interview, coming as it did immediately after the Oscar ceremony, was also interesting in that only an hour or two before, a seemingly cool, articulate, and sophisticated Julia had presented one of the Best Song nominations, "I Love to See You Smile," a Randy Newman composition from the film, *Parenthood*. The song had failed to win and so, again, had Julia. The Best Actress statuette that year went to Kathy Bates for her role in *Misery*. It was presented to her by Daniel Day-Lewis who in less than a year would reject a co-starring role with Julia.

In attempting to define Julia for their readership since her instant stardom in *Pretty Woman*, magazine writers have gone to great lengths to capture on paper the indefinable "it" that has made Julia one of Hollywood's most original and captivating stars since Audrey Hepburn had stepped into the limelight in *Roman Holiday* four decades before.

"Although she wears her regular-gal veneer like armour, she has surprisingly sharp edges and is fiercely protective of parts of herself," penned a writer. "She is reminiscent of those cool high school girls—the ones who are sophisticated before they're experienced, who go to rock clubs and chain smoke and who, for all their nonchalance, take themselves and their pursuits just a bit too seriously."

Other writers have described Julia as being everything from "free-spirited and coltish" to "a wolf, regal and a little feral with deep, uncompromising eyes." By late spring, 1991, however, Julia had begun to look more like a shy, frightened fawn than either a wolf or a colt. Perhaps

Garry Marshall had been extraordinarily insightful when he nicknamed her Bambi. But if this was Bambi, it was Bambi caught in the headlights of an on-coming car.

Photograph after photograph taken by the paparrazzi during this time show Julia invariably clutching Kiefer, as though seeking protection from some menacing unseen force, with an apprehensive, wary look on her face. "I hate being photographed," she explained. "I get so nervous—my heart starts to pound and I flip out." It was an interesting response from someone who only five years before had seriously contemplated earning a living as a model.

Heart palpitations aside, three months after Ian Blair had sat exchanging pleasantries with her, Julia's wariness of the media had turned into unmasked hostility. Everything at that point seemed to annoy her, especially the media scrutiny she'd endured since receiving the Golden Globe award for *Steel Magnolias*.

Unable to accept the fact that living a fishbowl existence is the price one pays for being a celebrity, Julia resented the intrusions into her life, her lifestyle, and her thoughts. Her romantic liaisons, she believed, were no one's business. Why, she would repeatedly ask, can't the public simply enjoy her work on film and then go about their own business?

"It's bizarre to deal with reports in the press about my romantic life," she scolded. "Why the fuck would anybody care?"

She was equally disgusted by the media's inference that her affairs of the heart had been mostly screen romances gone awry. "I've known many actors, including myself, who've been tortured by having gone out with somebody they've worked with," she admonished, adding, "and it doesn't matter if you go out with them for two years because people will still call it a location romance. Give me a fucking break. Who am I going to go out with? I don't work at a pet store."

It wasn't just the media coverage of her personal life that bothered her, either. She was equally disturbed by the media's continual comparison of her acting style with that of Eric's. "People seem surprised that Eric and I act so differently. Well, we're two different people. We share the same last name, but that's about it," she bluntly told an interviewer. "We also have a sister in between us, Lisa, who's an actor, who's at the stage now where she's looking for representation and doing plays, and she's as different as we are. Who'd want us to be the same? That would be boring."

Perhaps it was because she, herself, was bored by the topic or perhaps it was because Julia, once touted as Eric Roberts' younger sister, had decidedly come into her own. But, by January, 1992, Julia was no longer discussing Eric, even in the most remotest of terms, and had requested that Eric do likewise where she was concerned. What no one then knew, other than Julia and Eric, and those people closest to them, of course, was that by then the two siblings also were not speaking to each other.

As for the press in general, Julia had nothing kind to say, especially where the weekly tabloids were concerned. "When they completely fabricate something, it really blows your mind," she simmered. "I have seen years of my life summed up in five sentences, but it sounds like it all took place over the course of a wild weekend," she continued. "I've read flat out lies so hideous they made me cry. But I stopped because I wasn't going to let those people get to me."

It was this on-going testiness which, along with an Oscar nomination, earned her a 1991 Sour Apple Award nomination from the Hollywood Women's Press Club.

What had happened to the free-spirited Julia of yester-year who had run around New York and Los Angeles, barefoot in torn jeans and silver bracelets, chain-smoking Marlboro Lights, flashing the peace sign on Arsenio Hall's syndicated show, proudly showing off the tattoo on her left shoulder blade in a *Rolling Stone* photo, eating grilled salmon with her fingers at the posh Four Seasons restaurant, and espousing some vague mystical belief of wish flowers, angels, and in things becoming clear only when they're supposed to?

What had happened to that unshackled free-wheeling young woman who would show up for important break-fast meetings at the Polo Lounge in shapeless sweaters and tee shirts and wild hair, then proceed to yawn and smoke, one leg on her chair, the other on a chair of an acquaintance, a long arm draped over the back of a chair at the table behind her, while an elderly couple nearby quietly pondered the scene, wondering who this graceless creature was and why she merited so much space?

Had the rigors of instant stardom begun to take their toll? Had appearing in back-to-back films over four years finally physically and emotionally drained her? Or was it something else? And if so, what was that something?

Rumors of trouble between Julia and Kiefer had begun circulating through Hollywood shortly before Julia's March interview with Barbara Walters. The tabloids had reported that Kiefer was having difficulty handling Julia's Oscar nomination for *Pretty Woman*. An item in "The Insider" column in the March 4 issue of *People* magazine had even suggested Kiefer's agents were "encountering difficulty finding him a job" and pointed out that, of the four movies Kiefer had starred in last year—*Flatliners, Chicago Joe and the Showgirl, Flashback,* and *Young Guns II*—only *Flatliners,* co-starring Julia, had succeeded at the box office.

A *Los Angeles Times* article published around the same time had also speculated Kiefer might be having difficulty dealing with Julia's $5 million per picture salary, when his salary was a mere $1 million per flick. "There is definitely a problem and the problem is work-related," a source close to the couple had confided, adding "Kiefer is not getting offers for roles, and Julia's phone is ringing every two minutes. But she is madly in love with him, and wants the relationship to work."

There were unconfirmed stories that the couple had fought over finances and that Kiefer was upset that Julia was insisting he sign a prenuptial agreement. There was also a bit of unconfirmed gossip making the rounds that, unhappy living in Julia's star-studded shadow, Kiefer had undertaken a fling with a stripper while Julia had been in northern California filming *Dying Young.*

All the gossip came to a screeching halt on April 30, however, when Julia and Kiefer announced through their publicists that they had decided to marry and that the wedding would take place on June 14, 1991.

"I think she's reaching out to settle her life," Jeanne Wolf, hostess of a syndicated radio show covering Hollywood, observed a few days later. "She's trying to build a cocoon."

No one could have been happier about the Kiefer–Julia coupling than Joel Schumacher, who once humbly confided "If God said, 'Design the daughter you want,' it would be Julia."

"Julia's an original, in a category all to herself," Schumacher cooed, "which probably helps explain how she's captured everyone's attention so quickly. She's a brilliant actor—her presence lights up a room, yet there are these delicious contradictions. She's not really a sex symbol, but she's very sexy. She's got great comic timing but she can also make you cry. She seems very wise for her age sometimes, yet she's totally guileless, unpretentious."

But Schumacher didn't reserve all of his praise for Julia, he also had generous words to say about Kiefer, as well. In fact, the director felt a certain kinship with the actor, probably he explained because they shared a certain commonality. "He left home when he was fifteen and so did I," Schumacher said, pointing out, "What happens is you either grow up very fast or you don't. And so Kiefer is very, very, very, overly mature and responsible for his age. He had no time to be a kid. He left home very young, had a child very young and got divorced very young. If there's such a thing as an old soul, he has one."

Only two weeks after the couple had announced their mid-June wedding plans, however, all hell broke loose when *The National Enquirer* published a front-page article in which a stripper, Amanda Rice, detailed what she claimed had been an on-going love affair with Kiefer, beginning in January. The May 14 *Enquirer* cover story, which had been gleaned from a similar article published only a week before in *The London Sun*, included photos of the couple together at Disneyland and regaled readers with Kiefer's supposed complaints about his life with Julia.

According to Amanda, Kiefer's complaints about Julia had been that she was too pale and skinny, that she was perpetually unhappy with her body and that she was "a cold fish" in bed. Amanda also quoted Kiefer as having said that *Pretty Woman* had turned Julia into an "ice princess," and that making love to her was like making love "to a corpse."

Picking up on the gossip from La La Land, the *London Daily Express* quickly published an article on Donald Sutherland's reaction to his son's supposed infidelity, quoting a Sutherland insider as having confided that "Donald is very fond of Julia and he is angry that Kiefer has caused her so much grief. He telephoned a few days ago to say that if Kiefer didn't sort his love life out, Julia would probably walk out on him, and he'd lose the best girl he'd ever had."

"Julia is a proud woman, Donald knows that," the friend had continued. "She won't put up with this sort of behavior for long. But he also knows she loves Kiefer deeply and his son is the only person who can make things right."

Only weeks before, Sutherland had told the newspaper he was extremely happy about Kiefer's forthcoming marriage. "Kiefer is a very lucky man. Julia is a wonderful girl. I'm delighted they're going to be married. They are perfect for each other. I'll be a very happy man on the day of their wedding."

Whether or not Kiefer and Amanda actually had a romantic entanglement remains an unsolved mystery, except to the two of them. But this much is known and has been documented:

On January 22, 1991, a month after Julia had left for Mendocino, Kiefer packed a suitcase and moved from Julia's hilltop house into the St. Francis Hotel at the corner of Western Avenue and Hollywood Boulevard, a rough area on the eastern fringes of Hollywood dominated by hookers, drug pushers, and addicts. Across the street from the St. Francis is the Hollywood Billiards parlor which, established in 1928, is the oldest pool parlor in Los Angeles. It was here, in his favorite pool-playing basement haunt, that Kiefer met Amanda Rice who, after indulging in several games of pool, told him she was a dancer at Crazy Girls, a Hollywood club on La Brea Avenue, and invited him to drop by.

Kiefer took her up on the invitation several nights later. In fact, by the time he had checked out of his tiny, clean, cheaply furnished $105-a-week room at the St. Francis, he had visited Amanda at the club on two or three occasions, taken her out to an all-night Sunset Strip diner for breakfast, played pool with her and several of her friends, and had taken Amanda, her young son, and his daughter, Sarah, to Disneyland.

At no time, however, did Amanda ever visit Kiefer at the St. Francis. Nor did she ever telephone him there. In the two weeks that Kiefer resided there, ostensibly doing research for an upcoming film, he had only two calls—one from Julia, the second from Michelle Pfeiffer, who left the message: "Remember, there's always a rainbow after the storm."

These facts are verifiable only because the hotel has controlled access and requires all visitors to register at the front desk. Since none of the St. Francis rooms have telephones, all incoming calls are taken by the hotel switchboard, and all outgoing calls are made from a pay phone in the lobby.

When Kiefer checked out of the St. Francis on February 5, he returned to their Hollywood Hills home, only three days ahead of Julia's return from northern California. Not long afterward the couple traveled to Kiefer's 300-acre ranch in Whitefish, Montana, a resort town of about 5,000 people in the northwest corner of the state, which is where the couple were vacationing when Julia received word she had been nominated for an Oscar for her performance in *Pretty Woman*.

Obviously whatever problems had lead Kiefer to check in to the St. Francis hotel had been resolved by the time Julia had returned to Los Angeles. Had this not been the case, the couple would not have flown to Montana together. Nor would they have continued to plan a life together and been so foolish to announce their forthcoming marriage. Perhaps the most telling clue of what would soon occur can be found in a comment about Julia delivered by a friend around the time that the gossip about Kiefer first surfaced. "Julia," explained the friend, "adores Kiefer and wants the marriage to work. But she's a down-home Southern girl and wants her family to be her sanctuary."

Two days after that devastating issue of *The National Enquirer* hit the newsstands, Julia entered Cedar-Sinai Medical Center under a phony name. She was suffering from headaches and a high fever caused by "a severe viral infection," explained Ron Wise, the hospital spokesman.

At the time of her hospitalization Julia had only been working on *Hook* a total of three days. Yet word quickly leaked out from the Twentieth Century Fox set that those initial three days of filming had not gone well, that the dailies filmed of Julia had been deemed unsatisfactory, that her trademark radiance simply wasn't on the screen. Tinkerbell, it was reported, looked pale, drawn, unhappy and not at all spritely.

Dressed in surgical blues, Kiefer kept a twenty-four-hour vigil at Julia's bedside throughout her five-day hospitalization. He was also at her side when she was discharged on May 21, 1991. Despite the Amanda Rice scandal it appeared that the relationship was as solid as ever. In fact, the following day Army Archerd reported in his *Daily Variety* column the couple had been out on the town celebrating their engagement at The Moonlight Tango Cafe, where Julia had gotten up and led the conga line, and at another Ventura Boulevard establishment, The Great Greek Cafe, where they had joined the dancing waiters and partied into the wee small hours of the morning.

Julia returned to work on *Hook* the Monday after her release from Cedar-Sinai, and life again seemed to have returned to normal for the twosome. At least there was no further scent of scandal. Even if there had been, though, chances are the media would have been too involved in covering Julia's wedding plans to even notice.

On Sunday, June 2, Elaine Goldsmith opened the doors of her Marina del Rey residence and gave Julia an elaborate wedding shower, where the gifts included a selection of lacy undergarments and at least one garter belt. Betty Motes, as well as one of Julia's best friends from Smyrna, were among the twenty-five guests who attended the soiré. The bride-to-be, it was reported, appeared to be "extraordinarily happy and glowing."

By then Julia had designed and ordered her wedding cake, a four-tiered white cake, twenty inches in diameter, with pale green icing ribbons draped on its sides and topped with violet icing flowers, rather than the traditional bride and groom. She had been fitted for her specially designed $2,500 wedding gown by Richard Tyler, her favorite designer, from the trendy Melrose Avenue shop, Tyler-Trafficante. She had approved the design and color of her Tyler-designed bridesmaids' dresses and had even picked out their shoes—four pairs of $425 white

satin pumps from Fred Hayman's Beverly Hills shop—
which Elaine Goldsmith had picked up in early May and
taken to be dyed a light green to match the silk seafoam
green bridesmaids' dresses.

The wedding originally was to have been a small intimate gathering of family and friends at the Hollywood
Hills home Julia and Kiefer had shared throughout most
of their romance. Then Joe Roth decided that the least he
could do, both as a close friend and as the head of Twentieth Century Fox, a studio which had made millions from
Julia's films, was to underwrite the wedding.

The last big Hollywood wedding to harken back to the
Golden Era of Hollywood had been that of Bruce Willis
and Demi Moore, who reportedly had spent $875,000
decorating a Burbank Studios soundstage for their 1988
nuptials. Not to be outdone, it was decided that the June
14 Kiefer–Julia union would take place on the Twentieth
Century Fox lot on Soundstage 14, a cavernous dwelling
used for interiors, which would be turned into a replica
of an antebellum home, porch, and backyard garden ala
Steel Magnolias. The setting would be lush with greenery
and plush with finery. The wedding guests were to sit
at tables for four, each decorated with a dozen roses,
reportedly Julia's favorite flower, where they would be
waited upon by 150 already-hired waiters.

Although having the wedding on an enclosed soundstage solved the problem of hovering helicopters filled
with photographers, Twentieth Century Fox reportedly
had earmarked $100,000 for extra security to protect the
couple from the prying eyes of the media and uninvited
guests. Among the invited guests were some of Hollywood's most powerful players, on screen and off, as well
as such well-known friends of Julia and Kiefer as Joel
Schumacher, Garry Marshall, Richard Gere, Michael J.

Fox, Charlie Sheen, Bruce Willis, Dolly Parton, Shirley MacLaine, Sally Field, Daryl Hannah, Lou Diamond Phillips, and Emilio Estevez.

With less than a week left before the couple were to exchange vows, everything was neatly in place. The gold-engraved wedding invitations had been mailed weeks before. The food had been ordered. The rental company handling the tables, chairs, linens, dishes, and silverware had been put on alert and was busy readying their delivery. The cases of champagne were just about to be put on ice. Dozens of roses had been ordered, and the caterers had even decided what creative form the decorative ice sculptures on the bountiful buffet table would take.

On Wednesday, June 5, Kiefer returned to Los Angeles from his 300-acre spread in Whitefish, Montana, where he had gone to spruce things up for the forthcoming honeymoon. Two days later, on Friday, June 7, Julia and several members of her bridal party, all female, headed for the exclusive, expensive, and quite posh Canyon Ranch Spa in Tucson for what was supposedly a "bonding" weekend. And it was, but not the kind Julia and her girlfriends had originally envisioned.

Julia returned to Los Angeles sometime Monday, June 10, and in a brief telephone conversation with Kiefer alluded to "problems on the horizon." She did not elaborate, however, on just what those "problems" might be. She also did not spend the night at her Hollywood Hills home. Instead she and her mother, who had flown in from Atlanta ostensibly to help Julia prepare for the wedding, went to stay with Elaine Goldsmith at her Marina del Rey digs.

Early Tuesday morning Goldsmith reportedly called Sutherland to inform him Julia had decided to call off the wedding. Goldsmith then supposedly telephoned Pat

218

Kingsley, Julia's personal publicist at the time, and asked her to prepare a statement for immediate release to the media.

What a strange twist of fate that the nuptials were canceled on June 11, 1991. Was it coincidence or karma that twenty years before, on that very same date, Julia's mother, Betty, had separated from her father?

The news that the wedding was being "postponed" was a shot heard round the world, making front-page headlines from Afghanistan to Zimbabwe. Within twenty-four hours, worldwide speculation on the "why" behind the postponement was running rampant, especially in the U.S. and Britain where Julia had amassed a large following.

While Julia's camp took charge of cancelling all of the wedding plans and contacting the wedding guests, Kiefer's publicist, Annett Wolf, went into immediate damage control, dividing up media contacts with Julia's public relations agency, PMK, to alert the more important press people that the wedding, indeed, was off.

According to friends, Kiefer spent most of Tuesday trying to reach Julia, but he fared no better than the press. According to friends, Julia never returned his phone calls. As one of Julia's old New York friends would later explain, "When Julia's through, she's through."

In the days immediately following the announcement, the rumor mill had Julia disconsolate, sobbing her brown eyes red on Betty's shoulder, crying into her margarita glass. But it was soon discovered that Julia was anything but distraught. At that point, however, Julia was in seclusion, hiding from the press, and no one except her closest friends knew the truth.

"I took Julia to her agent's house, where we thought we'd be safe," Betty Motes would later explain, recalling the events of Monday night and Tuesday morning. "But we looked out the window in the morning and we could not believe it. There must have been 150 photographers ringing the house. They were flying over in helicopters. I went out there and said, 'C'mon, you guys! All she did was break off an engagement! People are starving in the world, you know? Go home!' "

No one in the crowd took her up on the suggestion.

"These people from the *National Enquirer* would call Julia's agent's house in Los Angeles and lie about where they were from," Julia's mother, Betty, complained. "Once they even said it was *The London Times* calling. But we checked and there was no such person there. Once they said the *U.S. News Agency*, and there is no such thing. Anytime you get a British accent from a Florida area code it's a tabloid," Betty said knowingly, adding she'd even had a call from the phone company, asking if it would be okay to give Mr. Motes her unlisted phone number.

"I told the operator 'There is no Mr. Motes. Do not speak to this man!' "

But the international news media remained undaunted in its ongoing pursuit of Julia and everyone around her, including her mother, Betty, who would later laughingly recall her experiences for friends in Smyrna, telling them, "At one point I found myself racing along in my car, with these tabloid people trying to follow me home. And I just pulled over and said to myself, 'Wait a minute. I don't make enough money to have to put up with this.' "

When the photographs of Kiefer and Amanda Rice had first appeared in a British tabloid, and then in *The National Enquirer*, Julia had been seen as the heartbroken bride-to-be, an object of sympathy. Less than a month later, however, she had become "Jilting Julia," when it was discovered she had broken off the wedding after a weekend tryst with Jason Patric, a fellow thespian, during her Canyon Ranch visit. Thus, in a surprising backlash, public reaction went from "Will Julia Be Okay?" to "Why Is Julia Okay?"

If Julia had simply called off her wedding to Kiefer, come forth, and admitted it had been a mistake and *then* disappeared from public view, the pressure from the media probably would have diminished within a few weeks. However, when it was discovered that Julia had spent most of her "bonding" weekend bonded to a young actor named Jason Patric, the Julia–Kiefer story took an unexpected turn.

With this added dimension, the media pressed forward with renewed vigor, and the cancelled wedding became something akin to a bad television comedy-mystery, with jokes flying every which way, such as when Jay Leno confided to his *The Tonight Show* audience that he planned to unload the blender he'd bought for Julia and Kiefer on Donald and Marla.

Not a day passed without some item, some story, running somewhere about Julia Roberts. *The London Daily Express* ran an interview with Julia, in which she, with her usual mystical aplomb, explained "The success you achieve on a professional level can have nothing and everything to do with your personal life." *The Daily Express* story had originally been meant to run during her honeymoon. When that failed to occur, no detail became too minute to report, from the $425 Manolo Blahnik dyed-to-match seafoam green shoes to the fact that Julia's wedding dress remained, unclaimed, at Tyler-Trafficante. Yet, while she was certainly not out of mind,

Julia definitely remained out of sight throughout the week.

Betty Motes guarded Julia's whereabouts, as well as the reasons behind the abruptly halted wedding, with the kind of patriotic fervor usually experienced only by prisoners-of-war. She begrudgingly offered only rank, name, and serial number, even under threat of duress.

"Julia's been working very hard. She has been under an incredible amount of pressure and stress. So many things have happened for her so quickly," she explained to one persistent reporter.

"She's talked this over with us and I think she feels she should allow a little more time before making such an important decision as marriage," she proffered to another.

Later, however, Betty told a reporter from her hometown newspaper, "Julia did not ask my advice about Sutherland and I wouldn't have had the vaguest idea of what to tell her if she had. Julia knows that I respect her decisions—that's why we're so close. She's handled this whole thing with maturity. She's ignored the press."

With, or without Julia's attention, however, the press was not about to be ignored. Within days it was revealed that Julia had dined on chicken piccata, peanut butter yogurt with graham cracker crust, and iced coffee, the night of Sunday, June 9, before quietly slipping out of the dining room with Jason, who appeared to be comforting her.

Other Canyon Ranch visitors confirmed the couple had spent the greater part of the weekend together. More importantly, after returning to Los Angeles on Monday, June 10, and dumping Kiefer on Tuesday, June 11, Julia and Jason had become inseparable.

Early Wednesday morning, the studio carpenters and gardeners began dismantling the antebellum porch and garden that was to have been the site of the reputed $500,000 wedding. Wednesday night the staff at Dominick's, the West Hollywood restaurant which was to have been the site of Kiefer's stag party, devoured the cake that had been ordered and delivered for the celebration. It was a confectionary replica of a fifteen-pound roasted tom turkey on a silver platter. "Kiefer," explained a friend, "has a thing for turkeys."

The following day, Thursday, June 13, Julia traveled to the Twentieth Century Fox lot where she posed for publicity stills with Stephen Spielberg on the *Hook* set wearing a baseball cap with "Notre Dame" emblazoned on it. A studio employee who was present during the photo session said "She seemed fine and was very happy, not mopey and sad, as she had been before." It wasn't until days later that the media discovered that Jason Patric was a life-long Notre Dame football fan.

Later that night, Julia was seen entering Jason's West Hollywood duplex. She was not seen again until Friday morning when she drove off in her BMW. Several hours later, on what was to have been her wedding day, Julia and Jason were spotted dining on turkey burgers at the Nowhere Cafe, a popular Melrose Avenue health food restaurant in West Hollywood. Kiefer, it was later learned, had spent *his* wedding day moving out of the Hollywood Hills home he had shared with Julia, and later playing pool at the Hollywood Billiards parlor.

The following day, Saturday, June 15, Julia and Jason flew to Ireland, where they had booked separate $250 per night rooms at the Sherbourne Hotel in Dublin. "The engagement ring was off her finger," reported a hotel staffer, adding "She was wearing jeans and looked very drawn. She had lost a lot of weight and her hair was a pale orange, like a dye job gone wrong." A fellow traveler, wishing to join in the international "Julia Watch," also reported that on the Aer Lingus flight to Dublin from London Julia and Jason were "practically making love" throughout the forty-minute flight.

On Sunday the twosome quietly slipped out of the Sherbourne before dawn and disappeared into the countryside, reportedly to seek refuge at the Galway cottage of Adam Clayton, the U-2 bassist. Meanwhile, back in Los Angeles, Kiefer spent Sunday, which was Father's Day, with his ex-wife, Camelia, and their three-year old daughter, Sarah, trying to figure out, like much of the world, what had happened . . . and why.

Chapter Twelve

Although Julia would claim Kiefer had been the one to call off the marriage, friends and associates of the actor have steadfastly denied this. In fact, they say, Kiefer never even had the opportunity to talk to Julia. The only phone call he had received, they claim, had been the one from Julia's agent, telling him that Julia had decided to cancel the nuptials.

Kiefer, claim his friends, tried for days to reach Julia, but she never returned his calls. Thus, like the rest of the world, he had been relegated to reading about his life—and Julia's merry romantic escapades with Jason—in the newspapers.

"He was despondent," confided a friend. "When someone you spent three years of your life with, someone who goes on every talkshow and tells the world how much she loves you does something like this, how could you *not* be upset?''

In the days immediately following the announcement that the wedding was off, media speculation about the causes behind this sudden turn of major events ran rampant, with virtually all fingers of guilt pointed squarely at the jilted bridegroom. The accusations against Sutherland ranged from his heavy drinking to his alleged jealousy of Julia's career and her $5 million movie fee to his purported refusal to sign a prenuptial agreement waiving his rights to her fortune if they broke up.

Yet none of these supposed reasons really holds up under close scrutiny. For one thing, Kiefer had never varied in his hearty-party, heavy-drinking ways in the two years he and Julia had been involved. Secondly, Kiefer was from a show business family and was well aware of the ups and downs of an acting career. Thirdly, Julia and Kiefer would have had plenty of time to work out any financial agreements so that the signing of a prenuptial could hardly have been an eleventh hour problem. Besides, both the Sutherland and Roberts camps denied there had ever been any talk of a prenuptial agreement. It was the only thing the two sides ever agreed on during the chaos following the cancellation.

''Kiefer supported Julia in everything,'' confided one of his friends. ''He's been the best thing that ever happened to Julia. He took a year off so they could focus on one of their careers. I know of at least two movies out now that he turned down. He's the reason she agreed to do *Hook*. Julia's decision to call off the wedding had nothing to do with their careers or money.''

''The problem was not money, or other women,'' echoed another insider. ''The problem was Julia. Everytime she gets close, she just shies away.''

In a press release dated June 19, 1991, Amanda Rice denied having had an affair with Kiefer. Of course, she also denied having given an interview to any of the tabloids, which is difficult, albeit if not impossible, to believe. Nevertheless Rice, who was then dancing under the name of Raven, went on record:

"I have never given any interviews about having an affair or a relationship with Kiefer Sutherland," she stated. "Kiefer is a friend. We have not had an affair. Everything that has appeared about us in print has been manufactured and blown out of proportion."

But it was too late for the truth or, for that matter, more lies, to be of any consequence. The damage had been done. Whatever ties that had bound Julia and Kiefer together had been ripped, shredded, torn asunder.

Months after the fact, Julia would attempt to explain why she had continued her dance toward the altar for almost a month following the revelations of the *National Enquirer* article in a November 22 interview with *Entertainment Weekly*. In the article she claimed she had "sort of swallowed her pride" by continuing the relationship with Kiefer after reading of his dalliance with "the stripper."

"I mean, this had been going on for a really long time," she said, regarding Amanda Rice. "So then I had to say, 'Well, I have made an enormous mistake in agreeing to get married. Then I made an even greater mistake by letting it all get so big. I'm not going to make the final mistake of actually getting married.' At that point I just realized that this had all turned into an enormous joke, and that it wasn't going to be respectable, it wasn't going to be honest, it wasn't going to be simple. And it could have been all those things."

According to a source close to Kiefer, however, Julia

had known about the *Enquirer* article before it was even published, had known that it was false, and yet had still gone ahead with the wedding plans. "There's nothing she didn't know about it," explained the source. "Whatever problems she had, whatever hesitations or issues they had, they had worked through. There were no secrets there. There's no explanation that has anything to do with Kiefer. He never denied that he met Amanda. He denied that he had a relationship with her."

If this scenario is true, then the only conclusion can be that Julia deliberately set Kiefer up for public humiliation, not only by launching into an affair with Jason Patric the very week of her wedding but by waiting until she had the entire world's attention and *then* dropping him. After all, she *did* continue the "wedding will go on as scheduled" charade for a month after *The National Enquirer* broke the news of Kiefer's alleged infidelity.

And, again, the same question arises. *Why?*

The answer has to be that, *if* Julia knew about the article and about Kiefer's "friendship" with Amanda, she did not know until she read the story that Kiefer had divulged intimate details of their life together, such as her insecurities about her body.

"I could sit here and tell you twenty things that annoy me about myself," Julia once explained, "but to say something critical is to bring it to other people's attention. If I say my fingernails are too short, people read that and say, 'You know, she's right. Her fingernails are hideous.' "

Interestingly, Julia is a nail biter. "She used to sit in the chair and bite her nails to the quick," confided one of her former hairdressers. "She's not your normal 'out there' star who wants to know every product you're putting on their hair. She just sits there and lets you do it because she wants to get out as soon as possible.''

Julia's major hangup, however, is not her fingernails. It's her body. ''Only my wardrobe people know how sick and paranoid I am about this,'' she once confided, referring to her body. ''With them I go bananas: 'I'm not going to wear *THAT!* Let's get one thing straight. These are the body parts I have a problem with. These are the ones we will hide, we will conceal, we will make look better. This is your job. This is your task!''

While it was one thing for Julia to discuss what she perceived to be her physical failings, however, it was another for Kiefer to have discussed them, especially with a stranger who would then tell the rest of the world. Having either read, or heard about, the tabloid story, Julia had to have known the truth—that Kiefer had, indeed, confided these things to a stranger. How else could Amanda Rice have known about her life-long insecurities?

At that point it probably didn't matter to Julia whether Kiefer had or had not slept with Amanda Rice. What mattered to Julia was that, in her eyes, she had been stripped naked and betrayed. So, since hell hath no fury like a woman scorned, what better revenge than in publicly humiliating Kiefer by, not only leaving him on the way to the altar, but by departing on the arm of a handsome new lover?

In an odd set of circumstances, while the paparazzi chased the couple from Los Angeles to Dublin and back again, TV commercials were heralding the opening of *Sleeping with the Enemy,* which was an important film for

Julia because it showed she could open a movie which, although mediocre, could still do box office. In fact, *Sleeping with the Enemy* grossed $31 million in its first eleven days at the box office, proving to be as big a film for Julia as *Cocktail* was for Tom Cruise. But for Julia, the film came and went without notice. She was too busy living her life . . . and trying to elude the media.

"There are people, photographers, who sit in their cars outside my house all day long who frighten me," Julia moaned. "I went out to dinner with my sister two weeks ago—I hadn't seen her in a couple of months—and we had a nice time and we were walking home. We turned a corner and six men jumped out of a dark parking lot at ten p.m. at night. You know, that is frightening—to anybody."

And, naturally, with the media spotlight focused squarely on Julia, Jason Patric suddenly found himself also dragged into the glare, his photo squeezed between those of Julia and Kiefer on the front pages of virtually every newspaper around the world. Who, the world wanted to know, is Jason Patric, and why did America's Pretty Woman run off with him only a few steps short of the matrimonial altar?

Determined to answer that question, the press hounded the couple. Photographers staked out Jason's West Hollywood duplex in twenty-four-hour shifts, telephoto lenses at the ready. Tabloid reporters with no lack of temerity went up and knocked on the door, hoping it would be opened by one or the other of the elusive lovebirds. In the ensuing year the couple could go nowhere, whether by foot or by car, without the tabloids in close pursuit.

"I want to be freed from this imprisonment of photographers outside my house, of people jumping out at me in the dark, simply because I am just a girl, and I am

230

twenty-four years old and I just want to have a nice life and be able to run around and laugh and have fun and not sit hunched down with a hat on all the time and my hair down in my face,'' Julia complained. ''I want to be able to look up and see everything instead of always feeling like I have to hide.''

With his privacy suddenly shattered, Jason also felt violated by the media. The constant surveillance was the antithesis of what he, too, wanted out of life. Known for being an intensely private, extremely reclusive young man, who liked to keep a low profile, Jason was shy and withdrawn even as a child. ''He's got a space in himself and he doesn't want it violated,'' his father, playwright Jason Miller, explained shortly after the Julia–Jason media blitz began.

Hence the unrelenting scrutiny of his relationship with Julia had to have turned Jason's life into a living nightmare. ''I don't want to be photographed. I don't want to be a celebrity,'' he had explained in a rare magazine interview only the year before his encounter with Julia. ''I'm an actor. I don't want to be trapped in a persona.''

Jason subsequently made his point about not wanting to be photographed when, in July, 1992, he became involved in a melee when he encountered a camera crew from *First Person*, the NBC hour-long magazine show hosted by Maria Shriver, stationed outside his duplex on a sunny Saturday morning. When the crew began following and filming Jason and an unidentified friend as they walked, Jason got into a physical confrontation with the camerawoman, who bit him on the arm, supposedly when he tried to wrest the camera from her. The police were called but the brouhaha quietly ended when Jason refused to press charges.

What had to have been equally distressing to Jason

were the many rumors that began cropping up when the elusive couple made themselves totally inaccessible to all but a very few friends. One of the first stories to surface in the aftermath of Julia's new coupling was that Jason and Kiefer had been close friends, that Jason had been invited to the wedding and then disinvited when Kiefer discovered the two had been secretly dating. Although this is a fabrication, it nevertheless gained a groundswell and was published in several prominent magazines.

The truth is that Kiefer and Jason *had* known each other because in 1986 they had co-starred in *The Lost Boys,* an intriguing chiller of a vampire movie which had been directed by Joel Schumacher, Julia's director-cum-father figure on *Flatliners* and *Dying Young.* In fact it is Schumacher who has been credited with having "discovered" Patric. So, if Julia knew Jason Patric prior to encountering him at Canyon Ranch, it's more likely she had been introduced to him by Schumacher than by Kiefer.

Ironically, shortly after the July 1987 release of *Lost Boys*, Jason began receiving numerous film offers, including a lead role in *Young Guns*, which, of course, turned out to be a Kiefer movie. Another ironic twist to the Julia-Kiefer-Jason story is that Jason reportedly turned down a leading role in *Flatliners*, claiming it was too commercial a project for his taste.

"I turned all that kind of crap down," Jason told a *Rolling Stone* writer. "I mean, who needs it?"

Despite having worked together and the strange intertwining of their careers, Kiefer and Jason had not maintained their on-the-set friendship, probably because the two are worlds apart in lifestyles. And, contrary to popular gossip, Jason had not been invited to attend Julia and Kiefer's wedding. Jason had been invited, however, to attend Kiefer's 1987 summer wedding to Camilla Kath, probably because it occurred around the time *The Lost Boys* was released.

For a person not wanting to be trapped by the trappings of celebrity, Jason's life obviously took a turn for the worse, at least in his eyes, when he suddenly found himself at the center of worldwide notoriety, not for his acting ability, but for having romanced America's Pretty Woman right out of her wedding gown.

"I'm not interested in talking about my lineage," Jason bluntly told a reporter, who'd had the chutzpah to inquire into his background. "I'd rather not talk about my personal life. You want to know about me. You want to know where I grew up. You want to know my ideas on things," Jason had continued with the verbal punch of a prizefighter. "Well, I can tell you the truth, or maybe not tell you the truth. You'll never know, and it doesn't matter. If it sounds good the people who read it want to believe it."

It's no doubt because of this attitude that very little has ever been published about Jason's personal life. But this much is known. He is the twenty-seven-year old son of Jason Miller, the Pulitzer Prize-winning author of *That Championship Season,* and his first wife, Linda, who is the daughter of the late TV comedian Jackie *The Honeymooners* Gleason. The couple met, and married, while both were drama students at Catholic University in Washington, D.C. and had three children—Jennifer, Jason, and Jordan—before divorcing in 1975. Both parents subsequently remarried and Jason has a younger half-brother, Joshua, eighteen, also an actor, from his father's mid-Seventies marriage to Susan Bernard, whom he divorced in 1979.

After his parents' divorce, Jason moved with his mother to southern California, graduating in 1984 from

Santa Monica High School where he had been involved with various school drama department productions. Despite his cross-country move, Jason has remained extremely close to his father, from whom he gleaned a love of reading and football, especially Notre Dame football games which, as a staunch Irish Catholic, he had been attending since he was five years old. It was also his father who convinced Jason to drop Miller and adopt his middle name, Patric, a Celtic spelling, as a last name; and who offered Jason his first taste of movie-making by hiring him as a production assistant on the screen version of his hit play, *That Championship Season*.

Jason subsequently made his film debut in the forgettable Mel Brook's spoof, *Solarbabies*, in 1986, a year after making his professional acting debut portraying the troubled son of Lee Remick and Bruce Dern in the 1985 television movie, *Toughlove*. In the intervening years, unlike Julia, he has made few films, enduring months of unemployment while waiting for what he considers to be a "meaningful" role.

As a result, despite critical praise for his performances in *Forever, My Love* and *Rush,* his last two films, Jason has acquired little of the fame and fortune enjoyed by Kiefer. But, of course, that's by design, not by default. Julia speaks of wanting to be known only for her acting ability. Jason lives the part. Which is, no doubt, why he is content to live so frugally.

An interesting footnote to the Julia-Kiefer-Jason story is that Kiefer reportedly was paid the $2.5 million he was to receive for his co-starring role in *Renegades*. When Julia offered Jason the opportunity to star opposite her in the film, he flatly turned it down.

According to people who have visited the duplex, it's a small one-bedroom home filled with beat-up, dingy, nondescript furniture. And, even though Jason has lived there for several years, bedsheets, rather than curtains, cover the windows. "He's into not seeming materialistic," explained an acquaintance, adding "*studiously* into not seeming that way. It's like he's a rich kid but doesn't want to appear like one, you know? So he goes out of his way to look and live like he's poverty-stricken."

"He doesn't live in a palatial place. There's an old, used couch. I go in there and I'm disgusted," admitted Jami Gertz, a former co-star and long time friend of Jason's.

Indeed, the small apartment in a modest single-story beige clapboard building on a well-traveled street, not far from the million dollar home she had shared with Kiefer, is a world apart.

But it apparently was a world Julia wanted, or needed, because, throughout their fourteen-month relationship, Julia rarely spent time at her own home high atop the Hollywood Hills. Instead, according to neighbors, she was always at Jason's place, enjoying domesticity by cooking and baking, happily spending her evenings curled up on the couch watching television or entertaining Jason's "hippie-looking young actor typefriends" who apparently dropped in whenever the mood suited them.

And then, of course, there was the responsibility of the pot-bellied pig, Ferguson, a gift from Julia to Jason shortly after their two lives became entangled as one. Julia took great pride in feeding and bathing Ferguson. In fact, at one point, she began warning neighbors they shouldn't be alarmed if they heard any screaming. It would just be Ferguson getting a bath, she would laughingly explain.

Pot-bellied pig aside, Julia's lifestyle with Jason was far removed from what one would expect of Hollywood's highest-paid actress. Not only was she living amid tatty furniture, she was dressing in tatty clothes, too. But that's the way Jason, with his scraggly beard and long hair, dresses. And Julia *does* tend to take on the chameleon-like coloration of whomever she's romantically linked with, be it Kiefer in Armani or Jason in rags.

It's not simply clothing that separates the two men. Whereas Kiefer is a hearty-partying, tequila-drinking, pool-shooting man about town, Jason is quiet and reserved, more into reading—everything from Edgar Allen Poe to John Cheever—than shooting pool. And, although he has been known to down a beer or two, Jason also is more into health foods than he is alcohol, which might explain why Julia, a chainsmoker, tried to give up cigarettes and coffee, especially capuccino, during their cohabitation. And why Julia, a notorious late sleeper, joined Jason in early morning workouts with a personal trainer, who would come to the house for an hour of exercise several times a week.

On her own, Julia liked to browse at the Beverly Hills Starbucks, no doubt in search of some exotic blends of coffee, which she likes to drink strong. In the company of Jason, however, she was more likely to be found browsing the shelves at Erewhon, a West Hollywood health food store, in search of organically grown produce. Not only had her romantic focus changed, her lifestyle had changed.

Gone were the wild nights of drinking and dancing at funky underground rock clubs in Los Angeles. In their place were quiet lunches at the Nowhere Cafe and intimate dinners at Morton's, a trendy bistro on L.A.'s westside, which has become the "in" spot for Hollywood's publicity-shy powerbrokers and stars, thanks to the restaurants firmly enforced policy of "No Photographs."

It was at Morton's that Julia Phillips claims to have first learned she'd probably "never eat lunch in this town again." And it was at Morton's, with its unlisted telephone number and its dimly lighted privacy, that Julia and Jason could relax over long dinners without worrying about the prying eyes and cameras of the town's papparrazi.

An industry powerbroker was having dinner at Morton's one night when Julia and Jason were also dining there. "She was a woman obviously in distress," he recalled, adding that this was shortly after the couple had returned from Ireland. "Her shoulders were slumped over, as if she was carrying the world on her," he confided. "It was almost as though she was hiding away. Or defeated."

During the time they were together, Julia and Jason were the antithesis of glamorous movie stars. Instead they shared a mutual love for disheveled-looking clothes and could frequently be found walking around West Hollywood—Julia in either her ill-fitting granny dresses or ripped jeans, Jason in his ragged tee shirts and baggy nondescript pants, a scraggly beard hiding his handsome Irish face—looking more like two of the area's homeless people than glittering screen images.

The couple's tendency toward a look of poverty even extended to their feet. Julia, for instance, prefers to be shoeless and is often barefoot even when driving her shiny expensive black Porsche Targa. Jason prefers to go sockless but, unlike Julia, he does wear shoes.

Considering the twosome were as different as night and day, and had little in common on either an intellectual or professional level, their relationship appeared to be an odd coupling. In retrospect, however, it was probably the perfect alliance at the time for Julia, a little girl lost who was very much in need, and chivalrous Jason, who needed to be needed. As his father once explained, Jason is "singular and loyal" when it comes to love. "He's a very solid guy. I've seen him with two girls he loved and he's like a knight errant from medieval times. He believes in chivalry."

Within days of returning from Ireland, Julia was back, literally, in harness, flying through the air with not the greatest of ease on the set of *Hook*.

Interestingly, Julia had originally been offered the role of Tinkerbell in the fall of 1990 and had leapt at the opportunity to work with Spielberg. But shortly after beginning work on *Dying Young,* she had changed her mind and had sent word through Elaine Goldsmith that she wasn't going to be able portray Spielberg's on-screen pixie.

The reasons behind Julia's decision to bow out of *Hook* had been solid. She was emotionally and physically drained, and the role of Tinkerbell would be strenuous, calling for her to fly through mid-air, wearing a harness, against a blue backdrop. Also when she first turned the role down, *Hook* was scheduled to begin in January, which would have given her virtually no down time between the two films. "I didn't think I had the muscle to do it," Julia later admitted, adding she had believed it would be "better to pull out than to go in halfhearted and let everyone else down."

But, in late December, 1990, Goldsmith had abruptly called Spielberg and his agent, Mike Ovitz, head of CAA, as well as the film's producer, Kathleen Kennedy, to inform them that Julia was reconsidering the role.

Why did Julia, knowing how exhausted she was and

how much pressure the role would put on her, decide to go ahead with *Hook?* The answer is money, and lots of it. With a reported salary of $7 million, Julia stood to make more money from that one film role than she'd made in all of her previous films combined. But joining the cast of *Hook* had been a mistake, something Julia realized within days.

From the moment she first stepped foot on the set of *Hook* reports had begun to circulate through the omnipresent Hollywood grapevine that Julia was "hell to work with," that she would "burst into tears and tonguelash" the people around her, that she didn't feel she was getting the attention she deserved, and that she was complaining Dustin Hoffman was being far more favored than she. Julia also was reported to be constantly complaining that 'flying' on the high wire made her dizzy."

"She's young," a studio executive explained. "She's incredibly shy and not confident meeting strangers. She doesn't have the wit or the confidence to parry with a Dustin Hoffman or a Robin Williams, so, instead of even trying to get involved with the cast and crew, Julia retreated to her trailer, staying pretty much on her own set, Stage 10, where she got along fine with her special effects people."

"Robin and I worked together sometimes," Julia would later say, "and I met Bob Hoskins once. I was also off-camera one time for Dustin Hoffman. But I spent ninety percent of the time on a stage by myself with no other actors anywhere to be seen. It was me, Steven, and the crew, because most of the time I was on blue screen."

In the beginning, before the wedding debacle, friends and co-workers had attributed Julia's behavior to a severe case of wedding jitters. "Her insecurities are at an all time high right now. She's just overwhelmed by everything in her life," they'd explained, adding, "Julia's at her wit's end. She's a wreck and she's taking it out on the cast and crew. No one will be happier when the wedding's over than the people she is working with.

"Dustin and Julia are probably both getting the star treatment," added a crew member, "but she is just overwhelmed by everything in her life. Maybe she felt that she needed a little more attention than she was actually getting."

Herbert Ross had even added his voice to the prenuptial chorus, confiding "Julia is timid, frightened, and inexperienced, but a talented young actress. Her sudden tirades and infrequent overbearing actions could be the result of overwork. She's had a lot to deal with this year."

By the end of the film, however, the crew had begun referring to Julia's days on the set of *Hook* as "Tinker Hell."

"I'm a normal person," Julia had responded. "If I sit in my trailer for six hours doing nothing, I'm going to say, 'What the fuck is going on?' I don't think that's an outrageous question, I don't think that's temperamental either," and added that the experience of portraying the seven-inch sprite had been unlike any other she'd ever had. "I don't think I'd do a search and destroy for other parts like this, to be hanging on a wire for hours," she sarcastically admitted.

Despite the sarcasm, it was the truth. Portraying Tinkerbell at that particular time in her life had been the absolute worst thing that could have happened to Julia Roberts who, even in the best of times, is not emotionally equipped to spend her days alone in front of a blue screen on a special effects sound stage, strapped into a flying harness for hours, delivering her lines to nonexistent co-stars.

Julia probably could have handled the fatigue, the emotional stress of Kiefer's well-publicized folly, and her distress about whether or not to go through with the wedding *if* she'd had the love, the support, the camaraderie, the bonding of cast and crew that she'd had on *Pretty Woman* or *Flatliners,* or any of her other films, for that matter. But she didn't. She was alone, without a film family, without on-set friends, isolated from not only the outside world but the world inside, without either a surrogate mother or a father to give her a hug and cheer her up.

Brilliant though he may be, Steven Spielberg is *not* a fatherly director like a Garry Marshall or a Joel Schumacher. The two failed to connect, which is why Spielberg would later confess, "It was not a great time for Julia and I to be working together," during a *Sixty Minutes* interview with Ed Bradley.

Tired, depressed, hurt and angry, confused and without any emotional support, except what Jason could offer her, Julia found herself in the beginning stages of a nervous collapse. It had started before she cancelled the wedding and it would continue for months afterward. And it wasn't just the Kiefer episode. It wasn't simply fatigue. It was everything. It was her life.

"Julia is all fucked up," a close family friend had confided at the time. "She doesn't know what's what. She's still not normal. Every time she thinks she's finally okay, someone will ask her for an autograph and she can feel herself ready to burst into tears. It's a good thing she got $7 million for *Hook* because, with the way she's feeling, it may have been her last film."

Adding to Julia's emotional upset were the reviews of *Dying Young,* which, while it did marginally well at the box office, was soundly panned by the nation's movie critics.

"They said Julia Roberts could open any film," wrote Martin Grove, industry analyst for *The Hollywood Reporter*. "They said she could open a phone book. *Dying Young* proved they were wrong."

"Perhaps what *Dying Young* really proved is that you don't call a picture *Dying Young*," offered *Time* magazine. "Roberts' rapid ascendancy taught Hollywood that she could sell innocence, glamour, pluck. But not even the movies most reliable female star since Doris Day could peddle leukemia—particularly not to a summertime audience that wants only the bad guys to die. So *Dying Young* did just that, and Roberts' pristine rep got terminated too."

Yet, even while *Dying* was slowly doing just that, the Julia Roberts phenomenon continued to flourish, with the nation's tabloids rushing to keep up with her personal life. "Julia gets more media attention *without* making a movie than most people do *making* a movie," chuckled an industry powerbroker. "She not only dropped out of her career, she seemed to drop out of her life. And, of course, that's what's made everybody so interested in her. It wasn't like she just chose not to work. It was that she'd broken up with someone and was now seeing someone else and she was hiding from the media around the world, not wanting to be a public persona. It was a classic celebrity crisis in which her life began to transcend any cinematic story."

For a young woman whose ambitions were based on a desire to be loved, the reviews of *Dying Young* had been a crushing blow. The negative reviews both she and the film, *Hook,* received when it opened the following year only deepened Julia's fear of appearing before the cameras again.

"I've seen this happen before," said Larry Thompson,

a well-known TV movie producer. "A lot of actors get successful fast. They want it and they get it. Then they think they don't deserve it. And when they don't think they deserve it, they realize that, in their effort to get to the top, they have told so many stories and had so many press releases written about them, that they'd started to believe them. At that point the distance between the truth and the image becomes something they have to deal with. What do I want? How did this happen? Who am I?''

Perhaps that's why, despite having regained her physical strength, as months passed Julia became increasingly fearful her career would be forever ruined if her next film, whatever and whenever that might be, were not a certified box-office hit. "The longer she stays away from films," confided a friend in late 1991, "the more pressure she feels to have a hit. She really thought she was going to have a nervous breakdown last summer. In fact, she thinks her life is destroyed and is over. It may be a long while before she's right again.''

Indeed, it would be more than eighteen months before Julia Roberts appeared on a soundstage. And when she *did* reappear it would be with a new mentor and one of Hollywood's most unusual production deals.

"They say I've had it easy," she said to a *Los Angeles Times* reporter in early summer, 1991, "but 'easy' based on whose account? True, I haven't slept in the park. I haven't struggled to the bone. But this is my journey, so who's to criticize or judge? Making movies, to me, is the best thing in the world. But, at the risk of sounding ungrateful, it's very, very hard.''

Chapter Thirteen

Julia finished her work on *Hook* on August 8, 1991, and promptly disappeared from public view. She was, announced Elaine Goldsmith, taking a year off as planned to "refuel and recharge." From that moment on, in a pattern that would continue for almost two years, Julia surfaced only infrequently, and then, usually only by fluke, and almost always in the company of Jason.

Since it's extremely unusual for a star of her magnitude to so completely disappear, the wheels of the Hollywood gossip mill began to grind again, this time suggesting that Julia was on drugs—heroin, to be exact. Another rumor was that she had forsaken movies forever. Yet another story had her in the midst of a nervous breakdown.

"I think the luckiest thing that ever happened to her was to cancel her marriage, although she was totally discombobulated by it. But I don't think it's calming when you're rushing from one love affair to the next. I think it would be great if she concentrated on her career and not on the men in her life,'' wrote Liz Smith, syndicated columnist.

''I think it was one of the smartest, healthiest, most self-protective moves she could have made,'' Joel Schumacher told a reporter. ''Celebrity is a bucking bronco, but I think she's very firm in the saddle. She's not impressed by it and she's not obssessed by it. She has a real mom. I'm not worried about Julia at all. She's got what it takes to deal with whatever life has to offer.''

Garry Marshall also pointed to what he believed was Julia's strong family background as the major reason why Julia would survive the ravages of fame and the adverse publicity that had followed her across two continents after the wedding debacle.

''I could see from meeting her mother that Julia would have the right values and balance to get her through the horrible treacherous waters of Hollywood,'' Marshall explained in August, 1990. ''If you are a hit like Julia is right now, everybody's after you. But I think she's going to be okay because she's so smart and comes from a good solid background.''

Yet other Hollywood powerbrokers were not so certain.

''It's not that the bloom is off Julia Roberts, it's just that she is going to have to gain momentum again,'' explained a producer. ''Hollywood really is a town of who's the flavor of the month. With each passing month, there is less and less demand for her services. I still think of her as bankable. But how long are the studios going to risk huge budgets on an unproven?''

''Her private life has become a movie in itself and that is very difficult for anyone to handle,'' conceded another

245

producer. ''The public really likes her, but I think they were shocked to find out she had slept with everybody. She pulled back and didn't do anything and the media wrote so much about it she became a celebrity. She went from being an ingenue to a celebrity. Now she has to come back and be a serious actress.

''I think she's still our homecoming queen. She may have broken up with the captain of the football team, but she's going to go on and graduate with honors,'' he concluded.

For months Julia remained in reclusive silence. So did Kiefer, except for a brief comment about the cancelled wedding two years later. ''If it wasn't (mutual) on the specific day the wedding was canceled, it was mutual shortly thereafter. There was a mutual appreciation for the fact that it didn't happen,'' he told *Details* magazine in a September, 1992, interview that, so far, has been the only time he's broken his silence on the events leading up to the non-wedding.

By the time Kiefer had begun doing interviews to publicize the release of *A Few Good Men,* which had been filmed in fall, 1991, he had also spent a year in self-imposed exile at his Montana ranch. Within months of having been left only steps from the matrimonial altar he also had sold the $30,000 powerboat Julia had purchased for him, collecting only $1500 in return for the expensive craft. ''It was top of the line,'' claims a source, ''but he dumped it because *she* had bought it.''

Whether by coincidence or design, Julia broke her self-imposed silence only two months after Kiefer's interview was published in *Details.* In an exclusive November, 1992, interview with *Entertainment Weekly,* Julia angrily denied she had a drug problem, and even bared her arms to show the writer she had no needle marks, which obviously meant she had heard the specific rumor of heroin, rather than cocaine, addiction.

Once that was accomplished, Julia had then launched into *her* version of the cancelled nuptials. It had been Kiefer, she said, who had called off the wedding.

"I had returned from a trip to Arizona intending to tell Kiefer I thought it would be best for both of us not to get married. But the next time I talked to Kiefer, he called me on the telephone. The only thing I said was, 'Where have you been?' And he proceeded to tell me what I was going to tell him, which is he did not want to marry me, he did not want this to happen," she said, adding that Kiefer had then called back a few hours later and, at that point, she had told him that, as far as she was concerned, the wedding was off.

This version, of course, is fascinating more for what it doesn't say than what it does. Despite her candor, the fact is that Julia's recall of the events leading to the cancelled nuptials did not correspond to what had been reported months before about who-did-what-to-whom-and-when.

However, when it came to discussing her relationship with Jason Patric and that fateful trip to Canyon Ranch, which she merely described as "a trip to Arizona," Julia was less than candid. In fact, she never once mentioned Canyon Ranch and made her Arizona sojourn sound as though she'd been there alone, possibly on business, perhaps even house hunting.

And yet that "trip to Arizona" had changed two lives and fired a salvo heard 'round the world.

When the magazine writer later asked Julia about her relationship with Jason, her response had been cold, calculating, and careful. How could it not be, considering her neatly crafted, nicely edited version of what led up to the wedding-that-never-was. "I think that at this point the things I am choosing to discuss are things I am willing to give the public," she said. "I choose at this moment *not* to speak about Jason for the reason that it is far more dignified and deserving of respect than to put it out there and to allow people to give their opinion on it at lunch." End of comment. End of story.

On December 11, 1991, Julia appeared before the nation's press during a junket at the Century Plaza Hotel to promote *Hook*. Asked how she had prepared for playing Tinker Bell, Julia had responded, "I don't know. She's just sort of this thing that happens. And," she added, a noticeable bite to her voice, "who wants to know anyway how Tinker Bell comes about? It's like knowing a magic trick. If people enjoy it, it doesn't matter how hard it was or how easy or anything."

Although Julia sat quietly with her head down through most of the twenty-minute interview, she continued fiddling nervously with a microphone cord and her voice sounded tired and edgy as she answered questions, not one of which did she apparently consider to be worthy of her time.

Thus, while Robin Williams bounced around the Century Plaza ballroom, alternating between schtick and introspection, while Spielberg explained why he believed in fairy tales, while Dustin Hoffman ruminated on the nature of evil, Julia spent her morning on the defensive, as though she were practicing for the ugly personal questions she knew eventually would come up. And, of course, they ultimately did.

248

"It's just absurd. It's ridiculous," Julia retorted, when the subject of her purported drug use arose. "I guess people are really bored with themselves."

A few minutes later, when asked how the barrage of adverse publicity had affected her, she snapped back, "I don't concern myself with it. I don't follow it. When it follows me around, that's when I sort of react to it. I just wish the public at large would concern themselves with their own lives, with their own personal business and affairs. And then probably divorce rates would be lower, there wouldn't be so many fractured families and troubled people, and things would be a lot easier for everybody."

The interview session then deteriorated into awkward silence until one daring reporter said, "You're not happy being here, are you?"

"I've learned the hard way to be more frugal with words around people like you," Julia replied, "which is not necessarily a bad thing to learn. You just sort of figure things out as you go along, I guess. I've made plenty of mistakes and everyone's made sure that I've known about them."

A few weeks later, after *Hook* had been released to disastrous reviews, Betty Motes told an Atlanta audience at a Monday night sneak preview of the film that "Julia saw it the night before last and wasn't very pleased with it."

Disappearing once again from public view, Julia spent hours reading, doing needlepoint, quilting, and enjoying quiet dinners at home with Jason. "She's an incredible cook," confided a friend, who was unaware that, if so, it was a skill she had honed since Thanksgiving, 1989, when she'd spent a small fortune in long distance telephone calls to her mother in Smyrna, frantically asking directions while roasting a turkey.

During her sabbatical Julia also spent a great deal of time traveling, with and without Jason by her side. Only infrequently would she venture out to a Hollywood happening, such as a premiere.

Shortly after the *Entertainment Weekly* article was published, for instance, Julia popped up in New York for a visit with her sister, Lisa. Then in early December, 1991, she showed up on Jason's arm at the Beverly Hills premiere of his film, *Rush*. The couple surfaced again in Stowe, Vermont, where they spent the Christmas holidays in a rented home, their nights in front of the fire and in the bedroom, their days visiting such local attractions as Ben and Jerry's Ice Cream factory in nearby Waterbury.

It would have been an idyllic, low-keyed vacation had Julia's publicist not called the Stowe police department in search of a limousine company to pick the couple up at the Burlington, Vermont, airport. Upon hearing that America's Pretty Woman was coming to town and needed a ride, however, Kenneth Libby, Stowe's police chief, decided he would personally escort the couple from the airport to their rented home. Chief Libby also decided to give the couple a lift in one of Stowe's squad cars.

When the local citizenry discovered Libby had traveled to Burlington in a city car during working hours to pick up a movie star, they were displeased, to say the least. Jumping on the bandwagon, the local newspaper carried the story, along with comments from irate taxpayers, and the national media picked up the story, which then ran throughout the country.

What *didn't* make the national news, however, was that when the couple's rental car broke down during Julia's trek to the Grand Union grocery store the following day, it was Libby she called for assistance. Undaunted by the criticism and notoriety heaped upon him, Libby immediately leaped to the rescue, only this time he used his own car, "And," the local paper reported, "it was on his own time."

In January, 1992, Julia was in Smyrna, having dinner with a group of friends, dropping by her alma mater, Campbell High School, with her mother to pick up her half-sister, Nancy, and to visit one of her favorite teachers, David Boyd, who taught her composition and literature during her sophomore year. "She seemed like her old self," Boyd later proclaimed. This thought was echoed by Julia's former high school pals.

"I don't think she has any qualms about herself," one said. "She's been through a lot of rough times with the media, but I think she's handled herself as best she could. I don't think she takes it personally. It's part of being who she is. I don't think she lets it bother her."

Several months later, in May, 1992, Julia without Jason popped up in Smyrna for yet another visit with her family. She also dropped by Miss Kitty's, a popular country western bar, to hear one of her favorite groups, The Confederate Railroad. According to club workers, Julia was wearing her usual outfit—black cowboy boots, jeans and a loose tee-shirt—and sat with friends at an upstairs table in the middle of the balcony, her usual spot at the club.

"She seemed a little insecure and sorta hid behind her hair like she didn't want anybody to recognize her," recalled a waitress. When that failed, and people began approaching her table, Julia and her friends left. That was unusual, recalled several of the club employees, because in the past Julia would laugh freely with her friends and even occasionally hit the dance floor for a Texas two-step.

What was really unusual about Julia's visit to Smyrna was that it marked the third time in six months that she'd returned to Georgia since her self-imposed exile from public view. Yet only two years before she'd told a reporter for *The Atlanta Constitution* she didn't have "any great desire to return to Smyrna."

As spring turned slowly into summer, rumors of Julia having suffered a nervous breakdown and of having forever abandoned her film career began to surface. As they grew more widespread through the entertainment industry, Julia's publicist, Nancy Seltzer, and her agent, Elaine Goldsmith, downshifted into damage control. While Seltzer began planting items on Julia's return to the screen, Goldsmith began contacting producers, asking "What have you got for Julia?"

"In Hollywood it's not unusual for a star or director to say 'I'm not working for the next year, or until the spring.' No one thinks that's strange. But with Julia Roberts," explained a well-known producer, "it was odd because about every three months I'd get a call from Elaine, asking if I had any projects for Julia. She'd tell me 'She wants to work. Have you got a comedy, a drama?' I'd send out the scripts and Julia would reject them all. Then like clockwork Elaine would call and the cycle would start again. This was strange, even by Hollywood standards."

Another rumor making its way through the gossip columns was an unsubstantiated story that Julia and Jason were in the final throes of their relationship. The two, it was reported, had been "bickering." This rumor came to an abrupt halt when, in June, 1992, Julia surprised

Jason with a five-day cruise to Cabo San Lucas in Baja, California to celebrate his twenty-sixth birthday.

The following month, Julia was back at Canyon Ranch, this time reportedly looking for a home to buy in the prestigious Foothills area of the gate-guarded estates in the area.

In August, 1992, Julia vacationed in Hawaii with Elaine Goldsmith and actress Susan Sarandon, who had become her newest "best friend," on another one of her for women only "bonding" trips.

It was immediately upon their return from the Hawaiian trip that the Hollywood trade papers, *Daily Variety* and *The Hollywood Reporter*, were suddenly flooded with stories heralding Julia's return to the screen in *The Pelican Brief*, a contemporary drama to be produced for Warner Brothers under Joe Roth's new banner, Caravan Pictures. The production was slated to begin in May, 1993, almost a year away.

It was also shortly after her Hawaiian sojourn that Julia turned up at the September christening of Susan Sarandon and Tim Robbins' son, Miles Guthrie, named for two of the couple's musical favorites, Miles Davis and Arlo Guthrie. The following day it was reported by several eagle-eyed guests that Julia was wearing a bandage on her left shoulder where the birthday tattoo from Kiefer had once rested. Although Julia had proclaimed her love for Kiefer would last as long as the tattoo, the tattoo had actually lasted several months longer.

Shortly after the christening, Julia also showed up at the Beverly Hills premiere of *Bob Roberts*, the political satire Tim Robbins had produced, directed, and starred in. As had been the case at the christening, Jason again was nowhere in sight. Then, just as tongues were beginning to wag, the twosome were spotted together at a Michigan/Notre Dame home game in South Bend, Indiana, where they sat on the fifty-yard line and loudly cheered on "The Fighting Irish."

On September 15, a front-page story in *The Hollywood Reporter*, announced that Julia would be making her movie comeback in *Shakespeare in Love*. The article also stated her agents were asking "a king's ransom," reported in excess of $4 million, for her services, a fee hardly appropriate for a film supposedly falling in the "art house" genre. Universal Pictures, it was reported, was therefore seeking co-financiers to help underwrite the production.

The article also revealed that Daniel Day-Lewis, who had earned an Oscar for his stunning performance in *My Left Foot,* had been approached to portray Shakespeare opposite Julia as Anne Hathaway in the Elizabethan romantic comedy and was Julia's first choice of co-stars.

"Julia would certainly like to do the role," confirmed a source close to the actress. "She loves the script. She's just waiting for the word."

While Julia awaited "the word," she and Jason attended the September 22, 1992, MTV Unplugged Bruce Springsteen taping at the Warner/Hollywood Studios. At the backstage party following the taping, Julia was talking to rocker Richie Sambora, Cher's boytoy at the time, when Jason apparently decided it was time to leave and, claim observers, began tossing tiny licorice pieces from his table at Julia to get her attention.

When that didn't work, he walked up, grabbed her hand, and tugged at her, saying "Let's go." Julie reportedly pulled her hand back and replied, "You don't own me." Jason then stood obediently by her side as she finished her conversation with Sambora. Despite this small sign of petulance, however, the twosome turned up in the audience of Springsteen's concert the next night at the Los Angeles Forum. But, although Jason returned for the remaining three nights of Springsteen's appearances at the Forum, Julia was nowhere to be seen.

Two weeks later "the word" Julia had been awaiting was that Day-Lewis, hot off his starring role in *The Last of the Mohicans*, a Twentieth Century Fox production put into play by Julia's friend, Joe Roth, did *not* want to star opposite Hollywood's Golden Girl in *Shakespeare in Love*. Thus, it was reported in the October 6, 1992, issue of *Daily Variety*, that Day-Lewis had "officially passed on the period romancer."

The reason given by the actor's representatives was that Day-Lewis was committed to star in the title role of *The Gerry Conlon Story*, a drama about four men wrongly charged and imprisoned in an IRA bombing in London who became known as the Guilford Four, which was to be produced by his mentor, Jim (*My Left Foot*) Sheridan.

In explaining the Day-Lewis decision, his agent, Gene Paraseghian, of Triad Artists, claimed the actor wanted more breathing room between his starring role in the just-finished *Age of Innocence* and *Conlon*. At that point, however, *Conlon* had no firm shooting date and had not even been greenlighted as a *go* picture.

Jumping on the story, the British press offered a more intriguing assessment of the situation. Day-Lewis, they wrote, was miffed that Julia would be paid more than three times his salary for her services. Adding to his disenchantment, they added, was his dislike of "a Yank playing the Bard's wife."

Whatever the reason behind Day-Lewis' decision *not* to portray Shakespeare, as the second week of October, 1992, rolled to an autumnal end, Julia/Juliet was still without a screen Romeo, despite the fact that every Shakespearean thespian in Great Britain, as well as few of its former colonies, was calling his agent, trying to get an audition for the role.

With 200 people already employed, sets under construction and preproduction in full swing at Pinewood Studios, Julia flew to London, where she reportedly had wig and costume fittings, and sat in on several auditions of her would-be leading male co-stars. Two weeks after arriving in London, however, she suddenly walked off the project, leaving publicist Seltzer and agent Goldsmith to explain her sudden departure and the resultant collapse of the film.

"I think the frustration comes with everyone wanting to go forward with this project and not being able to find the right person once Daniel Day-Lewis passed," Goldsmith said in a Friday, October 23, *Daily Variety* story published only a day after Julia's mystifying departure.

Seltzer was more blunt. "She has never been committed to *Shakespeare in Love*," she said, adding, "She ultimately decided it was a film she did not feel comfortable making."

Four days after having vanished from London, Julia was spotted in New York, celebrating her twenty-fifth birthday by attending *The David Letterman Show* and a Big Apple screening of *A Few Good Men*, the film which would re-start Kiefer's career. With Jason nowhere in sight, the rumor mill once again began churning, that the two, in Hollywood lingo, were "splitsville." Indeed, by mid-December, 1992, it had been noted in gossip columns on both coasts that Julia's black Porsche hadn't been seen in its once-regular berth outside Jason's West Hollywood duplex for several weeks.

"Although *Rush* star Jason Patric should have realized his *Pretty Woman* Julia Roberts' track record with men isn't exactly marathon material, Patric is one lost boy over stories that Roberts has dumped him for hawkeyed playboy Daniel Day-Lewis," wrote a "Page Six" columnist for the *New York Post* on December 1, 1992. The columnist then quoted Nancy Seltzer, Julia's publicist, as having said, "I spoke to Julia on Wednesday and she didn't mention anything. It's a surprise to me." Two hours later, however, Seltzer called the columnist back to report she hadn't been able to reach Julia because she was "out of the country".

Jason's long-time manager, Delores Robinson, was equally mum about the relationship, explaining "I don't know a thing about it. I just try to stay on the career side and let the personal side take care of itself."

As Thanksgiving, 1992, turned into leftovers and Julia's self-imposed sabbatical entered its fifteenth month, it became increasingly obvious to people close to her that, irrational though it might seem considering her track record at the box office, something had to be done to allay Julia's fears of returning to films. What Julia needed, it was decided, was some type of professional security. She needed someone whom she admired and trusted, someone with a knack for picking good projects, someone who could allay her phobia about returning to films and would look after her best interests in the movie-making process. That *someone* turned out to be Joe Roth.

While chairman of Twentieth Century Fox, Roth had not only hired Julia for *Sleeping with the Enemy* and *Dying Young,* but had also become one of Julia's revered father figures, someone Julia trusted and liked. An interesting blend of creativity and business acumen, power and sensitivity, Roth also has a great deal of respect within the film industry for his professionalism and his impressive track record in selecting commercial projects. In short, Joe Roth was the perfect solution to Julia's problem.

Adding to Roth's luster was that, after three years at the helm of Twentieth Century Fox, he had departed the studio in November, 1992, to launch his own independent production company, Caravan Pictures, at Disney Studios, where he had a five-year contract giving him the autonomy to greenlight five films a year.

Having Joe Roth in her corner would be an enormous comfort factor for Julia; and having Julia Roberts in his corner would be an enormous benefit to Joe Roth. It was a perfect blendship. So, shortly after Roth opened his production office on the Disney lot, Julia and Elaine formed YMA Productions and, in early December, 1992, it was announced that Julia had signed a two-year contract with Roth's Caravan Pictures, whereby Joe Roth would specifically be developing film projects for Julia either to star in or produce under her YMA logo.

The Hollywood powerbrokers were stunned by the uniqueness of Julia having made an agreement with a production company rather than a studio. After all, they pointed out, with her kind of box-office clout Julia Roberts didn't need a middle man, which is what Roth and Caravan technically became, to get her films produced. She could have hung out her YMA banner at any studio on her own. What they didn't understand, of course, was the psychology behind the deal.

"I have the utmost respect for Joe Roth and I trust his creative instincts," Julia said in a prepared statement. "I am delighted to be working with him again, and to be affiliated with his new company. I am equally pleased to be returning to the Disney Studios."

It was all true. Julia felt safe not only with Roth but with Disney. After all, it had been Touchstone Films, a Disney studio, that had produced and released *Pretty Woman*, the movie that had led her to instantaneous international stardom only two years before.

Within two weeks of Julia joining forces with Roth, it was disclosed she had committed to star in a comedy, *I Love Trouble*. A short while later it was announced Julia would, indeed, be making her return to the big screen in an adaptation of John Grisham's best-selling novel, *The Pelican Brief*.

Within weeks of having announced her joint venture, and subsequent return to films, however, Julia's personal life came under renewed scrutiny when in mid-December, 1992, *USA Today* repeated what was by then becoming an oft-asked question:

"Has Jason Patric become the 'Last of the Mohicans' on the trail of Julia Roberts? Are Roberts and Daniel Day-Lewis a new twosome?"

The columnist then reported that "Roberts is abroad," and that her publicist, Nancy Seltzer, had stated: "She and Daniel are friends, professional friends. They met when they were discussing doing *Shakespeare in Love*. To make more out of it is not fair.' "

Ah, but as the cliche goes, all *is* fair in love and war.

By the time the press had begun publishing rumors of a rift between the two, Jason and Julia had already broken up. In fact, by the time the *USA Today* item found its way into print, the twosome had already reunited after a loud and angry fight in late November, after which Julia had disappeared from Jason's tiny one-bedroom duplex for almost a month. It had, in fact, been during this period that Jason, despondent and distraught, had begun drinking far more than his usual one or two bottles of beer, a situation reported in another gossip column as having caused Julia to exit Jason's life.

Shortly before Christmas, however, Julia had magically reappeared at the ill-furnished duplex and life seemed to have returned to normal for the couple. Following Jason's lead of having given her a 1968 Volkswagen van in mint condition the previous Christmas, Julia presented him with an expensive, top of the line, Landcruiser. The two rang in the New Year together and toasted each other with hopes for a happy and successful 1993.

Any doubts concerning whether or not Julia was truly returning to public life, and whether her popularity had diminished, were erased the night of Sunday, January 10, 1993, when a sleek charcoal gray limousine slowly eased its way past a throng of roped off press and bystanders, straining to catch a glimpse of its passenger, and pulling to the curb, rolled to a stop.

The limo door opened and suddenly, as if by magic, Julia Roberts, beautiful and radiant, impeccably gowned and immaculately coiffed, tenuously stepped onto a red-carpeted tarmac, and with a brief, shy, wide smile, back into the spotlight.

"There was a moment of silence," recalled a bystander. "Everyone just stood still and looked at her. She was wearing a stunning emerald green velvet suit with white piping. Her hair and makeup were perfect. And then after a split second, everyone just rushed at her. She looked spooked and sort of fragile, but she handled it."

As fans thrust pads and pens toward her and photographers begged her to turn their way, Julia smiled that great wide, shy grin and, surrounded by security men, slowly made her way through the clamoring crowd until she'd disappeared into a sea of churning figures on her way into a Universal City hotel to accept the Screen Actor's Guild Lifetime Achievement Award on behalf of Audrey Hepburn.

Julia's appearance at the SAG annual business meeting lasted only twenty minutes. After Gregory Peck spoke of Ms. Hepburn's lifetime achievements, both as an actress and as a humanitarian, Julia stepped to the podium and accepted the award for the actress, who was then recuperating from colon cancer surgery at her home in Switzerland. Realizing she would be too ill to attend the meeting, Hepburn supposedly had asked Julia to accept the award for her when the two had met only months before.

Unfortunately, Julia's comments, which reportedly had been written by Hepburn, were not recorded for posterity because only television news crews from CNN and the three major TV affiliates had been allowed inside to film the proceedings.

Although SAG had issued press credentials several weeks before, only days prior to the event, Nancy Seltzer, Julia's publicist, had insisted that no press, other than the TV networks, be allowed access to the proceedings. When SAG officials protested, Seltzer threatened to pull her client from the event. Thus SAG press representatives found themselves faced with the unpleasant and embarrassing task of calling every news organization that had been cleared for press credentials to explain that "a mistake" had been made, that there was a "press blackout" and that all previously issued press credentials had been cancelled.

"If it were up to us," SAG officials confided to several members of the media, "the press would be there. We'd welcome as much coverage as possible."

But, of course, it hadn't been up to SAG. It had been up to Julia. Whether or not Seltzer's demands for a press blackout were at the behest of her client, or simply an ego gratifying bit of power brokering, will probably never be known. But what became known that night was that, despite a fifteen-month absence from public view, Julia had lost none of her sizzle, none of her power to elicit the admiration of her adoring public, and none of her mystique for the ever-inquisitive ubiquitous press.

Chapter Fourteen

Only eight days after Julia's glamorous re-emergence at the Audrey Hepburn tribute, whatever bliss she and Jason had achieved during the holidays came to an abrupt and nasty halt during a loud, drunken argument the night of January 18, 1993.

Although the quarrel had first begun inside Jason's tiny Stanley Street duplex, it reached its climax outside, with Julia and Jason standing in the middle of the street in front of TV star Jasmine Guy's house, several doors away, shouting obscenities at each other. At the core of the altercation, claim the couple's neighbors, none of whom could help but overhear the dispute, was Daniel Day-Lewis.

"Jason was almost falling-down drunk," confided a neighbor, "and although Julia wasn't drunk it was obvious she'd also been drinking. Anyway, Jason kept accusing her of having slept with Daniel Day-Lewis, yelling 'You fucked him. I know you fucked him.' Then Julia yelled back at him, 'I can fuck anyone I want to!' ''

With that final proclamation, Julia had climbed into her shiny black Porsche and vanished into the night. Since that winter night, neither Julia nor the Porsche have ever been seen in the neighborhood again.

In early 1992, *US* magazine, had published an intriguing look at Julia and Jason's relationship through their respective astrological charts in an article titled ''What's in the Stars for Them?'' The article had painted Julia as being ''earthy and nurturing,'' but somewhat uncommunicative, while suggesting that ''Jason does most of the talking and decision-making.''

''A mesmerizing speaker,'' the article concluded ''he has an almost Svengali influence over her.''

The magazine article declared that, although the two were attracted to each other ''like moths to a flame,'' their charts reflected few compatible aspects, making them unlikely candidates for everlasting happiness. ''It's Julia who will get hurt the most (if the couple breaks up),'' the article concluded.

But the charts had either lied or been misread. For it was Julia, not Jason, who called an end to the highly publicized affair. And it was Jason, not Julia, who was devastated when the relationship ended.

In fact, according to a family friend, Jason had been so distraught in the days following Julia's late night departure he had been unable to sleep in the bed he and Julia had once shared. He had then moved to the living room couch but, after being unable to sleep there as well, he had abandoned the tiny duplex for almost a month.

264

"Jason was terribly despondent and obsessed with Julia after they broke up," recalled a source close to the couple. In fact, he was so despondent he went to her house several times, apparently looking for love letters from Daniel Day-Lewis, or some evidence of her having slept with him. "I know at one point Jason even had one of Daniel Day-Lewis' ex-girlfriends over to his house. I don't know which one, or whether they were actually dating, but I do know they saw each other briefly, for whatever reason, right after he and Julia broke up."

In an ironic twist, Jason reportedly learned Julia had definitely decided to call a halt to the relationship in much the same manner Kiefer had discovered he was not going to become a bridegroom—through a telephone call from Elaine Goldsmith. In the call, Goldsmith supposedly broke the news that the affair was over and that Julia would *not* be returning, and then told Jason he would be hearing from Julia within an hour or two. A short while later, Julia did call—from New York—to personally deliver the final *coup de grace*.

"Naiveté rears its ugly head, and you find out that head is yours," Jason once told a reporter, adding "and you grow up quickly." As it turned out, Jason could have been speaking about Julia, as well.

Reports of Julia being head-over-heels in lust with the reclusive Daniel Day-Lewis had been surfacing in both British and American newspapers for months before Jason and Julia had their final fight in mid-January, 1993. They had arisen within days of Julia's sudden exodus from *Shakespeare in Love* in late October, 1992. Although the gossip had subsided during the ensuing months, it had never completely vanished.

265

Whether Jason had just cause to believe Julia had been unfaithful to him, or whether he was simply reacting to what he had read in the newspapers, remains unclear. However, Jason was not alone in his conviction that there was a romantic liaison of some kind going on between Julia and Day-Lewis. Virtually every gossip columnist covering Hollywood from near and afar had reached the same conclusion by March, 1993. Yet, curiously, no one ever actually saw the twosome together throughout their supposed affair.

Of course that probably can be explained by the actor's all-encompassing desire for privacy. Day-Lewis is a notoriously reclusive figure, who has been known to disappear for months, taking only a metal paintbox, his sepia ink, his running shoes, and banknotes with him. "I always prefer to leave before I feel unwelcome," he once explained. "I feel the urge to escape."

With this mind set, its not surprising to learn the intensely secretive actor has been known to frequently check into hotels under a variety of pseudonyms. When preparing for his role in *Age of Innocence*, for example, he checked into a New York hotel as Newland Archer, the name of the character he would be playing in the Edith Wharton screen adaptation.

As unfashionable off-screen as Julia, Day-Lewis is known for being shamelessly unkempt and for wearing tattered blue jeans, old boots held together by tape, and a faded bandana, none of which juxtapose with his upper-class British accent. Brilliant, intense, unorthodox, a staunch supporter of all that is Irish, Day-Lewis is a seething, complicated six-foot, two-inch mass of contradictions.

Although Julia and Daniel Day-Lewis are worlds apart on most levels, they do share the same fate of having had unhappy childhoods. Day-Lewis lost his father when he was quite young and, like Julia, was raised in a house divided. Whereas Julia cannot stand to be alone for any great length of time, however, Day-Lewis relishes seclusion. And, unlike Julia, Day-Lewis is able to articulate his feelings about the collapse of his family structure and response to his father's death.

Daniel Michael Blake Day-Lewis was born April 29, 1957, an event subsequently celebrated in a published poem written by his father, C.S. Lewis, who was Britain's poet laureate at the time and who died of pancreatic cancer when Daniel was only fifteen years old. "It's a source of great sadness to me that my father died without having seen me do anything worthwhile," Day-Lewis once noted.

"Through a passage of time I'd seen the astonishingly rapid disintegration of two households where I grew up—my parents' and my grandparents' houses both went," he explained. "The houses which had been apparently indestructible became nothing. I came to think of the concept of home as an elaborately constructed false front."

With this unhappy background and exposure to the world of theater and film, it was probably natural for Day-Lewis to choose acting as an outlet for his creative endeavors, even though he attributes the choice to a "desire to move away from my own life" instead. "My life was so intolerable that every night on stage was blissful because I was so happy to escape," he once explained, adding "I took up acting because I wasn't brave enough to stick with my own life."

Although the fifteen-year old Day-Lewis dropped out of school shortly after his father's death, it wasn't until years later in the mid-Eighties that he burst upon the film scene, portraying a tough gay street punk in the widely acclaimed British film, *My Beautiful Launderette*. He followed this by portraying the prissy suitor in *Room with a View* and then a neurosurgeon obsessed with women in the erotic *The Unbearable Lightness of Being*. But it wasn't until 1989, when he won an Oscar for his portrayal of the wheelchair-bound Irish writer Christy Brown in *My Left Foot*, that Day-Lewis gained international acclaim.

At that point, like Julia, Day-Lewis disappeared from public view for several years before resurfacing as Hawkeye, an English frontiersman raised by the Indians, in the screen adaptation of the James Fenimore Cooper classic, *The Last of the Mohicans* in June, 1991.

Since Joe Roth, who would later become her production partner, had produced *The Last of the Mohicans*, it's quite possible it was at Roth's suggestion that Julia and Daniel initially met while he was in Los Angeles, staying at the Bel Air Hotel, doing interviews for the soon-to-be-released *Mohicans*.

He had just completed the screen adaptation of Edith Wharton's American classic, *The Age of Innocence*, in late June and again had proven himself to be as reclusive as rumored. "He isolated himself from the rest of the group, crew *and* cast, never going to dinner with them, never partying with them," recalled a crew member. "Michele Pfeiffer went out, as did everyone else, but not Daniel. He never mingled with the cast. He either stayed in his trailer or disappeared back to his hotel. Daniel is very secretive, very close."

As a confirmed bachelor and demonstrated loner, Day-Lewis' only romantic involvement of any duration reportedly has been with the free-spirited, fast-living French actress Isabel Adjani, with whom he had been linked, but also never seen, despite a supposed three-year love affair.

"I'm like most human beings," Day-Lewis once explained. "I want what I don't have at the time. I want to be alone when I'm with someone and with someone when I'm alone."

Enter Julia Roberts, from whom Day-Lewis found himself sitting across the table in either late summer or early fall, 1992, discussing a starring role opposite her in *Shakespeare in Love*, the film which would have heralded Julia's re-entrance into the world of movies.

Instead, of course, *Shakespeare* came to an abrupt halt when, after having spent two weeks in London, Julia suddenly pulled out of the film, blithely leaving in her wake forty British actors and 200 crew members, who overnight found themselves unhappily unemployed only a month before principal photography was scheduled to begin.

The reasons given by Julia's publicist and agent were of little consolation to the British film industry which, along with the rest of the world, was puzzled as to why Julia would invest two weeks of her life in a project to which she was neither "committed" nor "comfortable." Within days of Julia's exodus, however, it became clear that her motivation in pursuing *Shakespeare* had far more to do with Daniel Day-Lewis than it did with the film.

"Julia's reason for not doing it is that she adores Daniel and doesn't want to do it without him," Julian Belfrage, Day-Lewis' agent, had explained only days after Julia had returned to the States. "I think she thought that by leaving she might persuade him to reconsider," Belfrage added in a *London Evening Standard* interview, "but now that Hollywood is blaming Daniel (for the demise of the film) he will never do the film."

But while that should have been the end of the story, it was reportedly only the beginning.

According to sources within the British film community, Julia had been pursuing Day-Lewis, not only as a *Shakespeare* co-star but as the object of her excessive affections. "It was the talk of the film industry," confided a source, adding Day-Lewis had made it known to all that he would be "very happy to do a screen test and go out with Julia, even sleep with her, but he was not going to put his professional career on the line and do a film with her."

Nothing was heard of the supposed romance for several months following Julia's break-up with Jason Patric. Instead, Julia's career moves took precedence, at least in the news.

In early February, Julia and Nick Nolte met to discuss, and then agreed, to co-stared in *I Love Trouble,* a romantic comedy about two newspaper reporters trying to outdo each other. Produced by Joe Roth's Caravan Pictures and released by Touchstone Films, the film was expected to go before the cameras in September, almost immediately after Julia completed *The Pelican Brief.*

In late February it was reported that Jason Patric had also returned to the business of making movies, and would be starring in *Geronimo* as the cavalryman who tracked down the legendary Indian warrior. It was *not* reported, however, that within a few weeks of having arrived on location in April, Jason had sent for pot-bellied Ferguson, the last living remnant of his romance with Julia.

In early March, 1993, it was announced that Denzel Washington had been set to star opposite Julia in Warner Brothers *The Pelican Brief,* which would be directed by Alan J. Pakula and would begin filming in New York in May. That same week stories of Julia's obsession with Day-Lewis surfaced again. "Julia Roberts has been in

London, visiting her old flame, Daniel Day-Lewis, and he *is* the man in her life these days," syndicated columnist Liz Smith reported on March 9, 1993.

Two days later the *London Daily Mirror* ran a similar item, adding that Julia had donned a series of "elaborate disguises" and "jumped aboard a series of first-class flights to London to try to keep her love for Day-Lewis under wraps."

The Mirror then quoted a supposed friend of Julia's as having confided: "She is besotted. Despite her fame, Julia is still only twenty-four years old and basically just a small-town girl from Georgia. The whole idea of this handsome man from across the Atlantic is all so terribly romantic to her. She is in awe of his talent, and overwhelmed by his sexual magnetism. But Daniel is trying to keep this thing quiet. He's very private. It's the real thing for Julia. She seems to spend half her life with jet-lag."

The Mirror then described a cottage Julia had purchased outside of Dublin in County Mayo, Ireland, where Daniel spent many of his childhood vacations and not far from a home owned by his sister, Tasamin. According to the newspaper, Julia allegedly spent $60,000 for the supposed "love nest" in an attempt to be near Day-Lewis.

The London Daily Express subsequently reported that Julia had "fallen head over heels for Day-Lewis" and had "spent a fortune on transatlantic telephone calls and flights from Hollywood to Ireland" in an attempt to win the reclusive actor's heart, but that Day-Lewis remained less than enamored of the actress, despite her pursuit.

Only a few days later, *The Dublin Evening Herald* reported that Julia had visited her new cottage with Day-Lewis.

Julia was "madly in love" with him, confided a Day-Lewis associate not long ago. "But Daniel's obsessed with his career. He doesn't *want* to get married. He doesn't *need* to get married." Indeed, only the year before, Daniel had confessed to an interviewer, "Marriage has no meaning to me as an idea. It's not a concept I think about."

Julia returned to Los Angeles and on May 8 dropped off an armload of clothes, mostly tweeds, at the Holloway Cleaners in West Hollywood. The following week Elaine Goldsmith threw Julia, who was heading to New York to begin filming *The Pelican Brief*, a send-off party attended by Nick Nolte, Billy Baldwin, Shirley MacLaine, Vincent D'Onofrio, Oliver Stone, and Joe Roth.

"I feel ready to blow the door open," Julia told columnist Army Archerd, adding she didn't have "a single regret" concerning her eighteen-month absence from films. When the subject of her personal life arose, Julia explained had been just "a homebody" trying to lead "a quiet, simple life. I'm not mean to anyone," she'd curiously added.

A short while later, filled with nervous anticipation about returning to the professional life she'd abandoned almost two years before, Julia flew to New York. She had no idea as she winged eastward that within six weeks she would be married . . . or to *whom*.

After almost a month of filming *The Pelican Brief*, in which she portrays a law student who uncovers evidence of foul play in the deaths of two U.S. Supreme Court justices and then discovers her life is also in jeopardy, Julia appeared at a press conference in Washington, D.C., on June 21, 1993. She was accompanied by her co-star, Denzel Washington, and the film's director, Alan Pakula.

Gone were the defensive attitude and the pallid personality Julia had exhibited during her travails of 1991. Whatever had occurred during her self-imposed exile of the previous two years, America's Pretty Woman was back in radiant splendor. Not only that, marveled those who saw her, Julia was relaxed and friendly, and had even regained her sense of humor.

Asked, for instance, if she felt rusty after not appearing in a film in the previous twenty-four-months, Julia had laughingly responded: "I don't feel rusty. Do I look rusty?" After a pause, she'd continued "I think I came back with some renewed vigor. . . . I've been giddy."

During the press conference Julia had also reiterated her hope that "Maybe the press will focus on the work instead of me and how many times a week I do my laundry." Quickly responding to Julia's remark, Denzel Washington had whipped out a notebook and, playing reporter, had laughingly asked "How many times a week *do* you do your laundry?"

Only a few days prior to the press conference Julia had even willingly, happily talked via telephone to Jeannie Williams, a *USA Today* columnist, about her twenty-four-month sabbatical. "I got to spend time with my friends, visit with my family, and travel around and just have a quiet time," she told Williams. "I had lots of nice days that were nothing more interesting than anybody else having a nice day."

Six days after the D.C. press conference, the source of Julia's self-confessed giddiness became apparent. His name was Lyle Lovett and he was about to fulfill Julia's last remaining fantasy by making her his bride.

Ten years older than Julia, the thirty-five-year-old

country western singer with a craggy face and pompadored hair piled so high it had earned him the nickname of "Eraserhead" in his hometown, was an astonishing choice of romantic partners for filmdom's "Pretty Woman," whose previous lovers had been handsome, invariably intense sexy actors.

Even more incredible was the fact that, instead of living with Lovett as she had with her former flames, Julia actually tied the knot with him, becoming Mrs. Lyle Lovett in a hush, hush wedding in the tiny town of Marion, Indiana, before anyone had managed to piece together that the two were anything other than friends.

In fact, according to Julia's mother, Betty, it was *because* the media was beginning to suspect there was more between Lyle and Julia than simply a shared love of country music that the couple had changed their wedding date from "sometime" in August to a definite June 27, miraculously pulling the people, flowers, and wedding ceremony together in a mere seventy-two hours.

"Julia has always wanted a traditional wedding, without all the fanfare and glitz of Hollywood," a source close to the actress later explained. "She's a Southern girl at heart, and Lyle's a downhome Texas boy. They worked together to plan the sweet, quiet ceremony."

Once in Marion, the couple had been so concerned about keeping the wedding ceremony private that they didn't arrive at the County Clerk's office to pick up their wedding license until 11:45 a.m., only a few hours prior to what was supposed to have been a 1:30 p.m. ceremony.

Although it was Sunday, Karen Weaver, the Grant County court clerk, had gone to her office immediately after her 10:30 a.m. church service and, in the name of love, had prepared a marriage license for the famous twosome, whom she found seated in the front row of a

274

huge tour bus parked beside the county courthouse in downtown Marion.

Whether by accident or by design, Indiana is the right place to go if you want to be married on the spot because, unlike most of the fifty other states, Hoosier land has no waiting period, and does not require either a blood test or an AIDS test. It does, however, require that women under fifty, provide proof that they have been vaccinated against German measles, which meant the only documentation Julia had to present was a doctor's certificate stating she'd been immunized.

Thus at three p.m. on June 27, 1993, a hot, humid, and rainy Sunday afternoon, Julia finally turned her last unfulfilled fantasy into a reality by marrying Lyle Lovett in a twenty-minute ceremony at the St. James Lutheran Church in Marion, Indiana, a rural town of 32,000 on the outskirts of Indianapolis.

The only wedding decorations in the small church sanctuary where the ceremony took place were bouquets of red, yellow, and purple flowers tied to the wooden pews lining the center aisle down which the bride and her attendants approached the altar.

Betty and Nancy Motes, who had flown in from Atlanta, sat in the second pew and watched as Julia's sister, Lisa, the maid of honor, marched down the aisle to the strains of Bach's ''Jesu, Joy of Man's Desiring'' followed by Elaine Goldsmith, actress Deborah Goodrich Porter, Susan Sarandon, and Paige Sampson, her best friend from Campbell High school, who had flown in from Chicago for the occasion.

Unlike Julia's other planned nuptial, there were no expensive bridesmaids' gowns with shoes to match. Instead, each of her attendants wore whatever they'd chosen, and were designated special members of the wedding

275

party only by their red rose corsages, Julia's favorite flower.

Then, as a cellist segued into Mendelssohn's "Wedding March," Julia's two tiny flower girls—Eva Amurri, Susan's eight-year-old daughter, and Alexandra Porter, Deborah's five-year-old daughter—slowly made their entrance, scattering rose petals from wicker baskets as they made their way down the aisle. Immediately behind them was Julia, who was escorted to the matrimonial altar on the arm of actor Barry Tubb, another longtime friend, who had flown in from Montana, where he was appearing in the sequel to the TV mini-series.

For this wedding, Julia wore a simple white dress, a loose hanging floor-length sheath, which Lovett had himself purchased at the upscale New York boutique, Commes des Garcons, for a reported $2,000. Julia's long, curly tresses were covered by a floor-length tulle scarf and she was barefoot, walking on the rose petals strewn in her path by the two flower girls in pale green dresses preceding her.

Awaiting her arrival at the altar was the bridegroom wearing a conservative dark suit. Standing beside him was his best man, Wayne Miller, a close friend and a film director, who had shot many of Lovett's music videos.

The ceremony lasted only twenty minutes and was jointly conducted by Lovett's childhood minister, Pastor DeWyth Beltz, from the Trinity Lutheran Church of Klein, Texas, and the Rev. Mark Carlson, pastor of St. James. As soon as the bride and groom were pronounced man and wife and had kissed, Francine Reed, backup singer with Lovett's Large Band, broke into an *a cappella* version of "The Lord's Prayer" from the choir loft, and the newlyweds and their seventy-five guests began filing out of the sanctuary.

Liz Smith, syndicated columnist, would later report it had been an emotional day for both the bride and bridegroom, and that "midway through the ceremony, Julia was suddenly awash with emotion and began to weep unashamedly. Rather than being annoyed or embarrassed by Julia's unfettered feelings, Lyle also got caught up in the moment and burst into tears himself."

Around 4:30 p.m., after the bride and bridegroom had posed with family members and the wedding party for the obligatory wedding photos, Julia, still barefoot, and Lyle, his arm around her, with an umbrella protecting them both from the rain, walked quickly out the door to where the three buses were waiting.

"Julia dashed from the church doorway to a waiting bus with dark windows," observed a bystander, adding "It was raining so hard she was ducking her head and running in bare feet."

An hour later the wedding party and guests reconvened at a reception in a large green and white striped tent outside the Deer Park Music Center Amphitheater, where everyone dined from a lavish buffet of roast turkey, prime rib, and fresh-grilled shrimp, and washed down the five-tier angelfood wedding cake with champagne.

"He makes me so happy," Julia gushed to her well-wishers after Lovett had gotten down on his knees to remove her pale-blue garter. "He's so good to me," she'd added, her voice trailing off in whoosh of emotion. A short while later Julia tossed her wedding bouquet into a crowd of clamoring female guests, where it was caught by her bachelorette agent, Elaine Goldsmith.

Then it was time for Lovett to prepare for that night's concert. There was no traditional first dance—"We were all too exhausted," explained a guest. Nor was there the usual table filled with wedding gifts—"Who had time?"

Indeed, tying the wedding together in three days had been a remarkable feat. "I can now add chartering planes to my resume," Elaine Goldsmith would later admit with a sigh. It had been Goldsmith who had handled the travel logistics of flying in seventy-five guests from all over the country by private and commercial jet.

"We were coming in from everywhere," Susan Sarandon would later laugh. "It was like Noah's Ark."

The choice of Marion as the site of the wedding, it was later learned, had been suggested by Larry Chandler, Lyle's tour-bus driver, who lives in Marion and is a member of the St. James Lutheran Church congregation. Since Marion was on the way to Nobelsville, where Lovett was scheduled to appear in a Sunday evening concert, and the St. James Lutheran Church is affiliated with the same Missouri Synod as the Trinity Lutheran Church Lovett regularly attends in his hometown of Klein, Texas, there was no finer place to wed than this small farming community just outside of Indianapolis.

In an attempt to keep the news from leaking out to the press, none of the invited guests were told in their Friday night phone calls any details of the wedding, other than that it was going to take place over the weekend, which could have meant it was taking place in Cleveland, where Julia and Lyle had been happily ensconced in a suite at the Ritz-Carlton Hotel on Saturday night, after having spent Friday night in Detroit. It wasn't until Saturday that everyone was clued in.

"We had no idea where or when it was taking place," a guest later confided. "We were just told they were going to get married and to be near a phone Saturday morning for the final details."

The next call, which came around ten a.m. Saturday morning, informed Lyle's relatives that a private jet would be waiting for them in Houston Sunday morning and that they would be flown to Indianapolis.

"It was like 'Boom, let's do it. You're here, I'm here. Whoever can come can come," explained Lovett's cousin Wanda Hill, who also confessed the family had been worried about whether or not the nuptials would actually take place, considering what happened at Julia's last wedding. "Our whole side was saying 'Oh, Lord, please don't let her back out, because that'd break his heart.' "

Originally scheduled for 1:15 p.m., the wedding had been postponed several hours while the bride and groom awaited the arrival of late guests. As a result, by the time the wedding did take place, the sight of the five tour buses and three limousines parked outside the church for several hours had alerted the townspeople that something was afoot.

When they saw Susan Sarandon, who had winged in from Memphis where she was starring with Tommy Lee Jones in the screen adaptation of John Grisham's novel, *The Client*, and Tim Robbins, who had flown in on a private Lear jet from Mansfield, Ohio, where he was filming *Rita Hayworth and the Shawshank Redemption*, the townspeople *knew* something major was happening. They just didn't know *what* until reports of the wedding swept across the television newscasts the following day.

If the world had been shocked by her eleventh hour decision not to marry Kiefer two years before, it was even more stunned to discover she'd married Lyle Lovett, a man they would soon learn she'd only been dating for a month.

Chapter Fifteen

Although it was five hours after her wedding, Julia was still barefoot and wearing her wedding dress when, with no introduction, she stepped into the spotlight of the Deer Creek Amphitheater shortly after eight p.m. and, in something like a scene straight out of *A Star is Born*, dramatically announced to the capacity crowd: "Ladies and gentlemen, my husband . . . *LYLE LOVETT . . . AND HIS LARGE BAND!*"

Julia then excited the stage amid thundering applause, only to reappear moments later when Lyle opened the show with "Stand By Your Man." As word of the couple's marriage only a few hours earlier spread like wild fire through the rows of whispering onlookers, Julia first stood behind her man, then swayed side by side with him to the music. When the song ended, the couple kissed to the roaring approval of the delighted crowd of 10,000 Lovett fans.

"Thank you very much," Lyle said, turning from Julia to the audience, "and welcome to the happiest day of my life."

With that Julia again left the stage, but reappeared an hour later wearing a short black-and-white dress for Lovett's closing song, an old-fashioned gospel, "Pass It Not Gentle Savior," which had the audience on its feet. Together the newlyweds stood on stage, holding hands and facing the crowd, even breaking into an impromptu dance at one point. When the show ended, Julia took a bow with Lyle and then the happy couple walked off stage, with Lyle crowning his bride with a white cowboy hat as they made their exit.

"I'm afraid I'm going to wake up, and this will all be just a dream," Julia later confessed.

"They are just so in love. Every time you turned around they were kissing and hugging," confided an observer.

After the concert the newlyweds returned to their honeymoon suite at the nearby Omni Hotel in Castleton, Indiana, where they had rented a $250-a-night suite complete with wet bar, king-sized bed, living room and luxurious bathroom with TV and telephone.

Within minutes of having arrived back at the hotel, Lovett reportedly ordered a bottle of Dom Perignon champagne, which was promptly delivered by a hotel worker who later recalled, "Lyle answered the door, and I could hear Julia giggling in the background. He tipped generously, and obviously couldn't wait to get back to his bride."

The following day, the twosome treated a group of special wedding guests to lunch in the hotel's private

Club Room, where more bottles of Dom Perignon were opened to wash down lobster-filled pasta and veal cutlets. At this point, Julia had returned to her casual street wear—a long, red Indian-print dress, sandals, and over-size denim jacket. Her hair was pulled back in a bun.

By this time, of course, the report of their wedding had already been announced to most of the world, thanks to Julia's publicist, Nancy Seltzer, who had telephoned the *Associated Press* within hours of the nuptials. It was, she would later recall, one of her "most frustrating moments as a publicist" because the *AP* desk would not believe she was not trying to create a hoax.

"I could not prove to them who I was," Seltzer later laughed. "The *AP* asked me to name my clients, so I did. Then I said 'What about Julia's agent, Elaine Goldsmith? She's right here.' But then we couldn't prove who she was, either."

In desperation, Seltzer had put Susan Sarandon on the phone and it was ultimately Sarandon who convinced the wire service that Julia Roberts had, indeed, married Lyle Lovett. "She had too many details," a wire service reporter finally conceded.

Late Monday afternoon, Lyle escorted his bride to the airport, where they lovingly bid each other goodbye, then he headed for Kettering, Ohio, and another concert on his summer tour, while she returned to New Orleans. "They wanted their last moments together to be private, so they sneaked out the back door through the kitchen to avoid the press," explained a hotel employee.

As news of the wedding began to surface Sunday night and Monday morning, the international media went crazy. No respectable publication dealing with the entertainment industry wanted to be left out in the cold on what was perceived as one of the hottest, most surprising, stories of the year. Thus the newstands the following week were filled with supposed exclusive magazine cover stories on "The Wedding." America's Pretty Woman was back, in full regalia, and Lyle Lovett had her.

People magazine managed to pull off a coup by securing exclusive photos of the wedding, as well details of the ceremony, through the cooperation of Julia and her handlers, namely publicist Seltzer and agent Goldsmith.

The nation's tabloids, *The Star* and *The National Enquirer*, also featured cover stories and a couple of amateurishly taken, out-of-focus photographs of the couple leaving the church and, later, on stage at the Deer Park concert. And, not to be outdone by its competitors, *The Globe* took a color slide of Julia's wedding scene from *Steel Magnolias* and, in a moment of glaring chutzpah, superimposed Lovett's face, complete with his enormous pompador haircut, onto the screen bridegroom's body. Ironically, the deleted bridegroom was none other than Dylan McDermott, Julia's former fiancé.

Two weeks after the wedding, *Time* ran a full-page story on the union, with three behind-the-scenes photographs. And that same week even *TV Guide*, which by its very name is devoted to another medium, saw fit to run a cover story on the unusual coupling, using the Roberts/Lovett union as a peg for a peek into the "Hot-Blooded Hollywood" couplings of everyone from Tom Cruise and Nicole Kidman to Ted Danson and Whoopi Goldberg to Elizabeth Taylor and Richard Burton.

In short, virtually every publication in the nation carried *something* on the wedding. Even the psychologists got into the media act.

"I call these whirlwind relationships Velcro Attachments," confided Dr. Irene Kassorla, a Hollywood psychologist, explaining her terminology was based on the fact, "They are easily attached and easily separated."

"Because show business is so precarious, sometimes people panic and want to reach out for a quick feeling of security," explained Carole Lieberman, a Beverly Hills psychiatrist. "The quest for fame can be so stressful that in a period of vulnerability, you may impetuously reach out and grab someone. I think that's what Julia did."

Next, of course, came items on the honeymooners, such as that Julia had again appeared on stage at hubby Lyle's Friday, July 2, Minneapolis concert, during which he had again crowned her onstage with a cowboy hat. By that time photographs of Julia's post-wedding return to *The Pelican Brief* set showing her being greeted by cast and crew members wearing t-shirts reading "Welcome Back, Mrs. Lovett" on the front, and "He's a lovely boy . . . but you really must do *SOMETHING* about his hair!" on the back, had also found their way into the news.

"There is not a single crew member who does not wish Julia a lot of happiness," director Alan Pakula had explained to the press during the Tuesday, June 29, late afternoon celebration honoring Julia on the *Pelican* set. Pakula, it turned out, had been one of the few people who had known about the wedding in its early stages, although he had not known exactly when the union was going to take place.

By the time filming ended late Tuesday, Julia had spent most of her time between takes and camera set-ups, talking on the phone to Lovett. One of the couple's phone conversations, however, was a surprise to the actress. As the story goes, Julia was supposed to talk to John Heard, one of her co-stars, on the phone in the first scene to be shot on Tuesday, but Pakula arranged for Lovett to phone from Ohio and read Heard's lines.

Julia immediately recognized Lyle's voice, a good sign under the circircumstances, but finished the scene, anyway. Then, after Pakula had yelled 'Cut,' Julia reportedly had turned to him and proudly gushed, "That's my husband!"

While Lyle proceeded with his concert tour and Julia remained busy being a thespian, their friends and business associates continued to be plagued with phone calls from the nation's inquiring minds, all of whom were trying to discover how the romance, and then the marriage, had somehow managed to elude their keen sense of news. However, no one seemed to be forthcoming about the details of the romance and the events leading up to the wedding. Instead they chose to dwell on the couple's happiness which, according to Lovett intimates, was vast. "Lyle's extremely excited. He couldn't be happier," confirmed Ken Levitan, Lovett's manager, adding, "It happened rapidly, very rapidly."

Indeed, as the chain of events leading to the wedding were ever so slowly revealed, Levitan began to look like a master of understatement in his use of the word "rapidly".

Ten years older than Julia, Lyle Lovett's childhood was serenely spent in the small Texas town of Klein, Texas, where he grew up in the midst of a large loving extended family of aunts, uncles, and cousins. Only a stone's throw northwest of Houston, Klein, in fact, is named after Lovett's maternal great-great-grandfather, Adam Klein, a German immigrant, who helped found the community in the mid-1800s.

Although he is surrounded by family, with six uncles

and aunts living within half a mile of his home, Lovett is an only child, a status he enjoyed while growing up. "It was my place," he once said. "My folks just came home at night."

Lyle's home was a brick ranch built on several acres of rich farmland inherited by his mother, Bernel, who has been married for the past thirty-eight years to Bill Lovett, both retired employees of the nearby Exxon plant. Staunch Lutherans, the Lovetts are strict Sunday churchgoers and so is their only child.

During his early childhood, Lyle took German lessons and, when he showed an aptitude for music, learned to play the banjo and the guitar. He was active in high school, is remembered as being well-liked and intelligent, and even worked summers to earn extra spending money.

It was while in high school that Lyle began occasionally performing in some of the small clubs around Klein, singing and playing the guitar. Like Julia, however, Lyle was seriously toying with the idea of majoring in journalism when he enrolled at Texas A & M College. Unlike Julia, however, Lovett graduated and holds a 1980 journalism degree. It was music, however, that was his first love.

"I don't think I had what it takes to be a journalist," he once confessed. "Journalists have to tell the truth. And I don't know if I could've worked that hard. What I do mostly is have fun; I get to do something for a living that I would do for fun. I get to travel to interesting places, meet interesting people, eat in great restaurants, and sing and play my guitar. I get to think about life and turn it into music. What could be more fun than that?"

It was while attending college that Lyle began performing professionally, first doing the coffee house circuit, then concerts. Four years after graduating from Texas A & M he landed an MCA Records contract and his first album, *Lyle Lovett*, was released the following year. Since then, thanks to his quirky tunes, peculiar looks, and off-the-wall sense of humor, Lovett has slowly gained popularity and enjoyed a strong musical cult following.

It wasn't until Lyle won a 1989 Grammy as Best Country Male Vocalist, however, that he began making his way up the mainstream ladder to success. In 1993 he earned a second Grammy nomination, this one for his gold-selling album, *Joshua Judges Ruth*, which is based on three books of the Bible and reflects Lovett's strong religious background.

Since appearing in Robert Altman's film, *The Player*, which he reportedly did as a favor to Tim Robbins, Lovett has become a close friend of Robbins and Sarandon, both of whom were on hand in May, 1992, when Lovett and his twelve-member Large Band performed at a New York City club, The Bottom Line. Also in the audience during Lovett's week-long gig were Robert Altman, another Lovett friend and devotee, as well as John F. Kennedy, Jr., Elizabeth McGovern, Matthew Modine, Roseanne Cash, and Helen Gurley Brown. "You've got to admire somebody who can rhyme ice water and fly swatter," Tim Robbins once explained, adding "He's a real Texas gentleman. His songs may be twisted, eccentric, and dark, and I was expecting the same in his personality but he is totally egoless and his music is art."

Despite the rarified air Lyle has begun breathing on both coasts in the last couple of years, however, he has never abandoned his rural Texas roots or the small town of Klein, where he is remembered by family friends as a skinny kid, bashful and sensitive, not much different than he is now.

Unlike Julia, he has continued to live in his hometown, where he has painstakingly restored his grandfather's 100-year-old German-style frame home, which he had moved across town to acreage next to that of his parents and within close proximity to his three aunts, one uncle, and five cousins.

According to friends, Lyle is a thoroughly charming and delightful down home country boy who likes to hang out with the guys, go fishing and drive his pickup truck around town. He is not impressed with money and fame and is a religious man with a deep sense of family values. He wants what Julia professes to want: children and a home.

In fact, both Julia and Lyle have been in a marrying mood over the last couple of years. Lovett had asked his girlfriend, Allison Inman, a twenty-two-year old senior at Tennessee Tech University, whom he had met in Nashville, in October, 1989, and had been dating seriously since then, to marry him on several occasions. However, unlike the actress, Allison wasn't ready to commit to matrimony. She wanted to finish college and, like Lyle, get her degree in journalism. She also was not enthralled with show business.

"I'm not crazy about show business," she explained shortly after Lovett's marriage. "I don't like the phoniness and I don't like to be nice to people I don't like. I just wasn't comfortable in that lifestyle. It's just not my cup of tea."

"I love Lyle dearly but we had too many problems and it wasn't worth it," she had explained to friends shortly after breaking off the relationship with Lovett only weeks before his walk down the aisle with Julia. "Lyle and I were emotionally exhausted," she added. "We'd gone through a lot because it had been pretty rocky the past year. So I can see why either of us would be vulnerable to fall in love with someone in a matter of weeks. That's why I don't feel betrayed. I understand."

According to Allison, Lovett telephoned her Friday, June 25, from Detroit, where he and Julia were ensconced in the Ritz Carlton hotel, and told her he had been seeing someone and didn't want her to learn about his new romance secondhand. He also told Inman that he and this "someone" had met only three weeks before, but that things were progressing and that it was serious. When Allison finally asked who it was, Lovett told her Julia Roberts. "I was surprised, but the whole showbiz thing has never ceased to amaze me."

Indeed, show business is amazing; but what is truly astonishing is Julia Roberts' ability to spin on a dime where her affections are concerned.

In the wake of the wedding news, Julia's publicist, Nancy Seltzer, had attempted to make her client appear less spurious in the true love department by implying the relationship between the two lovebirds had begun after the couple had met on the set of *The Player*, Robert Altman's highly acclaimed 1992 Hollywood satire. Had this been true it would have unquestionably been "the best kept secret in Hollywood," as Seltzer would have had everyone believe, because *The Player* was filmed during the summer of 1991, almost two years to the date of Julia's wedding.

Besides, Julia had filmed the cameo role, in which

she portrayed herself, during the week of her non-June-wedding to Kiefer Sutherland. Not only was she involved with Jason Patric at that time, she was so distressed she barely remembered working with Bruce Willis.

She had agreed to appear in the film, playing opposite Willis in a movie-within-a-movie sequence as a favor to Susan Sarandon and Tim Robbins, both of whom she had known from her days in New York. But that was *before* her cancelled wedding to Kiefer and all of the reverberations that followed.

"I thought there was a fifty/fifty chance Julia wouldn't show up," Altman would later confessed. "She was emotionally distraught. The press was after her. She had to poke fun at herself. She would have been perfectly justified to not show up, but she did it. She was very gutsy."

Thus Seltzer's campaign to make the relationship "the best kept secret in Hollywood" was brief and ill-fated. Within days it was learned that the couple had never "met," as Seltzer had implied, while filming *The Player*, but rather in early June, only weeks prior to their sudden nuptials. This was verified by Lovett's ex-girlfriend, Allison Inman, in a *People* magazine cover story published the week following the wedding.

"Lyle and I were looking forward to seeing her," Allison told the magazine, "but we were gone the day Julia shot her scene."

Then, in a Thursday, July 22, 1993, interview with Robert Hilburn, music critic of *The Los Angeles Times*, Lovett, a man noted for his honesty, also confirmed that the two had not met during *The Player*. In fact, Lovett admitted he and Julia hadn't met until early June, only a few weeks prior to their wedding. "Meeting her is unlike anything that had happened to me before," Lovett explained. "She's so wonderful. It was one of those immediate things that you hear about."

Lovett then recalled how he had been looking forward to meeting Julia ever since he'd heard that she had appeared on a TV show several years ago and, when asked who her favorite country singer was, she had mentioned him. "I thought that was really something and wanted to write her a note, but I was too chicken," he laughed.

Dazzled by Julia's on-screen persona, Lovett had carried a tape of *Pretty Woman* with him whenever he was out on tour. It was his favorite movie. "He must've watched her a hundred times before he ever met her," confided a Lovett associate.

Then fate entered the picture last May when, while on a press tour promoting his latest album, *Joshua Judges Ruth*, Lovett was told by Terry Tomalin, Susan Sarandon's brother and a journalist on the *St. Petersburg Times*, that he had just returned from a vacation in Costa Rica with Susan and Julia, and that Roberts had in her possession a complete collection of the works of Lyle Lovett. "This time," Lovett confessed, "I decided I should call her."

Lovett followed through on his pledge to telephone Julia, and the rest is now well-recorded history.

With a day off between concerts in Jacksonville, Florida, and Raleigh, North Carolina, Lovett had flown to New Orleans, no doubt at Julia's invitation, for a visit on Tuesday, June 8. "Lyle visited the set, but he just kind of stood back and watched Julia work," a crew member recalled.

Later that night, however, the twosome were spotted at the Cafe Brasil, where the New Orleans Klezmer All-Stars, an acoustic band specializing in funky Jewish folk music, was performing. According to several customers, the couple came in with a half-dozen other people, and Julia was sans make-up, barefooted and garbed in a loose, flowing cotton dress.

After awhile, apparently caught up in the music, Julia and Lyle took to the dance floor, where they dipped, skipped, and circled to a Jewish folk song with the rest of the crowd, oblivious to everyone else in the club and obviously enjoying themselves. "They were nuzzling and dancing together," a patron later reported, "and everyone knew something special was happening between them." From that night on the couple were as inseparable as two people with two different careers in two different cities could be.

(An interesting aside to Julia's stay in New Orleans while filming *The Pelican Brief* is that she rented a house on Robert Street, just around the corner from one of her favorite hangouts, Robert's Bar, a small run-down blue collar and student hangout with one pool table and a bar for about a dozen of its beer drinking patrons. Whether by coincidence, by design or by divine providence, both the house and the bar are less than two blocks from Tulane University where, almost thirty years before, her father had attended school and her mother had worked in a book store to underwrite his higher education.)

Four nights after their night on New Orleans, Julia showed up backstage at Lovett's June 12 Memphis, Tennessee, show remaining quietly behind the scenes in Lyle's dressing room throughout most of the Mud Island Amphitheater concert. The following week she was on hand for his June 20 concert at Wolf Trap Farm Park in Northern Virginia, even taking an entourage of crew members from *The Pelican Brief* with her. "Julia got tickets for all of us, and we went backstage afterwards," confided a crew member. ''We had a great time, but we thought they were just friends.''

Without knowing Julia's middle name, members of her entourage had no idea that the ''Fiona'' to whom Lovett dedicated the song, ''She Makes Me Feel Good,'' was in actuality their compatriot and fellow worker, America's Pretty Woman.

Two days later, during a June 22 concert at New York's Paramount Theater, Lovett again dedicated the song to ''Fiona,'' telling his audience, ''Fiona likes to think I wrote this song for her and, well, I won't tell her any different. I love you, Fiona.''

Yet it wasn't until news of the romance began to leak out, that the Big Apple media realized the mysterious androgynous figure in a black tux who had introduced Lovett's ''Stand By Your Man'' had actually been none other than Julia Roberts in drag. It had been within days of Lovett's New York concert, of course, that the two had downshifted into action and had begun quietly plotting for their wedding to take place five days later on June 27.

''We had absolutely no hint,'' confided a *Pelican Brief* crew member after learning of the wedding. ''We thought they were just friends. Everyone is totally surprised.''

According to sources involved with the production, the reason the film's cast and crew were so ''totally surprised'' by the marriage, was that they believed Julia was still grieving over Daniel Day-Lewis, who reportedly had rebuffed her during a final rendezvous in New York in late May, only five weeks prior to her marriage to Lyle Lovett. The unsubstantiated story is that returning to the set following the break-up, Julia had been disconsolate and in tears, and had confided to several of her co-workers

293

that she had been rejected by Day-Lewis and that the romance was definitely over.

Unless you can believe that Julia, a woman who cannot stand to be alone or without a man in her life for any length of time, was indeed without intimate male companionship for almost six months, there is no other explanation. So, although the Day-Lewis romance remains undocumented, it is really the only scenario that explains the unexplainable in terms of Julia's love life, from her break-up with Jason Patric to her subsequent marriage to Lyle Lovett, a man she clearly had only been dating for a few weeks.

And so Julia is now Mrs. Lyle Lovett, and the big question is, of course, will the marriage last?

While no one, not even Julia herself, can peer into the future and see all that it holds, the truth may be that Julia's marriage to Lovett quite possibly is the best thing that could have ever happened to her. Despite the rebound aspects of the union, Julia may have finally fulfilled her life-long quest to be a part of a solid family unit.

By having wed a grounded, stable, sensible, and mature non-Hollywood gentleman like Lovett, whose values are steeped in the small town American tradition of home, hearth, children, and church, Julia may have at long last found the stability, the love and the nurturing she so desperately has been seeking in all the wrong places through all the wrong faces.

"Lyle," explained an associate, "is a very shy, very sweet, and sincere fellow. He's very humble and very unHollywood, and not terribly ambitious. He just wants to do his music. He's also not great looking, which can only enhance her own security. So Lyle is a safe bet. He's not going to be leaving her. He's not going to compete with her."

If, on the other hand, the marriage was simply an acting out of yet another Julia Roberts' fantasy, Lyle Lovett and the folks in Klein, Texas, will quickly be left standing in the dust, scratching their heads and wondering what happened, just like all the other people who have loved, and lost, this very pretty but previously elusive woman.

ZEBRA'S MASTER STORYTELLER—
LEWIS ORDE

THE EAGLE AND THE DOVE　　　　　(2832, $4.95/$5.95)
In this sweeping panorama of unbridled ambition that stretches across two continents—from the regal trappings of London's St. James's Square to the posh, limousine-lined streets of New York City's wealthy East Side—the vibrant heiress to Roland Eagles' vast newspaper empire loses her heart to the one man whose self-centered ambition may bring ruin to the very world she cherishes.

HERITAGE　　　　　(2397, $3.95/$4.95)
This is the magnificent saga of beautiful, innocent Leah Boruchowicz and her two brothers who were forced by the shadow of the Holocaust to flee their parents' home. They were poor but determined immigrants, each battling for happiness, success and survival, each hoping to fulfill a dream. And in a city where the streets teamed with temptation, and where ambition, money and violence challenged the very core of their beliefs, this courageous family would fight for love, power and their very lifeline—their heritage.

THE LION'S WAY　　　　　(2087, $4.50/$5.95)
This is the compelling saga of men and women torn between family and tradition, ambition and fame, passion and need . . . a story of the troubled and talented Daniel Kirschbaum, whose struggle to rise above his poor immigrant heritage becomes the driving force in his life. It is a tapestry of lives interwoven and intermingled, a world of glamor and ghettos, crime and passion, love and hate, war and peace, triumphs and tears—and above all, of one man's unrelenting determination to survive.

THE TIGER'S HEART　　　　　(3303, $4.95/$5.95)
A family held together by tradition—and torn apart by love! As beautiful and unique as the natural gem she was named for, Pearl Resnick always stood out in the crowded world of New York City's Lower East Side. And as she blossomed into womanhood, she caught the eye of more than one man—but she vowed to make a better life for herself. In a journey that would take her from the squalor of a ghetto to the elegance of Central Park West, Pearl triumphs over the challenges of life—until she must face the cruel twisted fate of passion and the betrayal of her own heart!

Available wherever paperbacks are sold, or order direct from the Publisher. Send cover price plus 50¢ per copy for mailing and handling to Zebra Books, Dept. 898 , 475 Park Avenue South, New York, N.Y. 10016. Residents of New York and Tennessee must include sales tax. DO NOT SEND CASH. For a free Zebra/ Pinnacle catalog please write to the above address.